CLIFFS

Advanced Placement
# English Language and Composition
Examination

## PREPARATION GUIDE

*by*

**Barbara V. Swovelin, M.A.**

*Series Editor*
Jerry Bobrow, Ph.D.

Cliffs Notes
INCORPORATED

LINCOLN, NEBRASKA    68501

# ACKNOWLEDGMENTS

*This book is dedicated to my husband, Jerry, who assisted and inspired me when I needed it most. I would also like to thank Dr. Jerry Bobrow for believing in me and Dr. Allan Casson for his technical assistance. Finally, I would like to thank all of my students and acknowledge Bill Danielson, Jessica Grossman, Oliver Miao, and Cheya Pope for their invaluable help with the essays.*

Excerpts from the following have been reprinted with permission.

*Cities on a Hill* by Frances Fitzgerald. Copyright © 1986 by Frances Fitzgerald. Reprinted by permission of Simon & Schuster, Inc.

Excerpt from *The Writing Life* by Annie Dillard. Copyright © 1989 by Annie Dillard. Reprinted by permission of HarperCollins Publishers.

*A Considerable Town* by M. F. K. Fisher. Copyright © 1978 by M. F. K. Fisher. Reprinted by permission of Alfred A. Knopf, Inc.

*Gather Together in My Name* by Maya Angelou. Copyright © 1974 by Maya Angelou. Reprinted by permission of Random House, Inc.

Reprinted with the permission of Macmillan Publishing Company from *The Proud Tower: A Portrait of the World Before the War 1890–1914* by Barbara W. Tuchman. Copyright © 1962, 1963, 1965 by Barbara W. Tuchman. Copyright © 1966 by Macmillan Publishing Company.

Excerpted from *Illness as Metaphor* by Susan Sontag. Copyright © 1977, 1978 by Susan Sontag. Reprinted by permission of Farrar, Straus & Giroux, Inc.

# CONTENTS

## PART VI: SUGGESTED READING LIST

# PREFACE

WE KNOW THAT GETTING A GOOD SCORE ON THE AP EXAM IS IMPORTANT TO YOU! This AP study guide is direct, precise, and easy to use. The comprehensive test preparation program can be thoroughly completed in a reasonable time and provides everything you need to do your best on the AP English Language and Composition exam. The strategies, techniques, and material presented in this guide have been researched, tested, and evaluated to provide an effective program for you.

This guide focuses on

1. The Ability Tested
2. The Basic Skills Necessary
3. Understanding Directions
4. Analysis of Directions
5. Suggested Approaches and Strategies
6. Practice-Review-Analyze-Practice

This AP language exam study guide also features a glossary of terms you may encounter on the actual test and includes three full-length practice exams. Each of these practice exams provides answers and complete explanations for all multiple-choice questions and, for each essay test topic, two realistic sample essays written by high school AP students.

This guide was written to give you the edge, to help you do your best, and to give you the maximum return on your investment of study time. It is meant to augment, not substitute for, formal and informal learning in high school. If you follow the Study Guide Checklist and work through the book systematically, you'll be on your way to getting the best score you possibly can.

# STUDY GUIDE CHECKLIST

____ 1. Become familiar with the test format, page 3.
____ 2. Familiarize yourself with the answers to the Questions Commonly Asked about the AP English Exams, page 5.
____ 3. Carefully read Part II: Analysis of Exam Areas, beginning on page 11.
____ 4. Take the Mini-Test section by section, strictly observing time allotments, beginning on page 53.
____ 5. Check your answers, analyze your results, and read the sample essays and analysis, beginning on page 63.
____ 6. Familiarize yourself with the AP exam terminology by carefully reading the Glossary of Important Terms for the AP Language Exam, beginning on page 75.
____ 7. Review as necessary Analysis of Exam Areas, beginning on page 11.
____ 8. Take Practice Test 1 section by section, strictly observing time allotments, beginning on page 103.
____ 9. Check your answers and analyze your results, beginning on page 131.
____ 10. While referring to each item of Practice Test 1, study ALL the Answers and Explanations, including the student essays and analysis, beginning on page 133.
____ 11. Review as necessary Analysis of Exam Areas, beginning on page 11.
____ 12. Take Practice Test 2 section by section, strictly observing time allotments, beginning on page 165.
____ 13. Check your answers and analyze your results, beginning on page 195.
____ 14. While referring to each item of Practice Test 2, study ALL the Answers and Explanations, including the student essays and analysis, beginning on page 197.

____ 15. Take Practice Test 3 section by section, strictly observing time allotments, beginning on page 225.

____ 16. Check your answers and analyze your results, beginning on page 251.

____ 17. While referring to each item of Practice Test 3, study ALL the Answers and Explanations, including the student essays and analysis, beginning on page 253.

____ 18. Review the Suggested Reading List, beginning on page 285.

____ 19. Go over Final Preparation, page 305.

# Part I: Introduction

# FORMAT AND SCORING OF A RECENT
# AP LANGUAGE AND COMPOSITION EXAM

## Format

| | |
|---|---|
| Section I: multiple-choice questions (55–60) | 60 minutes |
| Section II: free-response sections (3 essays) | 120 minutes |
| | Total time: 180 minutes |

## Scoring

1. In the multiple-choice section, you earn one point for each correct answer. To eliminate random guessing, a quarter point is deducted from the total for each wrong answer. Unanswered questions do not count for or against your score. The multiple-choice section equals 45% of the total exam score.

2. The three essays are each scored holistically; the scores range from one to nine (or zero for a blank paper or one that does not attempt to answer the question). These scores are then calculated to equal 55% of the total exam score. You can find more detailed information on the scoring of essays in Introduction to the Essay in this book.

3. The multiple-choice section score is added to the free-response section score to produce a composite (or total) score. Finally, this composite is translated into a five-point scale which is reported in July to the student, the student's secondary school, and any college designated by the student.

4. AP final scores are reported as follows: 5 = extremely well qualified; 4 = well qualified; 3 = qualified; 2 = possibly qualified; 1 = no recommendation.

# GENERAL DESCRIPTION

The AP English Language and Composition exam is used by colleges to assess your ability to perform college-level work. Actual college credit (either for one semester or for an entire year) may be offered by colleges and universities. The test lasts three hours and consists of two major sections. The multiple-choice section includes fifty-five to sixty questions that address four reading passages. All the questions in this section have equal value. The second portion of the test is called the free-response section. You will be given three essay topics, and you must write an essay on each of the three in two hours. Each of the essays is of equal value in your final score.

The multiple-choice questions are designed to test your ability in analyzing prose passages; these passages are drawn from a variety of sources, rhetorical modes, historical or literary periods, and disciplines. You will be asked questions about the passages' style, content, and rhetoric.

The essays test your writing ability in a variety of modes and for a variety of purposes. These timed essays measure your expository and analytical writing skills, skills that are essential to success in many college exams.

Overall, the entire exam is designed to show student awareness of how an author creates meaning through language use, genre conventions, and rhetorical choices. A qualifying score demonstrates your ability to perform college-level work.

# QUESTIONS COMMONLY ASKED
# ABOUT THE AP ENGLISH EXAMS

Q: WHO ADMINISTERS THE TEST?

A: The Advanced Placement exams are sponsored by the College Entrance Examination Board.

Q: WHAT MATERIALS MAY I BRING TO THE TEST?

A: Bring your identification card and plenty of pens for the essays and pencils for the multiple-choice questions. You may *not* bring a dictionary, a thesaurus, or any other reference book.

Q: MAY I CANCEL MY SCORE FOLLOWING THE EXAM?

A: Yes. You always have this option.

Q: IS THERE A PENALTY FOR A WRONG ANSWER?

A: Yes. To discourage random guessing, a quarter point is deducted for each wrong answer. You should make only educated guesses.

Q: HOW CAN I PREPARE?

A: **Practice!** Become comfortable with the test and its format. Take several practice exams to work on your timing. Learn new or unfamiliar terms that you might be expected to know for the exam. Practice your essay planning and timed writing. Practice paraphrasing what you read so that this skill becomes second nature *before* the exam.

Q: HOW DO I REGISTER FOR AN AP EXAM?

A: See your school counseling office for registration information. Most schools register candidates in March for the upcoming May AP exams.

Q: IS PAPER PROVIDED FOR THE ESSAYS?

A: Yes. In fact, you'll write all of your essays in a special book that conceals your identity from the readers who score it.

Q: HOW MANY STUDENTS A YEAR TAKE THE AP ENGLISH EXAMS?
A: Every year, over a hundred thousand students take the English literature exam; more than thirty thousand take the English language exam.

Q: WHY ARE THERE TWO ENGLISH EXAMS?
A: Because not all colleges offer the same curriculum for freshman English. The two separate exams permit each college to designate the exam that best reflects its curriculum.

Q: WHAT'S THE DIFFERENCE BETWEEN THE TWO ENGLISH EXAMS?
A: Basically, the two tests are similar; they test your ability to analyze the written word and to prove that you can communicate intelligent ideas on a given subject. However, the language exam asks more questions about nonfiction; there is no poetry on the language exam. In contrast, the literature exam places greater emphasis on literature; it includes poetry, fiction, and drama. You should expect to analyze several poems on the literature test.

Q: HOW DO I KNOW WHICH EXAM TO TAKE?
A: The best way to be sure is to ask the college that you plan to attend. A college may offer either one or two semesters of credit, depending on its freshman English curriculum. Generally, a school that has a literary component combined with expository writing skills in its freshman English course gives up to a full year's course credit for the literature exam. Conversely, a school that has a full year of freshman writing in various rhetorical modes may give up to a full year's credit for the language exam. In addition, you must know your own strengths and weaknesses, your likes and dislikes. If you enjoy prose reading and persuasive, analytical writing, then the language exam is for you. If you have a strong literary background, especially in American and British literature and poetic analysis, then the AP literature exam will be your goal.

Q: IS EITHER EXAM EASIER THAN THE OTHER?
A: They are equally rigorous.

Q:  WHAT IS AN AVERAGE SCORE?

A:  To earn an average score of three, you must answer about 50% to 60% of the questions correctly on the multiple-choice section and also write three adequate essays. At a typical test administration, two-thirds of all test takers receive a grade of three or higher.

# SOME SUCCESSFUL TESTING STRATEGIES

1. **Read the test directions carefully!** Become familiar with the wording in advance so that you'll be as comfortable as possible on the day of your AP exam.

2. **Mark your answer sheet carefully.** If you skip an answer, mark it *in your test book* and then check to make sure that the next answer has been correctly entered on your answer sheet.

3. **Practice your pacing and timing skills.** For multiple-choice questions, complete the easiest ones first; in essay writing, follow your preplanned strategy.

4. **Overall, be prepared!** Become familiar with the test. Remember that increased comfort builds confidence and relieves anxiety. These skills can all be improved by practicing *frequently.*

# Part II: Analysis of Exam Areas

This section is designed to introduce you to each AP area by carefully reviewing the

1. Ability Tested
2. Basic Skills Necessary
3. Directions
4. Analysis of Directions
5. Suggested Approaches and Strategies

# INTRODUCTION TO THE
# MULTIPLE-CHOICE SECTION

The multiple-choice section is normally sixty minutes long and consists of about fifty-five to sixty questions. You should expect four reading passages that represent a variety of rhetorical modes (for example, narration, argumentation, persuasion, description). The passages may vary in length from about three hundred to about eight hundred words. Each passage is followed by ten to fifteen questions based on its content. These questions are not ordered by level of difficulty.

## Ability Tested

This section tests your ability to analyze the linguistic and rhetorical choices of an author. You are expected to show an awareness of the stylistic effects created by specific word choices. These questions also test your ability to examine prose passages critically, to understand the author's meaning and purpose, to comprehend structural organization, to recognize rhetorical modes, and to analyze syntax, figurative language, style, and tone. The level of difficulty reflects college-level study.

## Basic Skills Necessary

It is assumed that you have an adequate background in grammar and in literary analysis. Although the questions don't specifically ask for definitions of terms (such as "subordinate clause" or "syntax"), you should be familiar with terms that may show up in the question stems or as answer choices. See the Glossary of Important Terms for a review of the those you're likely to encounter on the test. However, don't merely memorize a list of literary terms; you must understand *how* they create meaning. In addition, you need the skill of careful reading for your analysis and interpretation of the passages. You can enhance this skill by active, visual reading.

11

## Directions

On the test, the directions are similar to this:

This section contains selections from prose works and questions on their content, form, and style. Read each selection carefully. Choose the best answer of the five choices.

*Questions 1– .* Read the following passage carefully before you begin to answer the questions.

### Analysis of Directions

1. **Use self-discipline to manage your time effectively during the test.** You can develop this skill through practice. You should divide your time for each passage accordingly. Do *not* let yourself fall further and further behind as the test progresses.

2. **Answer all the questions to the best of your ability *before* going on to the next passage.** This strategy avoids your having to return to each passage at the end of the test just to answer a few skipped questions. If you do have time left at the end and there are earlier unanswered questions, you'll have to go back and review the passages for their content, a process that's too time consuming and distracting.

3. **Read each passage carefully and critically.** First, paraphrase the author's ideas as you read; then, concentrate on effective word choice. Avoid getting bogged down on diction, whether it's a word you don't know or a sentence structure that's confusing. Simply keep trying to get the main point and then let the questions guide what you need to know.

4. **Read all the answer choices.** Remember that the directions call for the *best* answer choice, which means there can be more than one reasonable choice for each question. Eliminate wrong answer choices.

*Suggested Strategies for Reading Passages and Questions*

1. **First, skim the questions to find out what you should concentrate on.** This technique works well when you practice frequently enough before the test for it to become second nature. You should look for the specific content of each question. For example, don't merely note that a question asks you to draw an inference. You must also focus upon the specific content included in the inference. Prior practice is essential for you to become comfortable with this strategy of skimming the questions prior to reading the passage.

2. **Read each passage *actively* and *visually*.** Active reading means that you should underline and mark key words and ideas (just the few most important ones) as you read. Don't sit passively and merely let your eyes move across the page. Visual reading means that you should picture any action of the passage in your mind; create a movie, if you will. Both of these strategies enhance your immediate retention and concentration—just what you need the most. Practice these skills daily and watch them become more effective with continued use.

3. **Paraphrase while you're reading.** This technique also helps your immediate retention and understanding of the author's ideas. Practice by *writing down* your concise statement of an author's point immediately after reading a paragraph or a whole passage. Later, you can develop this skill so that it's internalized, and you can do it very quickly. You'll find that eventually you can do this effectively *while* you're reading.

4. **Read the questions carefully after you've read the passage.** Don't assume from an earlier skimming that you know each question well. You must understand exactly what you're being asked.

5. **Read *all* the answer choices carefully.** Eliminate wrong answer choices as you read them and cross out that letter *in the test book.* Never waste time rereading the wrong answers. Make sure that your answer choice is accurate according to the passage and that it answers the question.

6. **Leave the most difficult questions until the end of each section.** From your practice on the test, you can learn to recognize which questions are harder for you and which ones you can do accurately and quickly. Then use this knowledge as part of your personal strategy to get the most correct answers you possibly can.

7. **One way to increase your score is to always analyze the questions that you get wrong on the practice tests.** Try to find out why you selected each incorrect answer choice. Did you misread the question? Did you misread the answer? Did you work too quickly? Try to detect any trends; for example, a certain question type may always be the hardest for you. Then you can study, analyze, and understand why the correct answer is better than your choice. This analysis will help you to stop repeating the same mistakes.

8. **Practice!** With extensive practice, you'll increase your familiarity with the question types. Thus, you'll begin to think like the test makers, not the test takers, and your scores will improve.

### Reasons Answers May Be Wrong

Understanding how to eliminate incorrect answer choices saves time and increases accuracy. Remember to cross out each wrong answer in the test booklet; don't waste time rereading these wrong answers. These are the most common reasons to eliminate answer choices.

1. **Contradictory to the passage.** If you read the passage carefully, you won't be tricked into rereading it to find what the author really said.

2. **Irrelevant or not addressed in the passage.** Again, poor readers are tricked into rereading to look for ideas that weren't there in the first place.

3. **Unreasonable answer choice.** If the answer makes you shake your head and ask, "Where did they get that idea?" it's unreasonable. You should be able to spot these quickly.

4. **Too general or too specific for the question.** Understand the degree of specificity that you need for a correct answer. For instance, if the question asks for the best title of a passage, you need a general answer, one that encompasses the content of the entire essay. On the other hand, if you're asked about the author's use of a certain quotation, the correct answer is likely to be quite specific.

## QUESTION CATEGORIES TO EXPECT

In general, the test questions tend to fall into just a few categories. By becoming familiar with these areas, you can more quickly understand what you're being asked. Also, you'll be more comfortable with the test format and able to work faster. As with all testing strategies, your practice in recognizing the question types *before* the test is essential.

A brief analysis of these question types follows.

### Questions about Rhetoric

The majority of the questions on the test are of this type and test your ability to understand *how* language works in each passage. These questions ask you to analyze the syntax (word order and word choice), point of view, and figurative language and their effects. Your mere recognition of these elements is not enough; you must be able to understand precisely how and why the devices of rhetoric produce particular effects.

Some of the ways this question type may be worded on the test are

- The shift in point of view has the effect of . . .
- The syntax of lines _____ to _____ serves to . . .
- Which of the following choices best describes what "_____" symbolizes?
- The second sentence is unified by metaphorical references to . . .
- As lines _____ and _____ are constructed, "_____" is parallel to which of the following?
- The antecedent for "_____" is . . .
- The third sentence remains coherent because of the use of . . .
- The phrase "_____" has the effect of . . .
- The style of the passage can best be characterized as . . .
- The sentence "_____" is chiefly remarkable for its . . .

### Questions about the Author's Meaning and Purpose

These question types also appear frequently on the test. They measure your ability to interpret the author's theme, meaning, or purpose. As with the rhetorical questions, these questions are closely tied to specific word choices; however, now you must determine *why* the author chooses the wording, not what effect it produces. These questions demonstrate understanding of the author's thematic reasons for chosing certain phrases.

Some of the ways this question type may be worded are

- Which of the following best identifies the meaning of "_____"?
- Which of the following best describes the author's purpose in the last sentence?
- The main purpose of "_____" is to make clear . . .
- The author emphasizes "_____" in order to . . .
- The sympathy referred to in line _____ is called "_____" because it . . .
- What is the function of _____?
- By "_____," the author most probably means . . .
- In context, which of the following meanings are contained in "_____"?

### Questions about the Main Idea

These questions also appear quite frequently; they test your understanding of the author's ideas, attitude, and tone. To prepare for these questions, paraphrase everything that you read. First, make yourself practice this skill in writing—literally write down an author's point in a sentence or two. After such practice, you'll be able to do it internally while you read, and you'll have greater comprehension.

Some of the ways these questions may be worded are

- The theme of the second paragraph is . . .
- The speaker's attitude is best described as one of . . .
- The speaker interests the audience by stressing the idea that . . .

- It can be inferred from the description of _____ that which of the following qualities are valued by the author?
- In context, the sentence "_____" is best interpreted as which of the following?
- The atmosphere is one of . . .
- Which of the following would the author be LEAST likely to encourage?
- Which of the following is true about the various assertions made in the passage?
- All of the following ideas may be found in the passage EXCEPT . . .

### Questions about Organization and Structure

Appearing less frequently than the first three question types, these questions test your ability to perceive how the passage is organized. For example, you need to know if the passage follows a structure of comparison/contrast or if it gives a definition followed by examples. Other passages may be organized around descriptive statements that then lead to a generalization. These are just a few of the methods an author may use to organize ideas. You also need to understand how the structure of the passage works. For example, you must know how one paragraph relates to another paragraph or how a single sentence works within a paragraph.

Some of the ways this question type may be worded are

- The quotation "_____" signals a shift from . . .
- The speaker's mention of "_____" is appropriate to the development of her argument by . . .
- The type of argument employed by the author is most similar to which of the following?
- The speaker describes _____ in an order best described as moving from . . .
- The relationship between _____ and _____ is explained primarily by the use of which of the following?
- The author's discussion depends on which of the following structures?

- Which of the following best describes the function of the third paragraph in relation to the preceding two?

### Questions about Rhetorical Modes

You should expect only a few questions of this type on the test. These questions ask you to identify and recognize the various rhetorical modes that authors use. You must know the difference between narration, description, argumentation, and exposition. Understanding *why* a particular mode is effective for the author's ideas is also helpful.

Some of the ways these questions may be worded are

- The pattern of exposition exemplified in the passage can best be described as . . .
- The author's use of description is appropriate because . . .
- Which of the following best describes the author's method?
- Because the author uses an expository format, he is able to . . .

### Other Possibilities

Be aware that the question types listed above do not constitute a complete list. You will encounter questions that don't seem to fit into a category. However, by understanding what question types are asked most frequently, you will increase your familiarity with the test and improve your understanding of how to find correct answers. Don't be thrown off balance by questions that don't seem to fall into set categories.

## A SUCCESSFUL APPROACH TO THE MULTIPLE-CHOICE SECTION

Many who take the AP exam don't get their best score because they spend too much time dwelling on hard questions, leaving insufficient time to answer the easy questions they can get right. Don't let this happen to you. Use the following system to mark your answer sheet:

For each passage and its set of questions

1. Answer easy questions immediately.

2. On more difficult questions, take advantage of being able to mark in your testing booklet. As you eliminate an incorrect answer choice from consideration, mark it out in your *question booklet* as follows:

$$(\cancel{A})$$
$$?(B)$$
$$(\cancel{C})$$
$$(\cancel{D})$$
$$?(E)$$

Notice that some choices are marked with question marks, signifying that they may be possible answers. This technique will help you avoid reconsidering those choices you've already eliminated and will help you narrow down your possible answers. If you've managed to eliminate two or more answers from consideration but still are not sure of the answer, mark a guess answer at this point. If you wish to reconsider these guess answers before you go on to the next set, you'll be able to identify them from the marks you've made eliminating wrong answers.

3. On questions you find very difficult—those on which you cannot eliminate wrong answers, leave the answer blank (but be careful to place your next answer in the right place on the answer sheet), put a check mark in the margin next to the question, and go on. Sometimes, consideration of other questions in the set suddenly sheds light on the question you left blank, and you can then quickly return to it and choose an answer.

Note: You don't have to erase the marks you make in your *test booklet*. However, don't make extraneous marks on your *answer sheet* because in machine scoring, such marks can be counted as wrong answers.

## A PATTERNED PLAN OF ATTACK
### *Multiple-Choice Section*

Follow this procedure for each passage and set of questions.

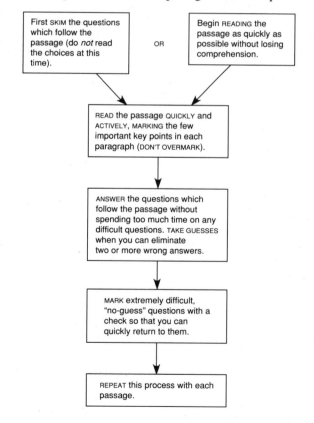

First SKIM the questions which follow the passage (do *not* read the choices at this time).

OR

Begin READING the passage as quickly as possible without losing comprehension.

READ the passage QUICKLY and ACTIVELY, MARKING the few important key points in each paragraph (DON'T OVERMARK).

ANSWER the questions which follow the passage without spending too much time on any difficult questions. TAKE GUESSES when you can eliminate two or more wrong answers.

MARK extremely difficult, "no-guess" questions with a check so that you can quickly return to them.

REPEAT this process with each passage.

# INTRODUCTION TO THE ESSAY SECTION

Sometimes called the free-response questions, this section of the AP exam requires that you write three essays. This essay section is normally two hours long. The suggested time for each essay is forty minutes. You must write your three essays in this time period, and you must write an essay on each of the three topics given; there are no alternative choices. You should expect one topic to be based on a fiction or nonfiction reading passage and to call for an analysis of style. A second topic, also based on a reading passage, calls for an argumentative essay. A third question may deal with a general topic related to language, or it may approach a passage from an angle different from that of the first question. For example, it may ask for a discussion of rhetorical purpose rather than an analysis of style. Remember that each of the three essays equals one-third of the total essay score and that the total for the essay portion equals 55% of the entire AP test score. A more detailed explanation of the essay scoring follows. You will be given an essay-writing booklet in which to write your essays; the test booklet includes blank space in which to plan your essays.

### Ability Tested

This section tests your ability to demonstrate an understanding of *how* language works while simultaneously demonstrating your ability to communicate intelligent ideas in essay form. You should read the prose passages very carefully and then quickly articulate ideas because each essay should be written in thirty-five to forty minutes. Your discussion of such literary aspects as tone, attitude, and persuasion is essential to obtaining a good score.

### Basic Skills Necessary

The basic skill necessary for the essay section is the ability to articulate and prove a thesis through concrete examples. You must be able to write on any assigned subject. Your paragraphs should be well developed, your overall essay organization should make sense, and your writing should demonstrate college-level thinking and style. The basic writing format of introduction, body, and conclusion is helpful, but to achieve a high score, you *must* demonstrate *how* language creates an effect. Analysis of diction, sentence style, and paragraph structure are vital tools in proving how a piece of writing works. Overall, you must show that you can read the question (and any subsequent passage) carefully, plan an intelligent thesis, organize and present valid and sufficient evidence while connecting such evidence to the thesis, and use college-level skill with your own language.

### Directions

Each essay topic has its own wording and therefore its own directions, but general instructions similar to the following are printed on the cover of the essay test booklet:

Three essay questions are printed in this booklet. Use this booklet to make your notes. You will be told when to open the essay-writing booklet and begin. Suggested writing time is given for each question.

### Analysis of Directions

Although each essay topic has its own specific requirements, use these general suggestions for all of your essays.

1. Use the test booklet to plan your essay. A poorly planned or an unplanned essay frequently reveals problems in organization and development.

2. Practice frequently so that you're comfortable with the timing.

3. Become familiar with the types of topics and comfortable with writing in a variety of modes.

4. Organize your ideas logically, and be careful to stay on the topic.

5. Write as legibly as possible; the readers have to be able to read your essay.

### Suggested Strategies for Essays

Remember the following as you practice the essay.

- Use a standard format: introduction—body—conclusion.
- Clearly divide ideas into separate paragraphs; clearly indent the paragraphs.
- Stay on the topic; avoid irrelevant comments or ideas.
- Use sophisticated language and sentences with syntactic variety.
- Be organized and logical in your presentation.

## ESSAY SCORING

Each of the three essays equals one-third of the total essay score, and the entire essay (free-response) section equals 55% of the total AP score.

Each essay is read by experienced, well-trained high school AP teachers or college professors. The essay is given a holistic score from one to nine. (A score of zero is recorded for a student who writes completely off the topic—for example, "Why I think this test is a waste of money." A student who doesn't even attempt an essay, who leaves a blank page, also receives a zero.) The reader assigns a score based on the essay's merits as a whole, on what the paper does well; the readers don't simply count errors. Although each essay topic has its own scoring rubric (scoring guide) based on that topic's specific information, a general sample breakdown of the scoring for a style-analysis question is as follows:

### High Score (9–8)

This essay clearly demonstrates a significant understanding of the passage, its style, and the essay question. The author of this essay shows a significant comprehension of how the language in a passage creates an effect. For a top-scoring essay, the language should be sophisticated; the sentences should have syntactic variety. Overall, this essay has intelligent ideas, sound organization, strong evidence, and articulate diction.

### Medium-High Score (7–6)

This essay completes the task of the essay topic well—it shows some insights but usually with less precision and clarity than the high-score papers. Some of the observations the author makes may be obvious instead of deeply insightful, or the observations may not be as fully substantiated as those of the top-scoring essays. There may be lapses in correct diction or sophisticated language, but the essay is generally well written.

### Medium Score (5)

The medium-score paper completes the essay, but with no special insights; the analysis is lacking depth, and it merely states the obvious. Because of these weaknesses, the ideas are predictable and the paragraphs weak. The writer does not demonstrate thorough understanding of the effects of rhetorical devices; he or she only observes that they are present in the passage. Language in the medium-score essay is usually acceptable but fairly simple, and sentences are frequently of the same length and pattern.

### Medium-Low Score (4–3)

This paper is weaker than the "5" score because its author misses important ideas in the passage. This essay summarizes the passage's ideas instead of analyzing them; it makes assertions without supporting them with evidence; it pays little attention to rhetorical devices. Any essay that merely paraphrases the passage will earn no score higher than a "3."

### Low Score (2–1)

This low-scoring, weak essay demonstrates minimal understanding of the topic or the passage. Perhaps unfinished, this essay has no analysis and little clarity. Usually little or no evidence is offered as a basis for the writer's ideas. Incorrect assertions may be made about the passage. Stylistically, the paper may show consistent grammatical problems, and sentence structure is usually simple and unimaginative.

## TYPES OF ESSAY TOPICS

Although the wording varies, there are only a few categories of essay questions. When you've become familiar with these, your planning should go much faster on the day of the test; this knowledge will also help you to stay on the topic.

1. **Agree or disagree.** This common question type can also be considered part of the general-statement category listed below. You can expect either a short sentence or two that have built-in controversy or a longer reading passage for which you are asked to evaluate the validity of the author's ideas. Persuasive writing is essential for this category.

2. **Author's attitude, tone, or point of view.** Common in recent AP tests, this question type is based on a reading passage in which you must read between the lines, read inferentially, to understand the author's attitude toward the subject. Literary analysis is the thrust of this essay type.

3. **Analyze effect.** There's a good chance that this type of question will be asked on your AP exam. Like questions on author attitude, these require an analytical essay based on a reading passage. However, here you must understand *how* word choice, diction, syntax, and rhetoric work together to produce an effect in a passage. Be sure that you understand the effect produced before you begin writing. Uncertainty results in muddled ideas.

4. **Author's purpose.** Appearing only occasionally, these questions ask you to discuss *why* an author writes what he or she does. You may, for instance, be asked to explain why a political speech is written as it is or why an author describes the physical world as he or she does.

5. **General statement about society or human nature.** This topic is rarely based on a reading passage. Frequently, it's placed as the final essay question. For example, you may be asked to describe a favorite location from the perspective of two times in your life, to compare the dialects of different groups of people, to comment

on humanity after reading a one-sentence aphorism, or to explain what importance knowledge has in your life. These topics are designed to let you use your own experience and observations as evidence while reflecting on all humankind.

6. **Comparison/contrast.** Although not often used, this type of topic does show up occasionally. These questions are frequently based on two reading passages—perhaps two authors on the same subject, two descriptions of a location, or two drafts of the same work from one author. If you get a comparison/contrast topic, be sure to read it carefully and analyze beyond the obvious similarities of and differences between the passages.

## PACING THE ESSAY

With an average time of only forty minutes per essay, you should divide your time as follows:

***Spend about ten minutes reading the topic and the passage carefully and planning your essay.***

This organizational time is crucial to producing a high-scoring essay. In this first ten minutes, your goals are to

1. read the topic's question carefully so that you know exactly *what* you're being asked to do

2. read the passage carefully, noting what evidence and rhetorical devices are relevant to the essay question

3. conceive your thesis statement, which will go in your introductory paragraph

4. organize your body paragraphs, deciding what evidence from the passage to use and what relevant remarks to make about the evidence

The importance of this planning phase cannot be overemphasized. When your essay has been well planned, your writing flows faster, the essay is on topic and well organized, and the paragraphs are well developed. You must practice this essential planning step several times before you take the actual AP exam.

***Take about twenty-five minutes to write the essay.***

If you've planned well, your writing should be fluent and continuous; avoid stopping to reread what you've written. Twenty-five minutes is sufficient time to produce all of the writing needed.

***Save about five minutes to proofread your essay.***

Reserving a few minutes allows you time to catch the "honest mistakes" that can be easily corrected, such as a misspelled word or punctuation error. In addition, it lets you set the essay to rest, knowing what you've written, so that you can go on to the next topic and give it your full attention.

## PLANNING THE ESSAY

Your planning and organizing should be done in the test booklet, in which space is provided for that purpose. Begin by reading the essay question carefully. Underline the key words and phrases of the prompt so that you *thoroughly* understand what your tasks are. Then read any accompanying passage analytically, always keeping the essay question in mind. As you read, underline important ideas and phrases that relate to the topic. Your goals while reading are to

—understand the author's point
—relate the passage to the essay question
—begin gathering evidence to support the points of your essay
—look for nuances of diction and syntax

After you've read both the question and the passage carefully, you're ready to plan and organize your essay. Again, use the space provided in the test booklet. Organize your thoughts using whatever method you're most comfortable with—outlining, clustering, listing, and so forth. Planning at this stage is crucial to producing a well-written essay and should produce the following:

1. your thesis statement

2. a list of supporting evidence

3. the order of presentation of that evidence

4. a list of logical paragraph units

5. notes on analysis or commentary to be added regarding the evidence (analysis which connects your evidence both to your thesis and to the essay question)

Be careful to manage your time during the planning stage. If you overplan, you may run out of time to commit all your ideas to paper; if you fail to plan sufficiently, you're likely to produce an unorganized essay or one that's not as thorough as it should be. Remember that you do *not* have time to write out full sentences for everything in the list above, with the possible exception of the thesis. Simply jot down phrases and ideas quickly. Your goal here is only to *plan* the essay; if you do that well, your writing will go much faster. You'll then need only to put it all down on paper, in complete sentences, and you'll have produced a well-written essay.

## WRITING THE ESSAY

A convenient format for essay writing uses the standard structure of introduction, body, and conclusion. The body should be made up of several paragraphs, but the introduction and conclusion require only one paragraph each.

In your introduction, make sure that you include a strong, analytical thesis statement, a sentence which explains your paper's idea and defines the scope of your essay. Also, be sure that the introduction lets the reader know that you're on topic; use key phrases from the question if necessary. The introductory paragraph should be brief, as only a few sentences are necessary to state your thesis.

The body paragraphs are the heart of the essay. Each should be guided by a topic sentence that is a relevant part of the introductory thesis statement. Always supply a *great deal* of relevant evidence from the passage to support your ideas; feel free to quote the passage liberally. However, be sure to connect your ideas to the thesis. Explain exactly how the evidence presented leads to your thesis. Avoid obvious commentary. A medium-low-score paper merely reports what's in the passage. A high-score paper makes relevant points about it. Remember to stay on the topic.

Your conclusion, like your introduction, shouldn't be long-winded or elaborate. Do attempt, however, to provide more than mere summary; try to make a point beyond the obvious, which will indicate your essay's superiority.

Remember to save a few minutes to proofread and to correct misspelled words, revise punctuation errors, and replace an occasional word or phrase with a more dynamic one.

### Some Suggestions about Style

On the actual exam, you won't have enough time during your proofreading to make major adjustments of style. However, as you practice, you can experiment with some stylistic devices that you can easily incorporate into your writing. Remember that top-scoring essays are stylistically mature and that your goal is to produce college-level writing. By answering the following questions and then practicing these suggestions, you'll improve your writing.

1. **How long are your sentences?** You should try for some variety in sentence length. Remember that the occasional concise, simple sentence can "pack a punch" and grab a reader's attention when it's placed among a series of longer sentences. If an essay's sentences are all of the same length, none of them stand out.

2. **What words do you use to begin your sentences?** Again, variety is desirable. Try to avoid "there is"or "there are" (or any other dull wording).

3. **Does every word you use help your essay?** Some bland, vague words to avoid include "a lot," "a little," "things," "much," and "very."

4. **How many linking verbs do you use?** The linking verb (to be) has no action, is vastly overused, and produces unimaginative prose. Replace as many of these as possible with action verbs.

5. **What sentence patterns do you use?** Again, you should aim for variety; avoid using the same pattern over and over. Also, try inverting the normal order; for example, try putting a direct object at the beginning of the sentence for emphasis.

6. **Are all your compound sentences joined in the same way?** The usual method is to use a comma and a coordinating conjunction (such as "and," "but," or "yet"). Try experimenting with the semicolon and the dash to add emphasis and variety (but be sure you're using these more sophisticated punctuation devices correctly).

7. **How many prepositional phrases do you use?** Eliminate as many as possible, especially the possessive prepositional phrase. Change "the words of Homer" to "Homer's words."

8. **Do you use any parallel construction?** Develop your ability to produce parallelisms and your writing will appear more polished and memorable.

9. **Do you use any figures of speech?** If you practice incorporating the occasional use of alliteration, repetition, imagery, and other figures of speech, your writing will be more vivid and engaging.

10. **What does your essay sound like?** Have a friend read your essay aloud to you and listen to how it sounds.

Finally, a word about vocabulary. Of course, the use of sophisticated language is one of your goals, but do *not* use words you're unfamiliar with. *Look up* new words in a dictionary before you use them, especially if you find them in a thesaurus. Variety in word choice is as essential as variety in sentences, so don't try to overload an essay with fancy, multisyllabic words. Use succinct words that specifically fit your purpose.

# SAMPLE TOPICS WITH STUDENT ESSAYS

Now let's examine some sample essays that were written by AP students under timed conditions. They are reproduced here as they were written, including some misused words and spelling and punctuation errors. You'll find a topic, scoring guide, and high- and medium-scoring essays with analysis for each of the two following passages.

## Question 1

The following passage is from George Eliot's novel *The Mill on the Floss*. After reading it carefully, write an essay that clearly defines the author's attitude and assumptions about human nature. Analyze the use of language to convince the reader of the author's assertions.

It was one of their happy mornings. They trotted along
and sat down together, with no thought that life would ever
change much for them: they would only get bigger and not
go to school, and it would always be like the holidays; they
(5) would always live together and be fond of each other. And
the mill with its booming—the great chestnut-tree under
which they played at houses—their own little river, the
Ripple, where the banks seemed like home, and Tom was
always seeing the water-rats, while Maggie gathered the
(10) purple plumy tops of the reeds, which she forgot and
dropped afterwards . . . these things would always be just the
same to them.
   Life did change for Tom and Maggie; and yet they were
not wrong in believing that the thoughts and loves of those
(15) first years would always make part of their lives. We could
never have loved the earth so well if we had had no
childhood in it,—if it were not the earth where the same
flowers come up again every spring that we used to gather
with our tiny fingers as we sat lisping to ourselves on the

(20) grass—the same hips and haws on the autumn hedgerows—
the same redbreasts that we used to call "God's birds,"
because they did no harm to the precious crops. What
novelty is worth that sweet monotony where everything is
known and *loved* because it is known?

(25)    The wood I walk in on this mild May day, with the young
yellow-brown foliage of the oaks between me and the blue
sky, the white star-flowers and the blue-eyed speedwell and
the ground ivy at my feet—what grove of tropic palms, what
strange ferns or splendid broad-petalled blossoms, could

(30) ever thrill such deep and delicate fibers within me as this
home-scene? These familiar flowers, these well-remem-
bered bird-notes, this sky, with its fitful brightness, these
furrowed and grassy fields, each with a sort of personality
given to it by the capricious hedgerows—such things as

(35) these are the mother tongue of our imagination, the
language that is laden with all the subtle inextricable
associations the fleeting hours of our childhood left behind
them. Our delight in the sunshine on the deep-bladed grass
to-day, might be no more than the faint perception of

(40) wearied souls, if it were not for the sunshine and the grass in
the far-off years which still live in us, and transform our
perception into love.

### Scoring Guide for Question 1 (George Eliot)

8–9 In a well-written essay, this writer clearly demonstrates an
understanding of the author's attitude and underlying assumptions about humankind while also demonstrating how the
author's language conveys that attitude. The writer presents a
clear, relevant thesis backed up with strong evidence from the
passage. Analysis of the evidence and how it demonstrates the
author's attitude about human nature is insightful. Not necessarily without flaws, the essay shows maturity in its use of
language and sentence structure.

6–7 Well presented, this essay accurately describes Eliot's attitude
about human nature but perhaps in a less explicit manner than
that of the high-scoring essay. Discussion of the author's

techniques may be less thorough, and evidence presented may be less specific. Connection between the evidence and the thesis may be less insightful. Overall, the essay shows satisfactory control over format and language, although some errors may be present.

5 The writer of the average paper recognizes the author's attitude about human nature but may be imprecise in discussing that attitude. Attempts to analyze the author's language may be simplistic, and evidence offered may be insufficient to prove the thesis adequately. Organization may be clear but not as sophisticated as that in the better-written paper. Inconsistencies in the command of language may be present.

3–4 This essay attempts to address the essay question but may fail to accurately address the author's attitude. It may not complete all of the tasks of the question. Inadequate evidence for the writer's ideas may be a problem. Insights may be inaccurate or superficial. The essay may convey ideas, but weak control over language may distract the reader's attention. Frequent errors in mechanics may be present.

1–2 This essay fails to respond sufficiently to the question or the passage. It may fail to recognize the author's attitude and may misread the passage so as to distort it. With little or no evidence offered, the essay may fail to persuade the reader, and the connection between the evidence and the thesis may be shallow or nonexistent. Persistent weaknesses may be evident in the basic elements of composition or writing skills.

### High-Scoring Essay

George Eliot's passage from The Mill on the Floss paints an appealing portrait of country life and a sunny picture of the human disposition. Eloquent yet readable, enthralling and complex, her assertions about temperament and perception strike a chord of familiarity in the reader without turning to tragedy or exploring the darker elements of human nature. Eliot uses loving, nostalgic descriptions of the natural world as seen through the eyes of a child to illustrate man's affection for that which is safe and known. She demonstrates that the perceptions formed in our childhood stay with us and influence our adult lives, convincing the reader of her assertions through skillful images of childhood harmony and the subsequent mature joy in those remembered fragments of youth.

Eliot first takes a nostalgic look at the carefree days of childhood. She explores the happy innocence of Maggie and Tom, assured that their lives will never change. She first makes the reader want to accept the notion that our childhoods form our futures, by making the scene idyllic and happy. The children "trot along" and "sit down together," content in their companionship, and happy to play in nature. With adult reflection, Eliot uses similar imagery later in the passage, placing the narrator in a splendid natural setting that is reminiscent of the childhood scene from earlier. This technique helps to show readers that adult life has many of the same elements of childhood, rather than simply telling them.

When young, the only change the children foresee is positive: they won't have to go to school any more; every day will be a holiday. Eliot implies that these expectations never fully die, even in adults. Unrealistic as they know it to be, adults do want every day to be a holiday, and they do wish, however faintly, that adult life could be more like an extended summer vacation, that "these things would always be just the same." These notions reinforce Eliot's assumption that humanity desires some degree of permanence in life, some memories that will remain peaceful and calm.

By tapping into subconscious childlike desires and recognizing the near universal optimism of childhood, Eliot wins readers over to her side. Few readers will be able to resist or deny her later assertion that "the thoughts and loves of those first years would always make a part of their lives" as she looks back from adulthood. She leads readers to believe that childhood is continually alive and well, coloring a view on the world, because she has discovered a self-fulfilling prophecy of human nature. Readers believe it to be true because they want it to be true, because they have no other option than to believe. If they cannot return to childlike openness from time to time in their adult lives, where is there hope in the world?

The Mill on the Floss takes the converse of Thomas Wolfe's position. Perhaps you can't go home again. But maybe home can come to you . . . indeed, perhaps home never really leaves us, even as we travel our distances and believe that our lives have changed beyond recognition. Through her resoundingly positive, almost archetypal images—of grass, of sunshine, of blue sky, of oak trees—Eliot seeks to reassure us that life has much goodness. After all, if the enormous eyes of childhood wonder shape each individual's paradigm, must not mankind be essentially good? Eliot has prepared a proscenium for Hope.

## Analysis of the High-Scoring Essay

This high-scoring essay is well presented, with effective wording to match its insightful comments. The first paragraph introduces Eliot's assertions about human nature, which are developed in greater detail in the later paragraphs. This student also includes a very nicely written statement about how fond memories of youth can bring "subsequent mature joy" to adults. The universal appeal is relaxing and comforting.

The student proceeds to explore Eliot's ideas on childhood memories and adult reflection on those memories, referring to appropriate sections in the text for example. The student also acknowledges the effect of credibility that comes with placing the narrator in a natural scene for reflection as opposed to simply telling the reader an insight. In the next paragraph, the student further clarifies Eliot's assumptions about human nature by explaining that humans desire something to hold on to, some permanent harmony in a somewhat chaotic world. The student shows skill in incorporating quotations into the essay so that they are integrated, not distracting.

The student realizes that one of Eliot's most effective techniques is "tapping into subconscious childlike desires" in all readers and then continues the discussion by doing the same. This handling is forceful; who hasn't wished, at some time, that a summer idyll could last forever? This student demonstrates a coherent understanding of the effect of Eliot's diction by inducing the same effect in the essay's reader.

The essay concludes with a nice allusion to Thomas Wolfe, showing that the student is well read. The last paragraph reinforces the concept that both the student and Eliot present so coherently—

that there is something warm and comfortable in the memories of youth, and reflecting on them, we can maintain hope for our future. This conclusion does much more than merely end the essay; it provides insight and optimism. This essay deserves a high score.

### Medium-Scoring Essay

The attitude of George Eliot about human nature is that people don't want the world to change very much. They like the way things are when they are children and they hope it will blissfully stay the same when they are adults. The problem with this is that they don't always stay the same. George Eliot discusses this in his passage from The Mill on the Floss.

The children think that they won't have to go to school, that all the good things of their childhood will remain constant. This is common with children, and Eliot defends this idea about human nature with his antidote about the children enjoying a happy morning, confident about their future. Later, when they are adults, they will appreciate what they see in nature because of the pleasant experiences they had when they were children.

Eliot uses a lot of pleasant descriptions of nature—trees, rivers, rats, flowers—to describe why they like things that are the same as when they were young. He uses diction to persuade the reader that this is something that all people share. He talks about exotic, tropical scenes as not being exciting after awhile because they are not as thrilling as home. But normal remembrances do last longer because they are comfortable and familiar. People like to have the same things and experiences again because it makes them feel safe.

The whole world may be changing, but not all of it. Some things in nature like "white star-flowers" and "yellow-brown foliage" don't change, and these things make his characters feel good. Eliot assumes that humanity needs the comfort and security of permanence.

So Eliot convinces the reader with his descriptive writing and his diction that childhood is an important time and the nature of children we should understand. We all have to change because that's what make's the world go round. So his attitude in writing The Mill on the Floss helps to convince us that's true. While we can still daydream, still reflect on the joyous days of youth.

*Analysis of the Medium-Scoring Essay*

This essay attempts to address the essay question; in a simplistic way, the first sentence provides a summation of Eliot's philosophy. There is no strong thesis, but the first paragraph is basically on topic. However, pronoun problems begin to appear in this first section; an example is the ambiguous word "they" in the third sentence. Additionally, the student mistakenly identifies George Eliot as a male, but students are not expected to be familiar with all authors from English literature.

The second paragraph reiterates the idea of permanence and also vaguely ties in the children's happy morning that begins the passage. Unfortunately, the student misuses the word "antidote" for "anecdote," probably a mistake made under time pressure.

The third paragraph discusses more of Eliot's ideas, still on topic, but it does not present substantial evidence to convince the reader. Phrases like "He uses diction" are not supported by examples or with any mention of how that diction affects the work.

The short fourth paragraph is repetitive; no new points are presented. It appears as if the student was determined to use a few quotations and tried to build a paragraph around these two phrases. There is no connection between these quotations and the thesis, and one wonders why the student thinks the flowers will never change. This paragraph suffers from poor development.

The conclusion merely summarizes the passage. Overall, this paper is hardly convincing, although it is adequate in its presentation. It needs more analysis and evidence and a proofreading for mechanical errors in order to achieve a higher score.

## Question 2

The following essay comes from Sir Thomas More's *Utopia* (1516). Read the passage carefully, and then write an essay that evaluates the validity of the speaker's ideas in light of contemporary standards. Use evidence from your own experience, reading, or observation to develop your essay and convince the reader of your ideas.

### On Communal Property

By this I am persuaded that unless private property is entirely done away with, there can be no fair distribution of goods, nor can the world be happily governed. As long as private property remains, the largest and far the best part of
(5) mankind will be oppressed with an inescapable load of cares and anxieties. This load, I admit, may be lightened somewhat, but cannot be entirely removed. Laws might be made that no one should own more than a certain amount of land nor possess more than a certain sum of money. Or laws
(10) might be passed to prevent the prince from growing too powerful and the populace from becoming too strong. It might be made unlawful for public offices to be solicited, or sold, or made burdensome for the officeholder by great expense. Otherwise officeholders are tempted to reimburse
(15) themselves by dishonesty and force, and it becomes necessary to find rich men for those offices which ought rather be held by wise men. Such laws, I say, may have as much effect as good nursing has on men who are dangerously sick. Social evils may be allayed and mitigated, but so long as private
(20) property remains, there is no hope at all that they may be healed and society restored to good health. While you try to cure one part, you aggravate the disease in other parts. In redressing one evil another is committed, since you cannot give something to one man without taking the same thing from another.

### Scoring Guide for Question 2 (Thomas More)

8–9 This well-written essay clearly takes a stand concerning More's ideas on communal property and substantially supports that stand. The thesis is articulate and relevant to the topic. The paper provides strong and relevant evidence intelligently connected to the thesis. The paper demonstrates an understanding of the needs of the essay. Although it need not be without errors, the paper shows a mature command of style and language.

6–7  This essay contemplates More's ideas on communal property but produces a less explicit thesis. Perhaps less relevant or insufficient evidence is offered, and the reader may not be as thoroughly convinced as with a top-scoring paper. Although well written, it may demonstrate some errors while still showing satisfactory control over diction and the essay requirements.

  5  The adequate presentation in this essay includes a thesis, but one that is perhaps not as well thought out as in higher-scoring essays. The ideas may be too hastily conceived after a cursory reading of More's concepts. Overall, the argument may not be as strong or convincing. It may appear more opinionated without sufficient evidence to support the opinions. Acceptable organization may be evident, but the style may not be as sophisticated as in higher-scoring essays.

3–4  This low-scoring essay fails to convince the reader. The weak presentation in this essay may include an unsupported or unsubstantiated thesis, weak paragraph development, and/or poor organization. The paper may exhibit confusion in ideas and superficial thinking and evidence. Frequent mechanical errors may persist.

1–2  This poorly written essay lacks clarity and coherence. It may have an overly obvious thesis or no thesis at all. It may contain little or no evidence, and the connection between the evidence and the thesis may be shallow or nonexistent. The paper may be unusually short and exhibit poor essay skills. Weak sentence construction and persistent weaknesses in command of the language may be present.

### High-Scoring Essay

Sir Thomas More's Utopia discusses ideas and conflicts still relevant to society today. He manages to perceptively express the nature of wealth and material goods; and although written over 400 years ago, his essay still reveals essential truths about the attitudes in our contemporary society.

More primarily addresses the issue of ownership of private property and its hindrance upon the fair distribution of wealth. More points out that ownership of private wealth hurts those who have little or none themselves, which makes up the majority of the population. More perceives that "As long as private property remains, the largest and far the best part of mankind will be oppressed with an inescapable load of cares and anxieties." In today's society, More's idea still holds true. The majority of the population does control less than their fair amount of wealth and goods. This is evident not just in America, but also among competing nations of the world. Each day, in countries like Mexico, the poor struggle to keep from getting poorer, while the wealth of many of the rich grows more opulent. Because of this unfair distribution of wealth, the poor have little opportunity to change their worsening situations.

More's concerns also go beyond the poor and encompass another major realm of controversy: politics. More correctly predicts the nature of politics which exists in a society where not everyone is of the same economic class. He suggests that "it might be made unlawful for public offices to be solicited, or sold, or made burdensome for the officeholder by great expense. Otherwise officeholders are tempted to reimburse themselves by dishonesty and force, and it becomes necessary to find rich men for those offices which ought rather be held by wise men." This prediction has certainly come true in contemporary America, where the vast number of politicians tend to come from the upper echelons of society; conversely, one would be hard-pressed to name a top office-holder who rose from the ranks of the poor under-class. In addition, just as Plato saw the need for wise, rational men to fill the position of philosopher-king, More also realizes the danger of public offices held by rich men rather than wise men, an event fostered by a society in which unequal distribution of goods exists. Both Plato and More have made a valid point here, and the voting public should be constantly cautioned to question a potential leader's wisdom and rational thinking before they vote.

While More's essays define the evils that burden a private property owning society, More fails to see some of the problems that would follow with completely eradicating the system. More suggests several legal reforms to stop and prevent the amassing of goods by citizens. When this is stopped, however, all incentive to work is taken away. People rarely have the time, the energy, or the interest to work solely for the merit of working. In contemporary society, human nature drives people to work to earn something tangible—be it wealth, or goods, or love. More's reforms are also unfair. While upon a first glance they may sound fair and equal, in reality they are not. This system would be unfair to hard workers who do deserve a reward, and unfair to lazy workers who don't earn what they receive. Instead of promoting equality, this system would promote laziness and remove the incentive to work. In theory this would be a good system. But, in reality, Sir Thomas More's Utopia simply does not work. The recent breakdown of the Soviet Union alone disproves More's system.

More's essay perceptively observes some of the major injustices and corruptions within a private property owning society. While these are valid, pertinent issues, More overlooks some of the inherent pitfalls within the system of a society which bans the ownership of private property.

### Analysis of the High-Scoring Essay

This thoughtful essay immediately addresses the topic in its first sentence. The writer uses contemporary examples to buttress points and also insightfully comments that More addresses more concepts than money and land distribution. The writer's inclusion of Plato in the third paragraph relevantly extends this idea. In the fourth paragraph, the writer acknowledges that More fails to accurately predict all the consequences of his proposals—the problem that the need for reward is inherent in human nature. Showing both advantages and disadvantages of More's proposal demonstrates the skill of close reading and a high degree of maturity in this writer. To improve this essay, the writer could have worked on a stronger thesis that more accurately addresses the writer's points; notice that the thesis does not allude to any criticism of More's ideas. Some of the vague wording could be made more specific. In general, the essay's ideas are more sophisticated than their presentation.

This essay is well organized and the ideas are supported by examples from contemporary society. Overall, this essay deserves a high score for pointing out the validity of More's ideas for today's society as well as their perhaps mistaken assumptions.

### Medium-Scoring Essay

Sir Thomas More's Utopia discusses fair government and equal social status within our society, and identifies the need for people to give up their private property. His ideas (as written about in the essay) are valid in light of contemporary standards.

More's initial position that private property is an unnecessary evil within our society at first appears to be blatantly Communistic. His desires to redistribute wealth and property, and to make laws preventing people from earning too much money seem absurd at first glance. However, on further inspection, the reader realizes that some of More's views are valid and relevant to society. In lines 14–17 More predicts corruption of the government, something that our nation has been experiencing for several decades. This corruption is a result of politicians feeling obligated to remunerate themselves for the great expense they go through as a part of their job. More sums this up very nicely and accurately as he points out that rich men (instead of wise men) take over the offices of government.

Not only do we see the validity of More's views in our current day and age, but personally speaking, I agree with More's beliefs. The greed and self-interest associated with Capitalism are two symptoms of the sickness that comes with private property. It is wrong for a country's government to allow some people to starve on the streets while others are living like kings. More sympathizes for the great majority of people who do not have much private property, as shown in lines 3–6.

Throughout his essay More proposes solutions to the problem of private property. He advocates altruism and his ideas are shown to be relevant to our society. His essay is very valid in light of today's social standards.

### Analysis of the Medium-Scoring Essay

This medium-scoring essay attempts to address the topic. The first paragraph produces a thesis that claims that More's ideas are valid for contemporary society, but little else is presented here. The thesis is not highly thought provoking, and it contains some redundancy ("as written about in the essay").

The student spends almost half of the second paragraph explaining his or her first impression of More, only to reverse it after a deeper analysis. This student should be commended for looking below the surface, but no evidence is offered to support the student's opinions. This paragraph would be stronger if the student were to include some examples of government corruption, rather than merely alluding to them.

The third paragraph becomes a forum for the student's personal beliefs. Once again, the student presents relevant ideas but little evidence for them. The only example included, the idea that the government allows poor people to starve while others live like kings, may indeed be true but is not specific. In addition, the reader must twice return to the More essay to find what statement the student refers to, in "as shown in lines 3–6," for example, making the reader assume the student's task of relating the essay's ideas to More's.

The concluding paragraph merely summarizes the essay's only point, that the writer finds More's ideas valid. There's not much of substance here, and the conclusion doesn't help to convince the reader of the validity of the writer's opinions.

Although this essay does take a stand, it offers only weak support and sometimes simplistic and redundant wording. This essay would be stronger if the student were to include more of More's ideas and test their validity by today's standards. Overall, this essay is adequate, but it is not persuasive enough to merit a higher score.

# Part III: Diagnostic Mini-Test

The Mini-Test that follows is designed to familiarize you with some of the AP language exam question types. It will also assist you in assessing some of your strengths and weaknesses. This short assessment includes complete answers and explanations, two essays written by AP students, and analysis of those essays.

The format, levels of difficulty, and question structures are similar to those on the actual AP language exam. The acutal AP exam is copyrighted and may not be duplicated, and these questions are not taken directly from the actual test.

ANSWER SHEET FOR THE MINI-TEST
(Remove This Sheet and Use It to Mark Your Answers)

# SECTION I: MULTIPLE-CHOICE QUESTIONS

1 Ⓐ Ⓑ Ⓒ Ⓓ Ⓔ
2 Ⓐ Ⓑ Ⓒ Ⓓ Ⓔ
3 Ⓐ Ⓑ Ⓒ Ⓓ Ⓔ
4 Ⓐ Ⓑ Ⓒ Ⓓ Ⓔ
5 Ⓐ Ⓑ Ⓒ Ⓓ Ⓔ

6 Ⓐ Ⓑ Ⓒ Ⓓ Ⓔ
7 Ⓐ Ⓑ Ⓒ Ⓓ Ⓔ
8 Ⓐ Ⓑ Ⓒ Ⓓ Ⓔ
9 Ⓐ Ⓑ Ⓒ Ⓓ Ⓔ
10 Ⓐ Ⓑ Ⓒ Ⓓ Ⓔ

CUT HERE

51

# MINI-TEST

## SECTION I: MULTIPLE-CHOICE QUESTIONS

**Time: 12 Minutes**
**10 Questions**

This section contains a selection from a prose work and questions on its content, style, and form. Read each section carefully. Choose the best answer of the five choices.

*Questions 1–10.* Read the passage carefully before you begin to answer the questions.

On Route 301 south of Tampa, billboards advertising Sun City Center crop up every few miles, with pictures of Cesar Romero and slogans that read FLORIDA'S RETIRE- MENT COMMUNITY OF THE YEAR, 87 HOLES OF
(5) GOLF, THE TOWN TOO BUSY TO RETIRE. According to a real-estate brochure, the town is "sensibly located . . . comfortably removed from the crowded downtown areas, the highway clutter, the tourists and the traffic." It is twenty-five miles from Tampa, thirty miles from Bradenton,
(10) thirty-five miles from Sarasota, and eleven miles from the nearest beach on the Gulf Coast. Route 301, an inland route—to be taken in preference to the coast road, with its lines of trucks from the phosphate plants—passes through a lot of swampland, some scraggly pinewoods, and acre upon
(15) acre of strawberry beds covered with sheets of black plastic. There are fields where hairy, tough-looking cattle snatch at the grass between the palmettos. There are aluminum warehouses, cinder-block stores, and trailer homes in patches of dirt with laundry sailing out behind. There are Pentecos-
(20) tal churches and run-down cafés and bars with rows of pickup trucks parked out front.

Turn right with the billboards onto Route 674, and there is a green-and-white suburban-looking resort town. Off the

main road, white asphalt boulevards with avenues of palm
(25) trees give onto streets that curve pleasingly around golf
courses and small lakes. White ranch-style houses sit back
from the streets on small, impeccably manicured lawns. A
glossy four-color map of the town put out by a real-estate
company shows cartoon figures of golfers on the fairways
(30) and boats on the lakes, along with drawings of churches,
clubhouses, and curly green trees. The map is a necessity for
the visitor, since the streets curve around in maze fashion,
ending in culs-de-sac or doubling back on themselves. There
is no way in or out of Sun City Center except by the main
(35) road bisecting the town. The map, which looks like a child's
board game (Snakes and Ladders or Uncle Wiggily), shows
a vague area—a kind of no-man's-land—surrounding the
town. As the map suggests, there is nothing natural about
Sun City Center. The lakes are artificial, and there is hardly
(40) a tree or a shrub or a blade of grass that has any
correspondence in the world just beyond it. At the edges of
the development, there are houses under construction, with
the seams still showing in the transplanted lawns. From
there, you can look out at a flat brown plain that used to be a
(45) cattle ranch. The developer simply scraped the surface off
the land and started over again.

Sun City Center is an unincorporated town of about
eighty-five hundred people, almost all of whom are over the
age of sixty. It is a self-contained community, with stores,
(50) banks, restaurants, and doctors' offices. It has the advertised
eighty-seven holes of golf; it also has tennis courts, shuffle-
board courts, swimming pools, and lawn-bowling greens. In
addition to the regular housing, it has a "life-care facility"—a
six-story apartment building with a nursing home in one
(55) wing. "It's a strange town," a clinical psychologist at the
University of South Florida, in Tampa, told me before I
went. "It's out there in the middle of nowhere. It has a
section of private houses, where people go when they retire.
Then it has a section of condos and apartments, where
(60) people go when they can't keep up their houses. Then it has
a nursing home. Then it has a cemetery." In fact, there is no

cemetery in Sun City Center, but the doctor was otherwise correct.

Sun City Center has become a world unto itself. Over the
(65) years, the town attracted a supermarket and all the stores and services necessary to the maintenance of daily life. Now, in addition, it has a golf-cart dealer, two banks, three savings and loan associations, four restaurants, and a brokerage firm. For visitors, there is the Sun City Center Inn. The town
(70) has a post office. Five churches have been built by the residents and a sixth is under construction. A number of doctors have set up offices in the town, and a Bradenton hospital recently opened a satellite hospital with 112 beds. There is no school, of course. The commercial establish-
(75) ments all front on the state road running through the center of town, but, because most of them are more expensive than those in the neighboring towns, the people from the surrounding area patronize only the supermarket, the laundromat, and one or two others. The local farmers and
(80) the migrant workers they employ, many of whom are Mexican, have little relationship to golf courses or to dinner dances with organ music. Conversely, Sun Citians are not the sort of people who would go to bean suppers in the Pentecostal churches or hang out at raunchy bars where
(85) gravel-voiced women sing "Satin Sheets and Satin Pillows." The result is that Sun Citians see very little of their Florida neighbors. They take trips to Tampa, Bradenton, and Sarasota, but otherwise they rarely leave the green-and-white developments, with their palm-lined avenues and
(90) artificial lakes. In the normal course of a week, they rarely see anyone under sixty.

1. In the first paragraph, the author refers to the "fields where hairy, tough-looking cattle snatch at the grass between the palmettos" in order to

   I. deny the area any pastoral attractiveness
   II. underscore the loss when farmland is subdivided for retirement homes
   III. suggest the savagery of the natural world which can be ordered and made beautiful by human projects

   (A) I only
   (B) II only
   (C) I and III only
   (D) II and III only
   (E) I, II, and III

2. In the last three sentences of the first paragraph ("There are fields . . . parked out front"), the author uses all of the following EXCEPT
   (A) parallel structure
   (B) periodic sentences
   (C) specific details
   (D) direct statements
   (E) subject-verb inversions

3. In the quotation at the end of the third paragraph, the use of two sentences with "where" clauses and three sentences beginning with "Then" has which of the following effects?

   I. It provides a rhetorical parallelism for an unspoken chronological progression.
   II. It invites the reader to supply the "where" clauses for the last two sentences that begin with "There."
   III. It provides a series of transitions that direct the reader's attention to the speaker.

   (A) II only
   (B) I and II only
   (C) I and III only
   (D) II and III only
   (E) I, II, and III

4. In the last paragraph, the list of services available in Sun City Center itemized in the sentence in lines 66–69 ("Now, in addition . . . brokerage firm") effectively suggests the residents' concern with
   (A) avoiding the idea of death
   (B) physical comforts
   (C) impressing one another
   (D) relaxation
   (E) money

5. Which of the following does NOT accurately describe the sentence in the fourth paragraph "Conversely, Sun Citians are not the sort of people who would go to bean suppers in the Pentecostal churches or hang out at raunchy bars where gravel-voiced women sing 'Satin Sheets and Satin Pillows.'" (lines 82–85)?
   (A) It reinforces the idea of the preceding sentence.
   (B) It effectively contrasts the Sun City Center residents and their neighbors.
   (C) It recalls details of the description at the end of the first paragraph.
   (D) It attacks the values of the people who live in the area near Sun City Center.
   (E) It presents an image that is amusing in its incongruity.

6. The effect of the last paragraph of the passage is to call attention to the
   (A) age of the Sun City Center's residents
   (B) convenience of life in Sun City Center
   (C) political indifference of the Sun City Center's residents
   (D) isolation of the Sun City Center's residents
   (E) wealth of the Sun City Center's residents

7. Which of the following best describes the diction of the passage?
   (A) formal and austere
   (B) informal and documentary
   (C) abstract
   (D) artless and colloquial
   (E) highly metaphorical

8. Which of the following quotations from the passage best sums up its main idea?
   - (A) "As the map suggests, there is nothing natural about Sun City Center." (lines 38–39)
   - (B) "The developer simply scraped the surface off the land and started over again." (lines 45–46)
   - (C) "Sun City Center is an unincorporated town of about eighty-five hundred people, almost all of whom are over the age of sixty." (lines 47–49)
   - (D) "In fact, there is no cemetery in Sun City Center, but the doctor was otherwise correct." (lines 61–63)
   - (E) "The result is that Sun Citians see very little of their Florida neighbors." (lines 86–87)

9. A principal rhetorical strategy of the passage as a whole is to
   - (A) depict a small city by presenting information in a chronological narrative
   - (B) portray a place by comparison and contrast
   - (C) raise and then answer questions about the nature of a place
   - (D) progressively narrow the focus from a larger area to a smaller one and its residents
   - (E) develop a discussion of a unique location by using multiple points of view

10. All of the following are characteristics of the style of this passage EXCEPT
   - (A) variety in the length of its sentences
   - (B) infrequent use of the first person
   - (C) infrequent use of adjectives
   - (D) infrequent use of simile
   - (E) frequent use of specific details

## SECTION II: ESSAY QUESTION

**Suggested Time: 40 minutes**

The following passage comes from Michel-Guillaume-Jean de Crèvecoeur's *Letters from an American Farmer* (1782). Read the selection carefully, and then write an essay in which you analyze Crèvecoeur's attitude toward Europeans and Americans, concentrating on how his diction reflects his opinions.

In this great American asylum, the poor of Europe have by some means met together, and in consequence of various causes; to what purpose should they ask one another what countrymen they are? Alas, two thirds of them had no
(5) country. Can a wretch who wanders about, who works and starves, whose life is a continual scene of sore affliction or pinching penury; can that man call England or any other kingdom his country? A country that had no bread for him, whose fields procured him no harvest, who met with nothing
(10) but the frowns of the rich, the severity of the laws, with jails and punishments; who owned not a single foot of the extensive surface of this planet? No! Urged by a variety of motives, here they came. Everything has tended to regenerate them; new laws, a new mode of living, a new social
(15) system; here they are become men: in Europe they were as so many useless plants, wanting vegetative mold and refreshing showers; they withered, and were mowed down by want, hunger, and war; but now by the power of transplantation, like all other plants they have taken root and flourished!
(20) Formerly they were not numbered in any civil lists of their country, except in those of the poor; here they rank as citizens. By what invisible power has this surprising metamorphosis been performed? By that of the laws and that of their industry....
(25)    What then is the American, this new man? He is either a European, or the descendant of a European, hence that strange mixture of blood, which you will find in no other country. I could point out to you a family whose grandfather was an Englishman, whose wife was Dutch, whose son

(30) married a French woman, and whose present four sons have now four wives of different nations. *He* is an American, who, leaving behind him all his ancient prejudices and manners, receives new ones from the new mode of life he has embraced, the new government he obeys, and the new rank
(35) he holds. He becomes an American by being received in the broad lap of our great *Alma Mater*. Here individuals of all nations are melted into a new race of men, whose labors and posterity will one day cause great changes in the world. Americans are the western pilgrims, who are carrying along
(40) with them that great mass of arts, sciences, vigor, and industry which began long since in the east; they will finish the great circle.

ANSWER KEY FOR THE MINI-TEST

## Section I: Multiple-Choice Questions

1. A
2. B
3. B
4. E
5. D
6. D
7. B
8. A
9. D
10. C

## Section II: Essay Question

An essay scoring guide, student essays, and analysis appear beginning on page 65.

# ANSWERS AND EXPLANATIONS FOR THE MINI-TEST

## SECTION I: MULTIPLE-CHOICE QUESTIONS

From *Cities on a Hill* by Frances Fitzgerald.

1. (A) The passage presents the area around Sun City Center as ugly: "scraggly pinewoods" and a "lot of swampland." Although the land is used for cattle ranching, the prose denies it any charm or beauty. The passage has no concern with making a case for the subdivision as ecologically good (III) or bad (II). In this passage, ecology is not an issue.

2. (B) These are all loose, not periodic, sentences. Each of the sentences could end after just three or four words. There is parallel structure in the repeated "There are." The sentences are direct statements made up chiefly of specific details. All three sentences place the verbs ("are") before the subjects ("fields," "warehouses," "churches").

3. (B) The repetition of "it has" and "then it has" is an example of parallel structure, and the chronological progress is from when the people first move to Sun City Center to a later time when health begins to fail, to a time of greater weakness, to death (I). The two "where" clauses invite us to supply two more for the last two sentences: "a nursing home, where they go when they can't keep up their condos" and "a cemetery, where they go when they die" (II). The series does not call attention to the speaker (III).

4. (E) There are five services listed, and three of the five (banks, savings and loan associations, brokerage firm) are specifically related to money. A fourth, the golf-cart dealer, is at least tangentially related to affluence. Choices (B), (C), and (D) are

plausible, but (E), although it may seem obvious, is the best choice.

5. (D) The sentence does reinforce the idea of the sentence before—the alienation of the Sun Citians from their neighbors (choices A and B). The bars and Pentecostal churches were mentioned in the last sentence of the first paragraph (C). The notion of a group of middle-class senior citizens sitting in a run-down cafe listening to country-western music is amusing in its incongruity (E). The passage is not satiric. Its point is not that the Sun Citians or their neighbors are flawed, but that they have nothing at all in common.

6. (D) Although the paragraph begins with an account of the stores and services of Sun City Center, even the first sentence insists on this development as "a world unto itself." And the last two-thirds of the paragraph (beginning with "There is no school, of course") gives evidence to support the notion of the residents' isolation from the rest of the world.

7. (B) While perhaps not an ideal answer, choice (B) is the best of the five choices here. The passage is not formal and austere, not abstract, not artless (although a few phrases could be called colloquial), and not at all highly metaphorical.

8. (A) Choices (B), (C), and (D) don't really sum up a central idea of the passage. Both (A) and (E) are good answers, but (A) can include the idea of (E), while (E) is more narrow. The whole passage is about the unnaturalness of Sun City Center, its oddness in this geographical area, and the segregation of its residents from their neighbors and from a world where many people are still under sixty. "Sun City Center has become a world unto itself" in the last paragraph would also be a good answer.

9. (D) The best choice here is (D). The passage begins with the geography of the central west coast of Florida but narrows to Sun City Center ("Turn right onto Route 674"). The second paragraph maps out the town, while the third and fourth

describe its residents. The passage is not a chronological narrative (A), uses contrast only in the last paragraph (B), asks no questions (C), and has only one point of view and one additional quoted comment (D).

10. (C) The passage varies its sentence length, uses the first person only once (paragraph three), uses very little figurative language, and uses a large number of specific details. It is very dependent on adjectives and without its adjectives would be barren and unrecognizable.

## SECTION II: ESSAY QUESTION

*Scoring Guide for the Essay Question (Michel de Crèvecoeur)*

8–9   This well-written essay clearly demonstrates understanding of Crèvecoeur's attitude toward Americans and a thorough comprehension of how his diction reflects his attitude. The thesis is articulate and thoughtful. Strong and relevant evidence from Crèvecoeur's essay is included. Thoroughly convincing, the essay shows a clear command of essay writing skills. Although it need not be without errors, the paper shows a mature style and use of language.

6–7   This essay shows the student's comprehension of Crèvecoeur's ideas, but its thesis may be less explicit than that of the top-scoring essay. The evidence offered may not be as convincing or thorough, making the essay less persuasive. Still, the essay is fairly convincing and shows clear thinking. The connection between the evidence and Crèvecoeur's attitude may not be as clear as in top-scoring essays. Although well written, it may demonstrate some errors while still showing satisfactory control over diction and the essay requirements.

5   This adequately written essay shows some understanding of Crèvecoeur's attitude but may not show clear comprehension of the relationship between his language and his attitude. The thesis may be simplistic and predictable and the evidence offered insufficient to prove the writer's points. Evidence presented for Crèvecoeur's attitude may be too brief or understated. Although the presentation of ideas may be acceptable, the paper as a whole is not strongly convincing. Acceptable organization and development may be evident, but the style may not be as sophisticated as that of higher-scoring essays.

3–4   This low-scoring essay fails to convince the reader. The weak presentation may not demonstrate a clear understanding of Crèvecoeur's ideas. Comprehension of how Crèvecoeur's language communicates his attitude may be lacking. The thesis may be unsubstantiated, paragraph development may be weak, and superficial thinking may be evident. Connection between Crèvecoeur's language and the paper's thesis may be nonexistent or trite. Frequent mechanical errors that distract the reader may be present.

1–2 This poorly written essay lacks coherence and clarity. It may present only a brief synopsis of Crèvecoeur's attitude with no mention of how his language reflects that attitude. The thesis may be overly obvious or missing. Little or no evidence may be offered, and the connection between the evidence and the thesis may be shallow or nonexistent. The paper may be unusually short and exhibit poor fundamental essay skills. Weak sentence construction may persist, and persistent weaknesses in mechanics may be present.

*High-Scoring Essay*

Many foreigners came to America during the republic's formative years to explore life in the new nation. The writings of de Tocqueville and Charles Dickens commented on the new American character and government in the nineteenth century. Michel-Guillaume-Jean de Crèvecoeur, who wrote *Letters from an American Farmer* in 1782, was not alone in his endeavor, though he was one of the first to visit the new United States. His writing generally reflects a positive image of Americans. While taking note of their humble origins and lack of cultural refinement, he praises the resilience of American citizens. Crèvecoeur's diction, and the positive connotations of the words he uses to describe Americans, clearly present his positive, though occasionally paternal and superior, attitude toward Americans.

Americans are defined by Crèvecoeur largely in terms of the land they left. Their new nation is a haven from a Europe of "severe laws, with jails and punishments." The common folk in England are faced by the "frowns of the rich." The new Americans have left the "refinement" of Europe behind, along with the class system and much else which had restricted them. These images tell as much about Crèvecoeur's attitude towards Europeans as it does towards Americans. The negativity attached to Americans' backgrounds perhaps emphasizes their ultimate determination and drive once they arrived on new soil. Crèvecoeur deliberately uses negative phrases in describing the Americans' pasts so that their change in the new country will be even more dramatic.

Crèvecoeur emphasizes the newness of the United States, thus implying a positive impression of the land. While he may look down somewhat on the breeding and manners of the Americans, noting that they come from the lower rungs of European social hierarchy, he certainly believes the new land is good for them. America is a place of "regenerative" powers, with "new laws, a new mode of living, a new social system." Crèvecoeur credits America with encouraging the "flourishing" of the world's poor and unwanted. Might he then be looking down on America, as the "asylum" he describes in the opening sentence, a refuge suitable only for the wretches of sophisticated European life? Perhaps. But he leaves no doubt about the successful attainment of such a goal, lauding it by writing that the "surprising metamorphosis" from wretches to citizens is thanks to American "laws and . . . industry."

Although Crèvecoeur generally presents Americans in laudable terms, a trace of condescension appears in some phrases. America was made up of "wretches" who had previously "wandered about." They had endured lives of "sore affliction or pinching penury." But despite the seeming elitism of Crèvecoeur's description, his word choices elicit sympathy rather than scorn in the attentive reader because he is referring to the Americans' previous lives in Europe. Crèvecoeur makes a careful point of the work ethic of these derelict new countrymen, essentially homeless among the world's nations. Such attention clearly shows that Crèvecoeur is sensitive to the plight of the new Americans.

Crèvecoeur writes as if America has surpassed his expectations as a melting pot of undesirables. He has an optimistic view of the country's role in the future. Compared to crusaders, the Americans he praises are the "western pilgrims" full of the "great mass of arts, sciences, vigor and industry" that once issued from the east. It is important to note that Crèvecoeur ends his essay on a positive tone, with phrasing that emphasizes greatness. Here, in his conclusion, Crèvecoeur's attitude toward Americans really shines with enthusiasm. They are the nation of the future he believes, and they will deeply influence the future of the world with their newborn splendor.

*Analysis of the High-Scoring Essay*

This thorough and well-written essay succeeds both in covering the topic and in convincing the reader. The student demonstrates a clear comprehension of the passage and does not merely present a one-sided view of Crèvecoeur. The first paragraph introduces and relates other foreign authors who also addressed the personality of the new Americans. Ultimately, it presents a thoughtful thesis that shows a full understanding of Crèvecoeur's attitude while also mentioning his diction.

In the second paragraph, the student addresses Crèvecoeur's negative statements about the Americans' background in Europe and does a nice job of placing this negativity in context by pointing out that it will be balanced with the "dramatic" changes that take place once the new citizens have become Americans. This paragraph, like those that follow, is thoughtful and articulate, presenting an ample number of specific examples for the student's points and providing connection to the thesis.

The next paragraph addresses the transformation that took place in the Americans after they arrived in the new country. This unified paragraph uses quotations from the passage well and presents interesting ideas from the student. This writer shows the ability to think about and interpret Crèvecoeur's ideas, not simply to present them.

The fourth paragraph describes the "condescension"in some of Crèvecoeur's phrasing; again the student does an admirable job of presenting Crèvecoeur's attitude while remembering that the topic asks for diction analysis. The student clearly sees that, although Crèvecoeur presents many negative ideas about the Americans' background, essentially, he praises Americans.

The essay ends positively, just as Crèvecoeur's does. The student's wording, like Crèvecoeur's, shows optimism and provides a clean ending to a fairly long essay. Influencing the future with "newborn splendor" sums up both Crèvecoeur's attitude and the student's ideas very nicely. Overall, the essay uses sophisticated wording and contains many intelligent ideas. It reads well because it's clear that the student has ideas of his or her own and is not merely listing Crèvecoeur's.

### Medium-Scoring Essay

Crèvecoeur was a French writer who wrote about life in the rural parts of America. He has a partly negative attitude about America, and cuts down the Americans many times in his essay. He also gives them some praise for starting over and doing something new. He also praises them for succeeding at something new.

He uses diction to obtain these results. A careful use of diction shows readers that he sometimes doesn't think much of the American people as a whole. He seems to think many of them just came from low class backgrounds. He points out that they were the "poor of Europe" who, as "wretches," lived a life of "sore affliction." He also says that "two thirds of them had no country."

This hardly sounds like Crèvecoeur admires the Americans background. He stereotypes Americans to all be like this.

Crèvecoeur continues his diatribe against Americans as he calls them "useless plants" in Europe. But finally, he has something more generous to say about Americans as he claims these plants have "taken root and flourished" here in American soil. So, although these Americans were low-life Europeans, once they became Americans they became "new." They became "citizens." Crèvecoeur also notices that Americans work hard and have good laws. I find it interesting that even though he has some good things to say about Americans, he still claims negative things; he believes that once the new Americans arrived, they left behind them all their "ancient prejudices . . . receiving new ones . . ." We in America today like to believe that we hold no prejudices; at least that's one of the principles that our country was founded on.

Thus it can be seen that Crèvecoeur seemed to have some good thoughts about Americans, but that he was by no means entirely impressed by them. He uses his diction to present his opinions, and very strong diction at that. His wording is surprisingly harsh at times, considering that he seems to want to praise Americans for what they have accomplished, yet he spends so much time degrading their background. His attitude toward Americans is best described as guarded; he certainly does not show Americans in nothing but glowing terms.

*Analysis of the Medium-Scoring Essay*

This essay, although well organized, clearly shows the student's problems in both reading and writing skills. It begins by attempting to address the topic, but it does so with such a vague thesis that all it essentially sets forth is the simplistic idea that Crèvecoeur is both positive and negative about Americans. How Crèvecoeur's diction establishes that attitude is not yet addressed.

The student then devotes a paragraph to proving how negatively Crèvecoeur viewed the Americans' backgrounds by supplying a fair amount of evidence from Crèvecoeur's text. The student cites several examples of negative wording but also makes mistakes. First, the student borders on a misreading of the passage. In explaining the despair that Americans felt before coming to this country, Crèvecoeur's purpose seems to be to show how much the Americans had to overcome, thus emphasizing their strength. However, this student concentrates on only the negative European experience and transfers that negativity to the Americans *after* they became Americans. The student's second mistake is failing to address the topic clearly, failing to comment on exactly *how* Crèvecoeur's attitude is presented through his diction. This student simply gives the evidence and leaves it to the reader to make the connection.

The next paragraph tries to establish Crèvecoeur's positive attitude toward Americans, but the evidence presented is weak; the student offers little more than that the country is "new" and that people are now "citizens." The student turns again to a negative reading of the text, focusing on Crèvecoeur's claim that Americans have prejudices. Because of this change in direction, the paragraph lacks unity.

The concluding paragraph finally mentions diction again, but again it makes no connection between Crèvecoeur's word choice and the attitude it reflects. Unfortunately, this paragraph is merely summary. Overall, the essay's weaknesses stem from a cursory reading of the passage, weak presentation of evidence, and a lack of attention to the topic or the thesis. Simplistic thinking and simplistic diction combine here to produce a bland essay that fails to convince the reader.

# Part IV: Glossary of
# Important Terms for the AP Language Exam

The following glossaries list technical terms, both literary and grammatical, that you should be familiar with before the AP exam. These are not exhaustive lists of every term you might encounter. For example, you won't find parts of speech defined, as it is assumed that AP students are familiar with them. The first glossary includes terms common in both multiple-choice and essay sections. The second includes terms used exclusively in the essay section.

# TERMS FOR THE MULTIPLE-CHOICE AND ESSAY SECTIONS

Some of the following terms may be used in the multiple-choice questions and/or answers or in essay section instructions. Others you might choose to incorporate into your essay writing—for example, to help explain the effect of a literary device mentioned in the essay prompt.

- **allegory**

  The device of using character and/or story elements symbolically to represent an abstraction in addition to the literal meaning. In some allegories, for example, an author may intend the characters to personify an abstraction like hope or freedom. The allegorical meaning usually deals with moral truth or a generalization about human existence.

- **alliteration**

  The repetition of sounds, especially initial consonant sounds in two or more neighboring words (as in "she sells sea shells"). Although the term is not used in the multiple-choice section, you can look for alliteration in any essay passage. The repetition can reinforce meaning, unify ideas, and/or supply a musical sound.

- **allusion**

  A direct or indirect reference to something which is presumably commonly known, such as an event, book, myth, place, or work of art. Allusions can be historical, (like referring to Hitler), literary (like referring to Kurtz in *Heart of Darkness*), religious (like referring to Noah and the flood), or mythical (like referring to Atlas). There are, of course, many more possibilities, and a work may simultaneously use multiple layers of allusion.

- **ambiguity**

  The multiple meanings, either intentional or unintentional, of a word, phrase, sentence, or passage.

- **analogy**

  A similarity or comparison between two different things or the relationship between them. An analogy can explain something unfamiliar by associating it with or pointing out its similarity to something more familiar. Analogies can also make writing more vivid, imaginative, or intellectually engaging.

- **antecedent**

  The word, phrase, or clause referred to by a pronoun. The AP language exam occasionally asks for the antecedent of a given pronoun in a long, complex sentence or in a group of sentences.

- **aphorism**

  A terse statement of known authorship which expresses a general truth or a moral principle. (If the authorship is unknown, the statement is generally considered to be a folk proverb.) An aphorism can be a memorable summation of the author's point.

- **apostrophe**

  A figure of speech that directly addresses an absent or imaginary person or a personified abstraction, such as liberty or love. The effect may add familiarity or emotional intensity. William Wordsworth addresses John Milton as he writes, "Milton, thou shouldst be living at this hour: England hath need of thee."

- **atmosphere**

  The emotional mood created by the entirety of a literary work, established partly by the setting and partly by the author's choice of objects that are described. Even such elements as a description of the weather can contribute to the atmosphere. Frequently, atmosphere foreshadows events. See *mood*.

- **clause**

  A grammatical unit that contains both a subject and a verb. An independent, or main, clause expresses a complete thought and can stand alone as a sentence. A dependent, or subordinate, clause cannot stand alone as a sentence and must be accompanied by an independent clause. Examine this sample sentence: "Because I practiced hard, my AP scores were high." In this sentence, the independent clause is "my AP scores were high," and the dependent clause is "Because I practiced hard."

- **colloquial/colloquialism**

  The use of slang or informalities in speech or writing. Not generally acceptable for formal writing, colloquialisms give a work a conversational, familiar tone. Colloquial expressions in writing include local or regional dialects.

- **conceit**

  A fanciful expression, usually in the form of an extended metaphor or surprising analogy between seemingly dissimilar objects. A conceit displays intellectual cleverness due to the unusual comparison being made.

- **connotation**

  The nonliteral, associative meaning of a word; the implied, suggested meaning. Connotations may involve ideas, emotions, or attitudes. See *denotation.*

- **denotation**

  The strict, literal, dictionary definition of a word, devoid of any emotion, attitude, or color. See *connotation.*

- **diction**

  Related to style, diction refers to the writer's word choices, especially with regard to their correctness, clearness, or effectiveness. For the AP exam, you should be able to describe an author's diction (for example, formal or informal, ornate or plain) and understand the ways in which diction can complement the author's purpose. Diction, combined with syntax, figurative language, literary devices, etc., creates an author's style. See *syntax.*

- **didactic**

  From the Greek, didactic literally means "teaching." Didactic works have the primary aim of teaching or instructing, especially the teaching of moral or ethical principles.

- **euphemism**

  From the Greek for "good speech," euphemisms are a more agreeable or less offensive substitute for a generally unpleasant word or concept. The euphemism may be used to adhere to standards of social or political correctness or to add humor or ironic understatement. Saying "earthly remains" rather than "corpse" is an example of euphemism.

- **extended metaphor**

  A metaphor developed at great length, occurring frequently in or throughout a work. See *metaphor.*

- **figurative language**

  Writing or speech that is not intended to carry literal meaning and is usually meant to be imaginative and vivid. See *figure of speech.*

- **figure of speech**

  A device used to produce figurative language. Many compare dissimilar things. Figures of speech include, for example, apostrophe, hyperbole, irony, metaphor, metonomy, oxymoron, paradox, personification, simile, synecdoche, and understatement.

- **generic conventions**

  This term describes traditions for each genre. These conventions help to define each genre; for example, they differentiate between an essay and journalistic writing or an autobiography and political writing. On the AP language exam, try to distinguish the unique features of a writer's work from those dictated by convention.

- **genre**

  The major category into which a literary work fits. The basic divisions of literature are prose, poetry, and drama. However, genre is a flexible term; within these broad boundaries exist many subdivisions that are often called genres themselves. For example, prose can be divided into fiction (novels and short stories) or nonfiction (essays, biographies, autobiographies, etc.). Poetry can be divided into lyric, dramatic, narrative, epic, etc. Drama can be divided into tragedy, comedy, melodrama, farce, etc. On the AP language exam, expect the majority of the passages to be from the following genres: autobiography, biography, diaries, criticism, essays, and journalistic, political, scientific, and nature writing.

- **homily**

  This term literally means "sermon," but more informally, it can include any serious talk, speech, or lecture involving moral or spiritual advice.

- **hyperbole**

  A figure of speech using deliberate exaggeration or overstatement. Hyperboles often have a comic effect; however, a serious effect is also possible. Often, hyperbole produces irony at the same time.

- **imagery**

  The sensory details or figurative language used to describe, arouse emotion, or represent abstractions. On a physical level, imagery uses terms related to the five senses; we refer to visual, auditory, tactile, gustatory, or olfactory imagery. On a broader and deeper level, however, one image can represent more than one thing. For example, a rose may present visual imagery while also representing the color in a woman's cheeks. An author, therefore, may use complex imagery while simultaneously employing other figures of speech, especially metaphor and simile. In addition, this term can apply to the total of all the images in a work. On the AP exam, pay attention to *how* an author creates imagery and to the effect of that imagery.

- **inference/infer**

  To draw a reasonable conclusion from the information presented. When a multiple-choice question asks for an inference to be drawn from a passage, the most direct, most reasonable inference is the safest answer choice. If an inference is implausible, it's unlikely to be the correct answer. Note that if the answer choice is directly stated, it is *not* inferred and is wrong.

- **invective**

  An emotionally violent, verbal denunciation or attack using strong, abusive language.

- **irony/ironic**

  The contrast between what is stated explicitly and what is really meant. The difference between what appears to be and what actually is true. In general, there are three major types of irony used in language: (1) In *verbal* irony, the words literally state the opposite of the writer's (or speaker's) true meaning. (2) In *situational* irony, events turn out the opposite of what was expected. What the characters and readers think ought to happen is not what does happen. (3) In *dramatic* irony, facts or events are unknown to a character in a play or piece of fiction but known to the reader, audience, or other characters in the work. Irony is used for many reasons, but frequently, it's used to create poignancy or humor.

- **loose sentence**

  A type of sentence in which the main idea (independent clause) comes first, followed by dependent grammatical units such as phrases and clauses. If a period were placed at the end of the independent clause, the clause would be a complete sentence. A work containing many loose sentences often seems informal, relaxed, and conversational. See *periodic sentence.*

- **metaphor**

  A figure of speech using implied comparison of seemingly unlike things or the substitution of one for the other, suggesting some similarity. Metaphorical language makes writing more vivid, imaginative, thought provoking, and meaningful. See *simile.*

## • metonomy

A term from the Greek meaning "changed label" or "substitute name," metonomy is a figure of speech in which the name of one object is substituted for that of another closely associated with it. A news release that claims "the White House declared" rather than "the President declared" is using metonomy. This term is unlikely to be used in the multiple-choice section, but you might see examples of metonomy in an essay passage.

## • mood

This term has two distinct technical meanings in English writing. The first meaning is grammatical and deals with verbal units and a speaker's attitude. The *indicative* mood is used only for factual sentences. For example, "Joe eats too quickly." The *subjunctive* mood is used for a doubtful or conditional attitude. For example, "If I were you, I'd get another job." The *imperative* mood is used for commands. For example, "Shut the door!" The second meaning of mood is literary, meaning the prevailing atmosphere or emotional aura of a work. Setting, tone, and events can affect the mood. In this usage, mood is similar to tone and atmosphere.

## • narrative

The telling of a story or an account of an event or series of events.

## • onomatopoeia

A figure of speech in which natural sounds are imitated in the sounds of words. Simple examples include such words as buzz, hiss, hum, crack, whinny, and murmur. This term is not used in the multiple-choice section. If you identify examples of onomatopoeia in an essay passage, note the effect.

## • oxymoron

From the Greek for "pointedly foolish," an oxymoron is a figure of speech wherein the author groups apparently contradictory terms to suggest a paradox. Simple examples include "jumbo shrimp" and "cruel kindness." This term does not appear in the multiple-choice questions, but there is a slight chance you will see it used by an author in an essay passage or find it useful in your own essay writing.

- **paradox**

  A statement that appears to be self-contradictory or opposed to common sense but upon closer inspection contains some degree of truth or validity. The first scene of *Macbeth*, for example, closes with the witches' cryptic remark "Fair is foul, and foul is fair. . . ."

- **parallelism**

  Also referred to as parallel construction or parallel structure, this term comes from Greek roots meaning "beside one another." It refers to the grammatical or rhetorical framing of words, phrases, sentences, or paragraphs to give structural similarity. This can involve, but is not limited to, repetition of a grammatical element such as a preposition or verbal phrase. A famous example of parallelism begins Charles Dickens's novel *A Tale of Two Cities:* "It was the best of times, it was the worst of times, it was the age of wisdom, it was the age of foolishness, it was the epoch of belief, it was the epoch of incredulity. . . ." The effects of parallelism are numerous, but frequently, they act as an organizing force to attract the reader's attention, add emphasis and organization, or simply provide a musical rhythm.

- **parody**

  A work that closely imitates the style or content of another with the specific aim of comic effect and/or ridicule. As comedy, parody distorts or exaggerates distinctive features of the original. As ridicule, it mimics the work by repeating and borrowing words, phrases, or characteristics in order to illuminate weaknesses in the original. Well-written parody offers enlightenment about the original, but poorly written parody offers only ineffectual imitation. Usually an audience must grasp literary allusion and understand the work being parodied in order to fully appreciate the nuances of the newer work. Occasionally, however, parodies take on a life of their own and don't require knowledge of the original.

• **pedantic**

An adjective that describes words, phrases, or general tone that is overly scholarly, academic, or bookish.

• **periodic sentence**

A sentence that presents its central meaning in a main clause at the end. This independent clause is preceded by a phrase or clause that cannot stand alone. For example: "Ecstatic with my AP scores, I let out a loud shout of joy!" The effect of a periodic sentence is to add emphasis and structural variety. See *loose sentence*.

• **personification**

A figure of speech in which the author presents or describes concepts, animals, or inanimate objects by endowing them with human attributes or emotions. Personification is used to make these abstractions, animals, or objects appear more vivid to the reader.

• **point of view**

In literature, the perspective from which a story is told. There are two general divisions of point of view and many subdivisions within those. (1) The *first person narrator* tells the story with the first person pronoun, "I," and is a character in the story. This narrator can be the protagonist (the hero or heroine), a partici-pant (a character in a secondary role), or an observer (a character who merely watches the action). (2) The *third person narrator* relates the events with the third person pronouns, "he," "she," and "it." There are two main subdivisions to be aware of: *omniscient* and *limited omniscient*. In the "third person omniscient" point of view, the narrator, with godlike knowledge, presents the thoughts and actions of any or all characters. This all-knowing narrator can reveal what each character feels and thinks at any given moment. The "third person limited omniscient" point of view, as its name implies, presents the feelings and thoughts of only one character, presenting only the actions of all remaining characters. This definition applies in questions in the multiple-choice section. However, on the essay portion of the exam, the term "point of view" carries a different meaning. When you're asked to analyze an author's point of view, the appropriate point for you to address is the author's *attitude.*

- **predicate adjective**

  One type of subject complement—an adjective, group of adjectives, or adjective clause that follows a linking verb. It is in the predicate of the sentence, and modifies, or describes, the subject. For example, in the sentence "My boyfriend is tall, dark, and handsome," the group of predicate adjectives ("tall, dark, and handsome") describes "boyfriend."

- **predicate nominative**

  A second type of subject complement— a noun, group of nouns, or noun clause that renames the subject. It, like the predicate adjective, follows a linking verb and is located in the predicate of the sentence. For example, in the sentence "Abe Lincoln was a man of integrity," the predicate nominative is "man of integrity," as it renames Abe Lincoln. Occasionally, this term or the term predicate adjective appears in a multiple-choice question.

- **prose**

  One of the major divisions of genre, prose refers to fiction and nonfiction, including all its forms, because they are written in ordinary language and most closely resemble everyday speech. Technically, anything that isn't poetry or drama is prose. Therefore, all passages in the AP language exam are prose. Of course, prose writers often borrow poetic and dramatic elements.

- **repetition**

  The duplication, either exact or approximate, of any element of language, such as a sound, word, phrase, clause, sentence, or grammatical pattern. When repetition is poorly done, it bores, but when it's well done, it links and emphasizes ideas while allowing the reader the comfort of recognizing something familiar.

- **rhetoric**

  From the Greek for "orator," this term describes the principles governing the art of writing effectively, eloquently, and persuasively.

- **rhetorical modes**

  This flexible term describes the variety, the conventions, and the purposes of the major kinds of writing. The four most common rhetorical modes and their purposes are as follows: (1) The purpose of *exposition* (or expository writing) is to explain and analyze information by presenting an idea, relevant evidence, and appropriate discussion. The AP language exam essay questions are frequently set up as expository topics. (2) The purpose of *argumentation* is to prove the validity of an idea, or point of view, by presenting sound reasoning, discussion, and argument that thoroughly convince the reader. *Persuasive* writing is a type of argumentation having an additional aim of urging some form of action. (3) The purpose of *description* is to re-create, invent, or visually present a person, place, event, or action so that the reader can picture that being described. Sometimes an author engages all five senses in description; good descriptive writing can be sensuous and picturesque. Descriptive writing may be straightforward and objective or highly emotional and subjective. (4) The purpose of *narration* is to tell a story or narrate an event or series of events. This writing mode frequently uses the tools of descriptive writing. These four writing modes are sometimes referred to as modes of discourse.

- **sarcasm**

  From the Greek meaning "to tear flesh," sarcasm involves bitter, caustic language that is meant to hurt or ridicule someone or something. It may use irony as a device, but not all ironic statements are sarcastic, that is, intending to ridicule. When well done, sarcasm can be witty and insightful; when poorly done, it's simply cruel.

- **satire**

  A work that targets human vices and follies or social institutions and conventions for reform or ridicule. Regardless of whether or not the work aims to reform humans or their society, satire is best seen as a style of writing rather than a purpose for writing. It can be recognized by the many devices used effectively by the satirist, such as irony, wit, parody, caricature, hyperbole, understatement, and sarcasm. The effects of satire are varied, depending on the writer's goal, but good satire, often humorous, is thought provoking and insightful about the human condition.

- **semantics**

  The branch of linguistics that studies the meaning of words, their historical and psychological development, their connotations, and their relation to one another.

- **style**

  The consideration of style has two purposes. (1) An evaluation of the sum of the choices an author makes in blending diction, syntax, figurative language, and other literary devices. Some authors' styles are so idiosyncratic that we can quickly recognize works by the same author (or a writer emulating that author's style). Compare, for example, Jonathan Swift to George Orwell or William Faulkner to Ernest Hemingway. We can analyze and describe an author's personal style and make judgments on how appropriate it is to the author's purpose. Styles can be called flowery, explicit, succinct, rambling, bombastic, commonplace, incisive, or laconic, to name only a few examples. (2) Classification of authors to a group and comparison of an author to similar authors. By means of such classification and comparison, one can see how an author's style reflects and helps to define a historical period, such as the Renaissance or the Victorian period, or a literary movement, such as the romantic, transcendental, or realist movement.

- **subject complement**

  The word (with any accompanying phrases) or clause that follows a linking verb and complements, or completes, the subject of the sentence by either (1) renaming it or (2) describing it. The former is technically called a predicate nominative, the latter a predicate adjective. See *predicate nominative* and *predicate adjective* for examples of sentences. This term is occasionally used in a multiple-choice question.

- **subordinate clause**

  Like all clauses, this word group contains both a subject and a verb (plus any accompanying phrases or modifiers), but unlike the independent clause, the subordinate clause cannot stand alone; it does not express a complete thought. Also called a dependent clause, the subordinate clause depends on a main clause, sometimes called an independent clause, to complete its meaning. Easily recognized key words and phrases usually begin these clauses—for example: although, because, unless, if, even though, since, as soon as, while, who, when, where, how, and that.

- **syllogism**

  From the Greek for "reckoning together," a syllogism (or syllogistic reasoning) is a deductive system of formal logic that presents two premises (the first one called "major" and the second "minor") that inevitably lead to a sound conclusion. A frequently cited example proceeds as follows:

  > *major premise:* All men are mortal.
  > *minor premise:* Socrates is a man.
  > *conclusion:* Therefore, Socrates is mortal.

  A syllogism's conclusion is valid only if each of the two premises is valid. Syllogisms may also present the specific idea first ("Socrates") and the general second ("All men").

- **symbol/symbolism**

  Generally, anything that represents, stands for, something else. Usually, a symbol is something concrete—such as an object, action, character or scene—that represents something more abstract. However, symbols and symbolism can be much more complex. One system classifies symbols in three categories: (1) *Natural* symbols use objects and occurrences from nature to

represent ideas commonly associated with them (dawn symbolizing hope or a new beginning, a rose symbolizing love, a tree
symbolizing knowledge). (2) *Conventional* symbols are those that
have been invested with meaning by a group (religious symbols,
such as a cross or Star of David; national symbols, such as a flag or
an eagle; or group symbols, such as a skull and crossbones for
pirates or the scales of justice for lawyers). (3) *Literary* symbols
are sometimes also conventional in the sense that they are found
in a variety of works and are generally recognized. However, a
work's symbols may be more complicated as is the whale in *Moby
Dick* and the jungle in *Heart of Darkness*. On the AP exam, try to
determine what abstraction an object is a symbol for and to what
extent it is successful in representing that abstraction.

- **syntax**

  The way an author chooses to join words into phrases, clauses,
  and sentences. Syntax is similar to diction, but you can differentiate them by thinking of syntax as the *groups* of words, while
  diction refers to the individual words. In the multiple-choice
  section of the AP language exam, expect to be asked some
  questions about how an author manipulates syntax. In the essay
  section, you will need to analyze how syntax produces effects.

- **theme**

  The central idea or message of a work, the insight it offers into
  life. Usually, theme is unstated in fictional works, but in nonfiction, the theme may be directly stated, especially in expository or
  argumentative writing.

- **thesis**

  In expository writing, the thesis statement is the sentence or
  group of sentences that directly expresses the author's opinion,
  purpose, meaning, or proposition. Expository writing is usually
  judged by analyzing how accurately, effectively, and thoroughly a
  writer has proven the thesis.

- **tone**

  Similar to mood, tone describes the author's attitude toward his or her material, the audience, or both. Tone is easier to determine in spoken language than in written language. Considering how a work would sound if it were read aloud can help in identifying an author's tone. Some words describing tone are playful, serious, businesslike, sarcastic, humorous, formal, ornate, and somber.

- **transition**

  A word or phrase that links different ideas. Used especially, although not exclusively, in expository and argumentative writing, transitions effectively signal a shift from one idea to another. A few commonly used transitional words or phrases are furthermore, consequently, nevertheless, for example, in addition, likewise, similarly, and on the contrary.

- **understatement**

  The ironic minimalizing of fact, understatement presents something as less significant than it is. The effect can frequently be humorous and emphatic. Understatement is the opposite of hyperbole.

- **wit**

  In modern usage, intellectually amusing language that surprises and delights. A witty statement is humorous, while suggesting the speaker's verbal power in creating ingenious and perceptive remarks. Wit usually uses terse language that makes a pointed statement. Historically, wit originally meant basic understanding. Its meaning evolved to include speed of understanding, and finally (in the early seventeenth century), it grew to mean quick perception including creative fancy.

# TERMS FOR THE ESSAY SECTION

The following words and phrases have appeared in recent AP language exam essay topics. While not a comprehensive list of every word or phrase you might find unfamiliar, it will help you to understand what you're being asked to do for a topic.

- **attitude**

  A writer's intellectual position or emotion regarding the subject of the writing. In the essay section, expect to be asked what the writer's attitude is and how his or her language conveys that attitude.

- **concrete detail**

  Strictly defined, "concrete" refers to nouns that name physical objects—a bridge, a book, a coat. Concrete nouns are the opposite of abstract nouns (which refer to concepts like freedom and love). However, as used in the essay portion of the AP test, this term has a slightly different connotation. The directions may read something like this: "Provide concrete detail that will convince the reader." This means that your essay should include details and evidence that relate to the topic. At times, you'll find the detail in the passage; at times, you'll be asked to provide detail from your own life (reading, observation, experience, etc.).

- **descriptive detail**

  When an essay question uses this phrase, look for the writer's sensory description. Descriptive detail appealing to the visual sense is usually the most predominant, but don't overlook other sensory detail. As usual, after you identify a passage's descriptive detail, analyze its effect.

- **devices**

  The figures of speech, syntax, diction, and other stylistic elements that collectively produce a particular artistic effect.

- **language**

  When you're asked to "analyze the language," concentrate on how the elements of language combine to form a whole—how diction, syntax, figurative language, and sentence structure create a cumulative effect.

- **narrative devices**

  This term describes the tools of the storyteller (also used in nonfiction), such as ordering events so that they build to a climactic moment or withholding information until a crucial or appropriate moment when revealing it creates a desired effect. On the essay exam, this term may also apply to biographical and autobiographical writing.

- **narrative technique**

  The style of telling the "story," even if the passage is nonfiction. Concentrate on the order of events and on their detail in evaluating a writer's technique.

- **persuasive devices**

  When asked to analyze an author's persuasive devices, look for the words in the passage that have strong connotations, words that intensify the emotional effect. In addition, analyze *how* these words complement the writer's argument as it builds logically. Speeches are often used in this context, since they are generally designed to persuade.

- **persuasive essay**

  When asked to write a persuasive essay, you should present a coherent argument in which the evidence builds to a logical and relevant conclusion. Strong persuasive essays often appeal to the audience's emotions or ethical standards.

- **resources of language**

  This phrase refers to all the devices of composition available to a writer, such as diction, syntax, sentence structure, and figures of speech. The cumulative effect of a work is produced by the resources of language a writer chooses.

- **rhetorical features**

   The tools of rhetoric, such as tone, diction, and imagery.

- **rhetorical structure**

   This phrase refers to how a passage is constructed. If asked to consider rhetorical structure, look at the passage's organization and how the writer combines images, details, or arguments to serve his or her purpose.

- **sentence structure**

   When an essay question asks you to analyze sentence structure, look at the type of sentences the author uses. Remember that the basic sentence structures are simple, compound, and complex and variations created with sentence combining. Also consider variation or lack of it in sentence length, any unusual devices in sentence construction, such as repetition or inverted word order, and any unusual word or phrase placement. As with all devices, be prepared to discuss the effect of the sentence structure. For example, a series of short, simple sentences or phrases can produce a feeling of speed and choppiness, which may suit the author's purpose.

- **stylistic devices**

   An essay question that mentions stylistic devices is asking you to note and analyze all of the elements in language that contribute to style, such as diction, syntax, tone, attitude, figures of speech, connotations, and repetition.

# Part V: Three Full-Length Practice Tests

This section contains three full-length simulated AP English language exams. The practice tests are followed by complete answers, explanations, and analysis of techniques. In addition, two sample essays written by AP students and analysis of the essays are included for each essay topic.

The format, levels of difficulty, question structures, and number of questions are similar to those found on the actual AP language exam. The actual AP exam is copyrighted and may not be duplicated, and these questions are not taken from the actual tests.

When taking these exams, try to simulate the test conditions by following the time allotments carefully. Remember, the total testing time for each practice test is three hours. Be aware of the time allotted for each section.

ANSWER SHEET FOR PRACTICE TEST 1
(Remove This Sheet and Use it to Mark Your Answers)

# SECTION I
## MULTIPLE-CHOICE QUESTIONS

| | | |
|---|---|---|
| 1 Ⓐ Ⓑ Ⓒ Ⓓ Ⓔ | 21 Ⓐ Ⓑ Ⓒ Ⓓ Ⓔ | 41 Ⓐ Ⓑ Ⓒ Ⓓ Ⓔ |
| 2 Ⓐ Ⓑ Ⓒ Ⓓ Ⓔ | 22 Ⓐ Ⓑ Ⓒ Ⓓ Ⓔ | 42 Ⓐ Ⓑ Ⓒ Ⓓ Ⓔ |
| 3 Ⓐ Ⓑ Ⓒ Ⓓ Ⓔ | 23 Ⓐ Ⓑ Ⓒ Ⓓ Ⓔ | 43 Ⓐ Ⓑ Ⓒ Ⓓ Ⓔ |
| 4 Ⓐ Ⓑ Ⓒ Ⓓ Ⓔ | 24 Ⓐ Ⓑ Ⓒ Ⓓ Ⓔ | 44 Ⓐ Ⓑ Ⓒ Ⓓ Ⓔ |
| 5 Ⓐ Ⓑ Ⓒ Ⓓ Ⓔ | 25 Ⓐ Ⓑ Ⓒ Ⓓ Ⓔ | 45 Ⓐ Ⓑ Ⓒ Ⓓ Ⓔ |
| 6 Ⓐ Ⓑ Ⓒ Ⓓ Ⓔ | 26 Ⓐ Ⓑ Ⓒ Ⓓ Ⓔ | 46 Ⓐ Ⓑ Ⓒ Ⓓ Ⓔ |
| 7 Ⓐ Ⓑ Ⓒ Ⓓ Ⓔ | 27 Ⓐ Ⓑ Ⓒ Ⓓ Ⓔ | 47 Ⓐ Ⓑ Ⓒ Ⓓ Ⓔ |
| 8 Ⓐ Ⓑ Ⓒ Ⓓ Ⓔ | 28 Ⓐ Ⓑ Ⓒ Ⓓ Ⓔ | 48 Ⓐ Ⓑ Ⓒ Ⓓ Ⓔ |
| 9 Ⓐ Ⓑ Ⓒ Ⓓ Ⓔ | 29 Ⓐ Ⓑ Ⓒ Ⓓ Ⓔ | 49 Ⓐ Ⓑ Ⓒ Ⓓ Ⓔ |
| 10 Ⓐ Ⓑ Ⓒ Ⓓ Ⓔ | 30 Ⓐ Ⓑ Ⓒ Ⓓ Ⓔ | 50 Ⓐ Ⓑ Ⓒ Ⓓ Ⓔ |
| 11 Ⓐ Ⓑ Ⓒ Ⓓ Ⓔ | 31 Ⓐ Ⓑ Ⓒ Ⓓ Ⓔ | 51 Ⓐ Ⓑ Ⓒ Ⓓ Ⓔ |
| 12 Ⓐ Ⓑ Ⓒ Ⓓ Ⓔ | 32 Ⓐ Ⓑ Ⓒ Ⓓ Ⓔ | 52 Ⓐ Ⓑ Ⓒ Ⓓ Ⓔ |
| 13 Ⓐ Ⓑ Ⓒ Ⓓ Ⓔ | 33 Ⓐ Ⓑ Ⓒ Ⓓ Ⓔ | 53 Ⓐ Ⓑ Ⓒ Ⓓ Ⓔ |
| 14 Ⓐ Ⓑ Ⓒ Ⓓ Ⓔ | 34 Ⓐ Ⓑ Ⓒ Ⓓ Ⓔ | 54 Ⓐ Ⓑ Ⓒ Ⓓ Ⓔ |
| 15 Ⓐ Ⓑ Ⓒ Ⓓ Ⓔ | 35 Ⓐ Ⓑ Ⓒ Ⓓ Ⓔ | 55 Ⓐ Ⓑ Ⓒ Ⓓ Ⓔ |
| 16 Ⓐ Ⓑ Ⓒ Ⓓ Ⓔ | 36 Ⓐ Ⓑ Ⓒ Ⓓ Ⓔ | 56 Ⓐ Ⓑ Ⓒ Ⓓ Ⓔ |
| 17 Ⓐ Ⓑ Ⓒ Ⓓ Ⓔ | 37 Ⓐ Ⓑ Ⓒ Ⓓ Ⓔ | 57 Ⓐ Ⓑ Ⓒ Ⓓ Ⓔ |
| 18 Ⓐ Ⓑ Ⓒ Ⓓ Ⓔ | 38 Ⓐ Ⓑ Ⓒ Ⓓ Ⓔ | |
| 19 Ⓐ Ⓑ Ⓒ Ⓓ Ⓔ | 39 Ⓐ Ⓑ Ⓒ Ⓓ Ⓔ | |
| 20 Ⓐ Ⓑ Ⓒ Ⓓ Ⓔ | 40 Ⓐ Ⓑ Ⓒ Ⓓ Ⓔ | |

CUT HERE

# ANSWER SHEET FOR PRACTICE TEST 2
(Remove This Sheet and Use it to Mark Your Answers)

## SECTION I
## MULTIPLE-CHOICE QUESTIONS

| | | |
|---|---|---|
| 1 Ⓐ Ⓑ Ⓒ Ⓓ Ⓔ | 21 Ⓐ Ⓑ Ⓒ Ⓓ Ⓔ | 41 Ⓐ Ⓑ Ⓒ Ⓓ Ⓔ |
| 2 Ⓐ Ⓑ Ⓒ Ⓓ Ⓔ | 22 Ⓐ Ⓑ Ⓒ Ⓓ Ⓔ | 42 Ⓐ Ⓑ Ⓒ Ⓓ Ⓔ |
| 3 Ⓐ Ⓑ Ⓒ Ⓓ Ⓔ | 23 Ⓐ Ⓑ Ⓒ Ⓓ Ⓔ | 43 Ⓐ Ⓑ Ⓒ Ⓓ Ⓔ |
| 4 Ⓐ Ⓑ Ⓒ Ⓓ Ⓔ | 24 Ⓐ Ⓑ Ⓒ Ⓓ Ⓔ | 44 Ⓐ Ⓑ Ⓒ Ⓓ Ⓔ |
| 5 Ⓐ Ⓑ Ⓒ Ⓓ Ⓔ | 25 Ⓐ Ⓑ Ⓒ Ⓓ Ⓔ | 45 Ⓐ Ⓑ Ⓒ Ⓓ Ⓔ |
| 6 Ⓐ Ⓑ Ⓒ Ⓓ Ⓔ | 26 Ⓐ Ⓑ Ⓒ Ⓓ Ⓔ | 46 Ⓐ Ⓑ Ⓒ Ⓓ Ⓔ |
| 7 Ⓐ Ⓑ Ⓒ Ⓓ Ⓔ | 27 Ⓐ Ⓑ Ⓒ Ⓓ Ⓔ | 47 Ⓐ Ⓑ Ⓒ Ⓓ Ⓔ |
| 8 Ⓐ Ⓑ Ⓒ Ⓓ Ⓔ | 28 Ⓐ Ⓑ Ⓒ Ⓓ Ⓔ | 48 Ⓐ Ⓑ Ⓒ Ⓓ Ⓔ |
| 9 Ⓐ Ⓑ Ⓒ Ⓓ Ⓔ | 29 Ⓐ Ⓑ Ⓒ Ⓓ Ⓔ | 49 Ⓐ Ⓑ Ⓒ Ⓓ Ⓔ |
| 10 Ⓐ Ⓑ Ⓒ Ⓓ Ⓔ | 30 Ⓐ Ⓑ Ⓒ Ⓓ Ⓔ | 50 Ⓐ Ⓑ Ⓒ Ⓓ Ⓔ |
| 11 Ⓐ Ⓑ Ⓒ Ⓓ Ⓔ | 31 Ⓐ Ⓑ Ⓒ Ⓓ Ⓔ | 51 Ⓐ Ⓑ Ⓒ Ⓓ Ⓔ |
| 12 Ⓐ Ⓑ Ⓒ Ⓓ Ⓔ | 32 Ⓐ Ⓑ Ⓒ Ⓓ Ⓔ | 52 Ⓐ Ⓑ Ⓒ Ⓓ Ⓔ |
| 13 Ⓐ Ⓑ Ⓒ Ⓓ Ⓔ | 33 Ⓐ Ⓑ Ⓒ Ⓓ Ⓔ | 53 Ⓐ Ⓑ Ⓒ Ⓓ Ⓔ |
| 14 Ⓐ Ⓑ Ⓒ Ⓓ Ⓔ | 34 Ⓐ Ⓑ Ⓒ Ⓓ Ⓔ | 54 Ⓐ Ⓑ Ⓒ Ⓓ Ⓔ |
| 15 Ⓐ Ⓑ Ⓒ Ⓓ Ⓔ | 35 Ⓐ Ⓑ Ⓒ Ⓓ Ⓔ | 55 Ⓐ Ⓑ Ⓒ Ⓓ Ⓔ |
| 16 Ⓐ Ⓑ Ⓒ Ⓓ Ⓔ | 36 Ⓐ Ⓑ Ⓒ Ⓓ Ⓔ | 56 Ⓐ Ⓑ Ⓒ Ⓓ Ⓔ |
| 17 Ⓐ Ⓑ Ⓒ Ⓓ Ⓔ | 37 Ⓐ Ⓑ Ⓒ Ⓓ Ⓔ | |
| 18 Ⓐ Ⓑ Ⓒ Ⓓ Ⓔ | 38 Ⓐ Ⓑ Ⓒ Ⓓ Ⓔ | |
| 19 Ⓐ Ⓑ Ⓒ Ⓓ Ⓔ | 39 Ⓐ Ⓑ Ⓒ Ⓓ Ⓔ | |
| 20 Ⓐ Ⓑ Ⓒ Ⓓ Ⓔ | 40 Ⓐ Ⓑ Ⓒ Ⓓ Ⓔ | |

CUT HERE

99

ANSWER SHEET FOR PRACTICE TEST 3
(Remove This Sheet and Use it to Mark Your Answers)

## SECTION I
## MULTIPLE-CHOICE QUESTIONS

1 Ⓐ Ⓑ Ⓒ Ⓓ Ⓔ
2 Ⓐ Ⓑ Ⓒ Ⓓ Ⓔ
3 Ⓐ Ⓑ Ⓒ Ⓓ Ⓔ
4 Ⓐ Ⓑ Ⓒ Ⓓ Ⓔ
5 Ⓐ Ⓑ Ⓒ Ⓓ Ⓔ

6 Ⓐ Ⓑ Ⓒ Ⓓ Ⓔ
7 Ⓐ Ⓑ Ⓒ Ⓓ Ⓔ
8 Ⓐ Ⓑ Ⓒ Ⓓ Ⓔ
9 Ⓐ Ⓑ Ⓒ Ⓓ Ⓔ
10 Ⓐ Ⓑ Ⓒ Ⓓ Ⓔ

11 Ⓐ Ⓑ Ⓒ Ⓓ Ⓔ
12 Ⓐ Ⓑ Ⓒ Ⓓ Ⓔ
13 Ⓐ Ⓑ Ⓒ Ⓓ Ⓔ
14 Ⓐ Ⓑ Ⓒ Ⓓ Ⓔ
15 Ⓐ Ⓑ Ⓒ Ⓓ Ⓔ

16 Ⓐ Ⓑ Ⓒ Ⓓ Ⓔ
17 Ⓐ Ⓑ Ⓒ Ⓓ Ⓔ
18 Ⓐ Ⓑ Ⓒ Ⓓ Ⓔ
19 Ⓐ Ⓑ Ⓒ Ⓓ Ⓔ
20 Ⓐ Ⓑ Ⓒ Ⓓ Ⓔ

21 Ⓐ Ⓑ Ⓒ Ⓓ Ⓔ
22 Ⓐ Ⓑ Ⓒ Ⓓ Ⓔ
23 Ⓐ Ⓑ Ⓒ Ⓓ Ⓔ
24 Ⓐ Ⓑ Ⓒ Ⓓ Ⓔ
25 Ⓐ Ⓑ Ⓒ Ⓓ Ⓔ

26 Ⓐ Ⓑ Ⓒ Ⓓ Ⓔ
27 Ⓐ Ⓑ Ⓒ Ⓓ Ⓔ
28 Ⓐ Ⓑ Ⓒ Ⓓ Ⓔ
29 Ⓐ Ⓑ Ⓒ Ⓓ Ⓔ
30 Ⓐ Ⓑ Ⓒ Ⓓ Ⓔ

31 Ⓐ Ⓑ Ⓒ Ⓓ Ⓔ
32 Ⓐ Ⓑ Ⓒ Ⓓ Ⓔ
33 Ⓐ Ⓑ Ⓒ Ⓓ Ⓔ
34 Ⓐ Ⓑ Ⓒ Ⓓ Ⓔ
35 Ⓐ Ⓑ Ⓒ Ⓓ Ⓔ

36 Ⓐ Ⓑ Ⓒ Ⓓ Ⓔ
37 Ⓐ Ⓑ Ⓒ Ⓓ Ⓔ
38 Ⓐ Ⓑ Ⓒ Ⓓ Ⓔ
39 Ⓐ Ⓑ Ⓒ Ⓓ Ⓔ
40 Ⓐ Ⓑ Ⓒ Ⓓ Ⓔ

41 Ⓐ Ⓑ Ⓒ Ⓓ Ⓔ
42 Ⓐ Ⓑ Ⓒ Ⓓ Ⓔ
43 Ⓐ Ⓑ Ⓒ Ⓓ Ⓔ
44 Ⓐ Ⓑ Ⓒ Ⓓ Ⓔ
45 Ⓐ Ⓑ Ⓒ Ⓓ Ⓔ

46 Ⓐ Ⓑ Ⓒ Ⓓ Ⓔ
47 Ⓐ Ⓑ Ⓒ Ⓓ Ⓔ
48 Ⓐ Ⓑ Ⓒ Ⓓ Ⓔ
49 Ⓐ Ⓑ Ⓒ Ⓓ Ⓔ
50 Ⓐ Ⓑ Ⓒ Ⓓ Ⓔ

51 Ⓐ Ⓑ Ⓒ Ⓓ Ⓔ
52 Ⓐ Ⓑ Ⓒ Ⓓ Ⓔ
53 Ⓐ Ⓑ Ⓒ Ⓓ Ⓔ
54 Ⓐ Ⓑ Ⓒ Ⓓ Ⓔ
55 Ⓐ Ⓑ Ⓒ Ⓓ Ⓔ

56 Ⓐ Ⓑ Ⓒ Ⓓ Ⓔ

# PRACTICE TEST 1

## SECTION I: MULTIPLE-CHOICE QUESTIONS

**Time: 60 Minutes**
**57 Questions**

This section consists of selections from prose works and questions on their content, style, and form. Read each selection carefully. Choose the best answer of the five choices.

*Questions 1–14.* Read the following passage carefully before you begin to answer the questions.

The written word is weak. Many people prefer life to it. Life gets your blood going, and it smells good. Writing is mere writing, literature is mere. It appeals only to the subtlest senses—the imagination's vision, and the imagina-
(5) tion's hearing—and the moral sense, and the intellect. This writing that you do, that so thrills you, that so rocks and exhilarates you, as if you were dancing next to the band, is barely audible to anyone else. The reader's ear must adjust down from loud life to the subtle, imaginary sounds of the
(10) written word. An ordinary reader picking up a book can't yet hear a thing; it will take half an hour to pick up the writing's modulations, its ups and downs and louds and softs.
　　An intriguing entomological experiment shows that a
(15) male butterfly will ignore a living female butterfly of his own species in favor of a painted cardboard one, if the cardboard one is big. If the cardboard one is bigger than he is, bigger than any female butterfly ever could be. He jumps the piece of cardboard. Over and over again, he jumps the piece of
(20) cardboard. Nearby, the real, living female butterfly opens and closes her wings in vain.
　　Films and television stimulate the body's senses too, in big ways. A nine-foot handsome face, and its three-foot-wide

smile, are irresistible. Look at the long legs on that man, as
(25) high as a wall, and coming straight toward you. The music
builds. The moving, lighted screen fills your brain. You do
not like filmed car chases? See if you can turn away. Try not
to watch. Even knowing you are manipulated, you are still as
helpless as the male butterfly drawn to painted cardboard.
(30)    That is the movies. That is their ground. The printed word
cannot compete with the movies on their ground, and
should not. You can describe beautiful faces, car chases, or
valleys full of Indians on horseback until you run out of
words, and you will not approach the movies' spectacle.
(35) Novels written with film contracts in mind have a faint but
unmistakable, and ruinous, odor. I cannot name what, in the
text, alerts the reader to suspect the writer of mixed
motives; I cannot specify which sentences, in several books,
have caused me to read on with increasing dismay, and
(40) finally close the books because I smelled a rat. Such books
seem uneasy being books; they seem eager to fling off their
disguises and jump onto screens.
    Why would anyone read a book instead of watching big
people move on a screen? Because a book can be literature.
(45) It is a subtle thing—a poor thing, but our own. In my view,
the more literary the book—the more purely verbal, crafted
sentence by sentence, the more imaginative, reasoned, and
deep—the more likely people are to read it. The people who
read are the people who like literature, after all, whatever
(50) that might be. They like, or require, what books alone have.
If they want to see films that evening, they will find films. If
they do not like to read, they will not. People who read are
not too lazy to flip on the television; they prefer books. I
cannot imagine a sorrier pursuit than struggling for years to
(55) write a book that attempts to appeal to people who do not
read in the first place.

1. Which of the following terms can be used to describe the imagery of the last sentence in the first paragraph ("An ordinary . . . and softs")?

   I. Simile
  II. Metaphor
 III. Synesthetic

  (A) I only
  (B) II only
  (C) I and III only
  (D) II and III only
  (E) I, II, and III

2. In the second paragraph of the passage, the author employs
  (A) a concession to an opposing point of view
  (B) a cause and effect relationship
  (C) a simile
  (D) a metaphor
  (E) an extended definition

3. Which of the following best describes how the second and third paragraphs are related?
  (A) The second paragraph makes an assertion that is qualified by the third paragraph.
  (B) The second paragraph asks a question that is answered by the third paragraph.
  (C) The second paragraph describes a situation that is paralleled in the third paragraph.
  (D) The second paragraph presents as factual what the third paragraph presents as only a possibility.
  (E) There is no clear relationship between the two paragraphs.

4. The "nine-foot handsome face" (line 23) refers to
  (A) the female butterfly
  (B) literary creativity
  (C) a television image
  (D) an image in the movies
  (E) how the imagination of a reader may see a face

5. In the fourth paragraph, the author argues that

   I. action scenes are better in films than in books
   II. novels written with an eye on future film adaptation stink
   III. novels specifically written to be adapted into films do not make superior films

(A) II only
(B) I and II only
(C) I and III only
(D) II and III only
(E) I, II, and III

6. The last sentence of the fourth paragraph ("Such books . . . onto screens") contains an example of
(A) personification
(B) understatement
(C) irony
(D) simile
(E) syllogism

7. According to the passage, literature is likely to be characterized by all of the following EXCEPT
(A) colloquial language
(B) imagination
(C) verbal skill
(D) moral sense
(E) intelligence

8. In the last sentence of the last paragaraph, the phrase "sorrier pursuit" can be best understood to mean
(A) more regretful chase
(B) poorer occupation
(C) more sympathetic profession
(D) sadder expectation
(E) more pitiful striving

9. In the last paragraph, the phrase "a poor thing, but our own" is adapted from Shakespeare's "a poor . . . thing, sir, but mine own." The change from the singular to the plural pronoun is made in order to
   (A) avoid the use of the first person
   (B) include all readers of this passage who prefer literature
   (C) avoid direct quotation of Shakespeare and the appearance of comparing this work to his
   (D) suggest that the number of readers is as great as the number of moviegoers
   (E) avoid overpraising literature compared to films, which are more popular

10. The sentences "The written word is weak" (line 1), "An ordinary reader . . . a thing" (lines 10–11), and "The printed word . . . should not" (lines 30–32) have in common that they
   (A) concede a limitation of the written word
   (B) assert the superiority of film to writing
   (C) do not represent the genuine feelings of the author
   (D) deliberately overstate the author's ideas
   (E) are all ironic

11. With which of the following statements would the author of this passage be most likely to disagree?
   (A) Life is more exciting than writing.
   (B) People who dislike reading should not be forced to read.
   (C) Good books will appeal to those who do not like to read as well as to those who do.
   (D) The power of film is irresistible.
   (E) Novels written for people who hate reading are folly.

12. The passage in its entirety is best described as about the
   (A) superiority of the art of writing to the art of film
   (B) difficulties of being a writer
   (C) differences between writing and film
   (D) public's preference of film to literature
   (E) similarities and differences of the novel and the film

13. Which of the following best describes the organization of the passage?

   (A) A five-paragraph essay in which the first and last paragraphs are general and the second, third, and fourth paragraphs are specific

   (B) A five paragraph essay in which the first two paragraphs describe writing, the third and fourth paragraphs describe film, and the last paragraph describes both writing and film

   (C) Five paragraphs with the first about literature, the second about butterflies, and the third, fourth, and fifth about the superiority of film

   (D) Five paragraphs with the first and last about writing, the third about film, and the fourth about both film and writing

   (E) Five paragraphs of comparison and contrast, with the comparison in the first and last paragraphs and the contrast in the second, third, and fourth

14. All of the following rhetorical features appear in the passage EXCEPT

   (A) personal anecdote
   (B) extended analogy
   (C) short sentence
   (D) colloquialism
   (E) irony

*Questions 15–28.* Read the following passage carefully before you begin to answer the questions.

These are the times that try men's souls. The summer soldier and the sunshine patriot will, in this crisis, shrink from the service of their country; but he that stands it now deserves the love and thanks of man and woman. Tyranny,
(5) like hell, is not easily conquered; yet we have this consolation with us, that the harder the conflict, the more glorious the triumph. What we obtain too cheap, we esteem too lightly: it is dearness only that gives everything its value. Heaven knows how to put a proper price upon its goods; and
(10) it would be strange indeed if so celestial an article as

freedom should not be highly rated. Britain, with an army to enforce her tyranny, has declared that she has a right not only to tax, but "to bind us in all cases whatsoever," and if being bound in that manner is not slavery, then is there not

(15) such a thing as slavery upon earth. Even the expression is impious; for so unlimited a power can belong only to God....

I have as little superstition in me as any man living, but my secret opinion has ever been, and still is, that God Almighty

(20) will not give up a people to military destruction, or leave them unsupportedly to perish, who have so earnestly and so repeatedly sought to avoid the calamities of war, by every decent method which wisdom could invent. Neither have I so much of the infidel in me as to suppose that He has

(25) relinquished the government of the world, and given us up to the care of devils; and as I do not, I cannot see on what grounds the King of Britain can look up to heaven for help against us: a common murderer, a highwayman, or a housebreaker has as good a pretense as he....

(30)    I once felt all that kind of anger, which a man ought to feel, against the mean principles that are held by the tories: a noted one, who kept a tavern at Amboy, was standing at his door, with as pretty a child in his hand, about eight or nine years old, as I ever saw, and after speaking his mind as

(35) freely as he thought was prudent, finished with this unfatherly expression, "Well! give me peace in my day." Not a man lives on the continent but fully believes that a separation must some time or other finally take place, and a generous parent should have said, "If there must be trouble,

(40) let it be in my day, that my children may have peace"; and this single reflection, well applied, is sufficient to awaken every man to duty. Not a place upon earth might be so happy as America. Her situation is remote from all the wrangling world, and she has nothing to do but to trade with

(45) them. A man can distinguish himself between temper and principle, and I am as confident, as I am that God governs the world, that America will never be happy till she gets clear of foreign dominion. Wars, without ceasing, will break out till that period arrives, and the continent must in the end

(50) be conqueror; for though the flame of liberty may sometimes cease to shine, the coal can never expire. . . .
The heart that feels not now is dead: the blood of his
children will curse his cowardice who shrinks back at a time
when a little might have saved the whole, and made them
(55) happy. I love the man that can smile in trouble, that can
gather strength from distress, and grow brave by reflection.
'Tis the business of little minds to shrink; but he whose heart
is firm, and whose conscience approves his conduct, will
pursue his principles unto death. My own line of reasoning
(60) is to myself as straight and clear as a ray of light. Not all the
treasures of the world, so far as I believe, could have
induced me to support an offensive war, for I think it
murder; but if a thief breaks into my house, burns and
destroys my property, and kills or threatens to kill me, or
(65) those that are in it, and to "bind me in all cases whatsoever"
to his absolute will, am I to suffer it? What signifies it to me,
whether he who does it is a king or a common man; my
countryman or not my countryman; whether it be done by an
individual villain, or an army of them? If we reason to the
(70) root of things we shall find no difference; neither can any
just cause be assigned why we should punish in the one case
and pardon in the other.

15. The essay appears to be addressed to
    (A) the British government
    (B) British citizens
    (C) Americans
    (D) the American government
    (E) all oppressed people

16. When the author addresses the "summer soldier and the
    sunshine patriot," he is most likely referring to
    (A) the American army's reserve soldiers
    (B) those citizens who are infidels
    (C) the British soldiers stationed in America
    (D) those who support the revolution only when convenient
    (E) the government's specialized forces

17. The author's style relies on heavy use of
    (A) allegory and didactic rhetoric
    (B) aphorism and emotional appeal
    (C) symbolism and biblical allusion
    (D) paradox and invective
    (E) historical background and illustration

18. Which of the following does the author NOT group with the others?
    (A) Common murderer
    (B) Highwayman
    (C) Housebreaker
    (D) King
    (E) Coward

19. The "God" that the author refers to can be characterized as
    (A) principled
    (B) vexed
    (C) indifferent
    (D) contemplative
    (E) pernicious

20. Which of the following rhetorical devices is NOT one of the author's tools?
    (A) Anecdote
    (B) Simile
    (C) Aphorism
    (D) Understatement
    (E) Symbolism

21. According to the author, freedom should be considered
    (A) that which will vanquish cowards
    (B) one of the most valuable commodities in heaven
    (C) that which can be achieved quickly
    (D) desirable but never attainable
    (E) an issue only governments should negotiate

22. The author's purpose in using the phrase "with as pretty a child
. . . as I ever saw" (lines 33–34) is most likely to
(A) prove that the tavern owner has a family
(B) display his anger
(C) add emotional appeal to his argument
(D) symbolically increase the tavern owner's evil
(E) dismiss traditional values

23. Which of the following would NOT be considered an aphorism?
(A) "Tyranny, like hell, is not easily conquered" (lines 4–5)
(B) "the harder the conflict, the more glorious the triumph"
(lines 6–7)
(C) "What we obtain too cheap, we esteem too lightly" (lines
7–8)
(D) "Not a place upon earth might be so happy as America."
(lines 42–43)
(E) "though the flame of liberty may sometimes cease to shine,
the coal can never expire" (lines 50–51)

24. As seen in lines 42–51, the author feels that, in an ideal world,
America's role in relation to the rest of the world would be
(A) only one of commerce
(B) one of aggressive self-assertion
(C) more exalted than Britain's
(D) sanctified by God
(E) one of complete isolationism

25. The rhetorical mode that the author uses can best be classified
as
(A) explanation
(B) description
(C) narration
(D) illustration
(E) persuasion

26. Which of the following best describes the author's purpose in the sentence "The heart that feels not now is dead . . ." (lines 52–55)?
    (A) To suggest that children should also join the revolution
    (B) To plant fear in people's hearts
    (C) To plead to the king once again for liberty
    (D) To encourage retreat in the face of superior force
    (E) To encourage support by an emotional appeal to all men

27. All of the following rhetorical devices are particularly effective in the last paragraph of the essay EXCEPT
    (A) aphorism
    (B) simile
    (C) deliberate ambivalence
    (D) parallel construction
    (E) analogy

28. The author's main purpose in the essay can best be described as
    (A) a summons for peace and rational thinking
    (B) overemotional preaching for equality
    (C) a series of unwarranted conclusions
    (D) a patriotic call to duty and action
    (E) a demand for immediate liberty

*Questions 29–43.* Read the following passage carefully before you begin to answer the questions.

It was a hazy sunrise in August. . . . The sun, on account of the mist, had a curious sentient, personal look, demanding the masculine pronoun for its adequate expression. His present aspect, coupled with the lack of all human forms in
(5) the scene, explained the old-time heliolatries in a moment. . . . The luminary was a golden-haired, beaming, mild-eyed, God-like creature, gazing down in the vigour and intentness of youth. . . .
     His light, a little later, broke through chinks of cottage
(10) shutters, throwing stripes like red-hot pokers upon cup-

boards, chests of drawers, and other furniture within; and awakening harvesters who were not already astir.

But of all ruddy things that morning the brightest were two broad arms of painted wood, which rose from the
(15) margin of a yellow cornfield hard by Marlott village. They, with two others below, formed the revolving Maltese cross of the reaping-machine, which had been brought to the field on the previous evening to be ready for operations this day. The paint with which they were smeared, intensified in hue
(20) by the sunlight, imparted to them a look of having been dipped in liquid fire. . . .

Two groups, one of men and lads, the other of women, had come down the lane just at the hour when the shadows of the eastern hedge-top struck the west hedge midway, so
(25) that the heads of the groups were enjoying sunrise while their feet were still in the dawn. . . .

Presently there arose from within a ticking like the lovemaking of the grasshopper. The machine had begun, and a moving concatenation of three horses and the
(30) aforesaid long rickety machine was visible over the gate, a driver sitting upon one of the hauling horses, and an attendant on the seat of the implement. Along one side of the field the whole wain went, the arms of the mechanical reaper revolving slowly, till it passed down the hill quite out
(35) of sight. In a minute it came up on the other side of the field at the same equable pace; the glistening brass star in the forehead of the fore horse first catching the eye as it rose into view over the stubble, then the bright arms, and then the whole machine.

(40)    The narrow lane of stubble encompassing the field grew wider with each circuit, and the standing corn was reduced to smaller area as the morning wore on. Rabbits, hares, snakes, rats, mice, retreated inwards as into a fastness, unaware of the ephemeral nature of their refuge, and of the
(45) doom that awaited them later in the day when, their covert shrinking to a more and more horrible narrowness, they were huddled together, friends and foes, till the last few yards of upright wheat fell also under the teeth of the

unerring reaper, and they were every one put to death by
(50) the sticks and stones of the harvesters.

The reaping-machine left the fallen corn behind it in little
heaps, . . . and upon these the active binders in the rear laid
their hands—mainly women, but some of them men in print
shirts, and trousers supported round their waists by leather
(55) straps, rendering useless the two buttons behind, which
twinkled and bristled with sunbeams at every movement of
each wearer, as if they were a pair of eyes in the small of his
back.

But those of the other sex were the most interesting of
(60) this company of binders, by reason of the charm which is
acquired by woman when she becomes part and parcel of
outdoor nature, and is not merely an object set down therein
as at ordinary times. A field-man is a personality afield; a
field-woman is a portion of the field; she has somehow lost
(65) her own margin, imbibed the essence of her surrounding,
and assimilated herself with it. . . .

There was one wearing a pale pink jacket, another in a
cream-coloured tight-sleeved gown, another in a petticoat
as red as the arms of the reaping-machine. . . . This morning
(70) the eye returns involuntarily to the girl in the pink cotton
jacket, she being the most flexuous and finely-drawn figure
of them all. But her bonnet is pulled so far over her brow
that none of her face is disclosed while she binds, though
her complexion may be guessed from a stray twine or two of
(75) dark brown hair which extends below the curtain of her
bonnet. Perhaps one reason why she seduces casual attention is that she never courts it, though the other women
often gaze around them.

At intervals she stands up to rest, and to retie her
(80) disarranged apron, or to pull her bonnet straight. Then one
can see the oval face of a handsome young woman with deep
dark eyes and long heavy clinging tresses, which seem to
clasp in a beseeching way anything they fall against. The
cheeks are paler, the teeth more regular, the red lips thinner
(85) than is usual in a country-bred girl.

29. In describing the sun, (lines 1–8) the author most frequently employs which of the following rhetorical devices?
    (A) Apostrophe
    (B) Personification
    (C) Onomatopoeia
    (D) Paradox
    (E) Parallel clauses

30. Of the following, which best illustrates the time that passes in the passage?
    (A) "The luminary was a golden-haired, beaming, mild-eyed, God-like creature" (lines 6–7)
    (B) "His light . . . broke through chinks of cottage shutters" (lines 9–10)
    (C) "awakening harvesters who were not already astir" (line 12)
    (D) "which rose from the margin of a yellow cornfield" (lines 14–15)
    (E) "the heads of the groups were enjoying sunrise while their feet were still in the dawn." (lines 25–26)

31. In lines 27–50, the steady movement of the reaping-machine as it cuts the wheat and reduces the animals' territory serves to reinforce the
    (A) positive aspects of technological progress
    (B) politicalization of pastoral areas
    (C) relentless momentum of industrialization
    (D) alacrity with which the task can be completed
    (E) comparison between the machine and the sun's movement

32. From the author's description of the "unerring reaper" in the sixth paragraph (lines 40–50), the machine can best be characterized as
    (A) a genuine improvement for humans
    (B) a benevolent companion to humans
    (C) a high-technology device run astray
    (D) an inevitable aspect of the future
    (E) a menacing destroyer of natural habitats

33. The effect of moving from a description of the sun to a description of the reaping-machine is to
    (A) diminish the power of the sun
    (B) connect the sun to something human
    (C) emphasize the lifelike quality of both objects
    (D) suggest the power of the machine
    (E) comment on the negative aspects of the two

34. Which of the following best explains the author's purpose in describing the animals of the field?
    (A) To demonstrate the effect of industrialization on nature
    (B) To illustrate the ruthlessness of the humans who kill them
    (C) To satirize the animals' flight from the terrifying machine
    (D) To suggest the senselessness of animals' deaths
    (E) To reduce any sympathy the reader may have for the animals

35. In context, "the ephemeral nature of their refuge" (line 44) most probably means the
    (A) sturdiness of their burrows
    (B) universality of their fear
    (C) human-like quality of their thoughts
    (D) animal instinct common to all creatures
    (E) transitory character of their environment

36. The description of the two buttons on the men's trousers has the effect of
    (A) metaphorical seriousness
    (B) humorous visual appeal
    (C) symbolizing the men's self-consciousness around women
    (D) superfluous detail
    (E) ironic hyperbole

37. According to the passage, the women and men in the field differ from each other because
    (A) the men take more care with their work
    (B) society's attitude inadvertently inhibits the women's productivity
    (C) it is one place where the women can excel over men
    (D) the women become a component of the field
    (E) the women's individual personalities become stronger

38. It can be inferred that the beauty of the girl in the pink jacket
    (A) is flaunted by means of her clothing
    (B) is impossible to detect
    (C) draws unsolicited attention
    (D) reveals her aristocratic background
    (E) is harmonious with nature

39. Which of the following best describes the tone of the passage?
    (A) Engrossed
    (B) Condescending
    (C) Optimistic
    (D) Ironic
    (E) Cavalier

40. It can be inferred from the passage that the girl in the pink jacket is
    (A) popular with the locals
    (B) flirtatious with the field-men
    (C) overwhelmingly attractive
    (D) more reserved than her coworkers
    (E) older than most of the other girls

41. The author's main purpose in describing the girl in the pink jacket is to
    (A) demonstrate her kinship to others
    (B) reveal how dissimilar she is to the other villagers
    (C) concentrate on her composure and dignity
    (D) contrast her sophistication with the others' naiveté
    (E) explain what a nonconformist she is

42. Which of the following rhetorical devices is NOT present in the essay?
    (A) Parallelism
    (B) Allegory
    (C) Personification
    (D) Allusion
    (E) Simile

43. The structure of the passage can be described as
    (A) becoming increasingly more abstract paragraph by paragraph
    (B) comparing and contrasting animals to humans while providing commentary about humanity
    (C) giving specifics to support generalizations about the Industrial Revolution
    (D) illustrating the same scene from differing points of view
    (E) moving from a visual overview of the village down to specific people

*Questions 44–57.* Read the following passage carefully before you begin to answer the questions.

Studies serve for delight, for ornament, and for ability. Their chief use for delight is in privateness and retiring; for ornament, is in discourse; and for ability, is in the judgment and disposition of business; for expert men can execute, and
(5) perhaps judge of particulars, one by one; but the general counsels, and the plots and marshaling of affairs come best from those that are learned. To spend too much time in studies is sloth; to use them too much for ornament is affectation; to make judgment wholly by their rules is the
(10) humor of a scholar. They perfect nature, and are perfected by experience; for natural abilities are like natural plants, that need pruning by study; and studies themselves do give forth directions too much at large, except they be bounded in by experience. Crafty men condemn studies, simple men
(15) admire them, and wise men use them; for they teach not their own use; but that is a wisdom without them and above

them, won by observation. Read not to contradict and
confute, nor to believe and take for granted, nor to find talk
and discourse, but to weigh and consider. Some books are to
(20) be tasted, others to be swallowed, and some few to be
chewed and digested; that is, some books are to be read only
in parts; others to be read but not curiously; and some few to
be read wholly, and with diligence and attention. Some
books also may be read by deputy, and extracts made of
(25) them by others; but that would be only in the less important
arguments and the meaner sort of books; else distilled
books are, like common distilled water, flashy things.
Reading maketh a full man; conference a ready man; and
writing an exact man. And therefore, if a man write little, he
(30) had need have a great memory; if he confer little, he had
need have a present wit; and if he read little, he had need
have much cunning, to seem to know that he doth not.
Histories make men wise; poets, witty; the mathematics,
subtle; natural philosophy, deep; moral, grave; logic and
(35) rhetoric, able to contend: *Abeunt studia in mores!*[1] Nay,
there is no stand or impediment in the wit but may be
wrought out by fit studies; like as diseases of the body may
have appropriate exercises. Bowling is good for the stone
and reins, shooting for the lungs and breast, gentle walking
(40) for the stomach, riding for the head, and the like. So if a
man's wit be wandering, let him study the mathematics; for
in demonstrations, if his wit be called away never so little, he
must begin again. If his wit be not apt to distinguish or find
differences, let him study the schoolmen; for they are *cymini*
(45) *sectores!*[2] If he be not apt to beat over matters, and to call up
one thing to prove and illustrate another, let him study the
lawyers' cases. So every defect of the mind may have a
special receipt.

[1]"Studies form character." Ovid
[2]Literally, "cutters of cumin seed," or hair splitters

44. The audience that might benefit the most from the author's ideas is likely to be those who
   (A) have returned to university study
   (B) think studies are unnecessary
   (C) are poor readers
   (D) already have university degrees
   (E) are successful in business

45. The word "humor," (line 10) can be best defined as
   (A) mirth
   (B) benefit
   (C) excuse
   (D) aspiration
   (E) temperament

46. According to the passage, reading is beneficial when supplemented by
   (A) academic necessity
   (B) literary criticism
   (C) personal experience
   (D) brief discussion
   (E) historical background

47. A prominent stylistic characteristic of the sentence "Read not to . . . weigh and consider" (lines 17–19) is
   (A) understatement
   (B) metaphor
   (C) hyperbole
   (D) parallel construction
   (E) analogy

48. The sentence "They perfect nature . . . by experience" (lines 10–14) most probably means that
    (A) professors should emphasize reading over personal experience
    (B) the message in some books is too complex to be understood by the common person
    (C) the ideas in books are readily accessible to one who reads widely
    (D) people misspend valuable time in the pursuit of evasive knowledge
    (E) that everything one learns in books cannot necessarily be applied directly to real-life situations

49. In context, the word "observation" (line 17) is analogous to
    (A) "experience" (line 11)
    (B) "directions" (line 13)
    (C) "studies" (line 14)
    (D) "wisdom" (line 16)
    (E) "believe" (line 18)

50. According to the passage, which of the following are reasonable uses for one's studies?

    I. For private enjoyment
    II. For intelligent conversation
    III. For sound judgment

    (A) I only
    (B) II only
    (C) III only
    (D) II and III only
    (E) I, II, and III

51. What paradox about studies does the author present?
    (A) Crafty men may be tempted to ignore studies.
    (B) Those who are too consumed by studies become indolent.
    (C) Some books can never be completely understood.
    (D) Not all books are approached the same way.
    (E) Some "defects of the mind" can never be remedied.

52. Which of the following does the author imply is the greatest error a reader can commit?
   (A) Reading voraciously
   (B) Reading only excerpts
   (C) Reading only what professors recommend
   (D) Reading without thinking
   (E) Reading only for pleasure

53. Which of the following phrases may be seen as rhetorically similar to "Some books are to be tasted . . . chewed and digested" (lines 19–21)?

   I. "natural abilities . . . need pruning by study" (lines 11–12)
   II. "Some books also may be read . . . by others" (lines 23–25)
   III. "like as diseases . . . have appropriate exercises" (lines 37–38)

   (A) I only
   (B) II only
   (C) II and III only
   (D) I and III only
   (E) I, II, and III

54. In context, the phrase "not curiously" (line 22) means
   (A) with questions in mind
   (B) with great interest
   (C) without much scrutiny
   (D) without strong background
   (E) with personal interpretation

55. Stylistically, the sentence "Reading maketh a full man . . . writing an exact man" (lines 28–29) is closest in structure to
   (A) "To spend too much time . . . the humor of a scholar." (lines 7–10)
   (B) "They perfect nature, and are perfected by experience . . . bounded in by experience." (lines 10–14)
   (C) "Some books also may be read by deputy . . . flashy things." (lines 23–27)
   (D) "Nay, there is no stand or impediment . . . exercises." (lines 35–38)
   (E) "So if a man's wit be wandering . . . begin again." (lines 40–43)

56. The word "wit," as it is used in line 41, can be interpreted to mean
    (A) wisdom, intuition
    (B) mind, intelligence
    (C) humor, caprice
    (D) opinion, sentiment
    (E) geniality, jocundity

57. Which of the following ideas is contradicted in the essay?
    (A) Specific ailments have specific cures.
    (B) Reading should be adjusted to suit one's purpose.
    (C) An educated man makes sound business decisions.
    (D) All books should be read in the same manner.
    (E) Excessive studying can be counterproductive.

**STOP.** IF YOU FINISH BEFORE TIME IS CALLED, CHECK YOUR WORK ON THIS SECTION ONLY. DO NOT WORK ON SECTION II.

# SECTION II: ESSAY QUESTIONS

**Time: 2 Hours**
**3 Questions**

## Question 1

(Suggested time—40 minutes. This question counts one-third of the total essay section score.)

In the following two passages, Virginia Woolf describes two different meals that she was served during a university visit; the first meal was served at the men's college, while the second meal was served at the women's college. Read the two passages carefully; then write an essay in which you analyze Woolf's underlying attitude toward women's place in society as she describes the two meals. Discuss how such elements as narrative structure, manipulation of language, selection of detail, and tone contribute to the effect of the passage.

### I

It is a curious fact that novelists have a way of making us believe that luncheon parties are invariably memorable for something very witty that was said, or for something very wise that was done. But they seldom spare a word for what
(5) was eaten. It is part of the novelist's convention not to mention soup and salmon and ducklings, as if soup and salmon and ducklings were of no importance whatsoever, as if nobody ever smoked a cigar or drank a glass of wine. Here, however, I shall take the liberty to defy that conven-
(10) tion and to tell you that the lunch on this occasion began with soles, sunk in a deep dish, over which the college cook had spread a counterpane of the whitest cream, save that it was branded here and there with brown spots like the spots on the flanks of a doe. After that came the partridges, but if
(15) this suggests a couple of bald, brown birds on a plate you are mistaken. The partridges, many and various, came with all their retinue of sauces and salads, the sharp and the sweet, each in its order; their potatoes, thin as coins but not so

hard; their sprouts, foliated as rosebuds but more succulent.
(20) And no sooner had the roast and its retinue been done with
than the silent serving-man, the Beadle himself perhaps in a
milder manifestation, set before us, wreathed in napkins, a
confection which rose all sugar from the waves. To call it
pudding and so relate it to rice and tapioca would be an
(25) insult. Meanwhile the wineglasses had flushed yellow and
flushed crimson; had been emptied; had been filled. And
thus by degrees was lit, halfway down the spine, which is the
seat of the soul, not that hard little electric light which we
call brilliance, as it pops in and out upon our lips, but the
(30) more profound, subtle and subterranean glow, which is the
rich yellow flame of rational intercourse. No need to hurry.
No need to sparkle. No need to be anybody but oneself. We
are all going to heaven . . . in other words, how good life
seemed, how sweet its rewards, how trivial this grudge or
(35) that grievance, how admirable friendship and the society of
one's kind, as, lighting a good cigarette, one sunk among the
cushions in the window-seat.

## II

Here was my soup. Dinner was being served in the great
dining-hall. Far from being spring it was in fact an evening
(40) in October. Everybody was assembled in the big dining-
room. Dinner was ready. Here was the soup. It was a plain
gravy soup. There was nothing to stir the fancy in that. One
could have seen through the transparent liquid any pattern
that there might have been on the plate itself. But there was
(45) no pattern. The plate was plain. Next came beef with its
attendant greens and potatoes—a homely trinity, suggesting
the rumps of cattle in a muddy market, and sprouts curled
and yellowed at the edge, and bargaining and cheapening,
and women with string bags on Monday morning. There was
(50) no reason to complain of human nature's daily food, seeing
that the supply was sufficient and coal-miners doubtless
were sitting down to less. Prunes and custard followed. And
if any one complains that prunes, even when mitigated by
custard, are an uncharitable vegetable (fruit they are not),

(55)  stringy as a miser's heart and exuding a fluid such as might run in misers' veins who have denied themselves wine and warmth for eighty years and yet not given to the poor, he should reflect that there are people whose charity embraces even the prune. Biscuits and cheese came next, and here the

(60)  water-jug was liberally passed round, for it is the nature of biscuits to be dry, and these were biscuits to the core. That was all. The meal was over. Everybody scraped their chairs back; the swing-doors swung violently to and fro; soon the hall was emptied of every sign of food and made ready no

(65)  doubt for breakfast next morning.

## Question 2

(Suggested time—40 minutes. This question counts one-third of the total essay section score.)

Read the following excerpt from Ralph Waldo Emerson's speech "The American Scholar," which was delivered at Cambridge on August 31, 1837. Then write a well-reasoned essay that defends, challenges, or qualifies Emerson's ideas about books and their usefulness. Use evidence from your own experience, reading, or observation to develop your essay.

The theory of books is noble. The scholar of the first age received into him the world around; brooded thereon; gave it the new arrangement of his own mind, and uttered it again. It came into him—life; it went out from him—truth.
(5) It came to him—short-lived actions; it went out from him—immortal thoughts. It came to him—business; it went from him—poetry. It was—dead fact; now, it is quick thought. It can stand, and it can go. It now endures, it now flies, it now inspires. Precisely in proportion to the depth of
(10) mind from which it issued, so high does it soar, so long does it sing.

Or, I might say, it depends on how far the process had gone, of transmuting life into truth. In proportion to the completeness of the distillation, so will the purity and
(15) imperishableness of the product be. But none is quite perfect. . . . Each age, it is found, must write its own books; or rather, each generation for the next succeeding. The books of an older period will not fit this.

Yet hence arises a grave mischief. The sacredness which
(20) attaches to the act of creation,—the act of thought,—is instantly transferred to the record. The poet chanting, was felt to be a divine man. Henceforth the chant is divine also. The writer was a just and wise spirit. Henceforward it is settled, the book is perfect; as love of the hero corrupts into
(25) worship of his statue. Instantly, the book becomes noxious. The guide is a tyrant. . . . The sluggish and perverted mind of the multitude, always slow to open to the incursions of

Reason, having once so opened, having once received this book, stands upon it, and makes an outcry, if it is dispar-
(30) aged. Colleges are built on it. Books are written on it by thinkers, not by Man Thinking; by men of talent, that is, who start wrong, who set out from accepted dogmas, not from their own sight of principles. Meek young men grow up in libraries, believing it their duty to accept the views which
(35) Cicero, which Locke, which Bacon, have given, forgetful that Cicero, Locke and Bacon were only young men in libraries when they wrote these books.

Hence, instead of Man Thinking, we have the book-worm. . . .
(40)    Books are the best of things, well used; abused, among the worst.

## Question 3

(Suggested time—40 minutes. This question counts one-third of the total essay section score.)

Samuel Johnson wrote, "Our desires increase with our possessions. The knowledge that something remains yet unenjoyed impairs our enjoyment of the good before us."

Write a persuasive essay that either qualifies, agrees with, or disagrees with Johnson's assertion. Use personal experience, reading, or observation to develop your ideas.

### END OF EXAMINATION

ANSWER KEY FOR PRACTICE TEST 1

## Section I: Multiple-Choice Questions

*First Passage*

| | | |
|---|---|---|
| 1. D | 6. A | 11. C |
| 2. B | 7. A | 12. C |
| 3. C | 8. B | 13. D |
| 4. D | 9. B | 14. E |
| 5. B | 10. A | |

*Second Passage*

| | | |
|---|---|---|
| 15. C | 20. D | 25. E |
| 16. D | 21. B | 26. E |
| 17. B | 22. C | 27. C |
| 18. E | 23. D | 28. D |
| 19. A | 24. A | |

*Third Passage*

| | | |
|---|---|---|
| 29. B | 34. A | 39. A |
| 30. E | 35. E | 40. D |
| 31. C | 36. B | 41. B |
| 32. E | 37. D | 42. B |
| 33. D | 38. C | 43. E |

*Fourth Passage*

| | | |
|---|---|---|
| 44. B | 49. A | 54. C |
| 45. E | 50. E | 55. A |
| 46. C | 51. B | 56. B |
| 47. D | 52. D | 57. D |
| 48. E | 53. D | |

## Section II: Essay Questions

Essay scoring guides, student essays, and analysis appear beginning on page 145.

## PRACTICE TEST 1 SCORING WORKSHEET

Use the following worksheet to arrive at a probable final AP grade on Practice Test 1. While it is sometimes difficult to be objective enough to score one's own essay, you can use the sample essay answers that follow to approximate an essay score for yourself. You might also give your essays (along with the sample essays) to a friend or relative to score if you feel confident that the individual has the knowledge necessary to make such a judgment and that he or she will feel comfortable in doing so.

### *Section I: Multiple-Choice Questions*

$$\frac{}{\substack{\text{right}\\\text{answers}}} - (\tfrac{1}{4} \text{ or } .25 \times \frac{}{\substack{\text{wrong}\\\text{answers}}}) = \frac{}{\substack{\text{multiple-choice}\\\text{raw score}}}$$

$$\frac{}{\substack{\text{multiple-choice}\\\text{raw score}}} \times 1.18 = \frac{}{\substack{\text{multiple-choice}\\\text{converted score}}} \text{(of possible 67.5)}$$

### *Section II: Essay Questions*

$$\frac{}{\substack{\text{question 1}\\\text{raw score}}} + \frac{}{\substack{\text{question 2}\\\text{raw score}}} + \frac{}{\substack{\text{question 3}\\\text{raw score}}} = \frac{}{\substack{\text{essay}\\\text{raw score}}}$$

$$\frac{}{\substack{\text{essay}\\\text{raw score}}} \times 3.055 = \frac{}{\substack{\text{essay}\\\text{converted score}}} \text{(of possible 82.5)}$$

### *Final Score*

$$\frac{}{\substack{\text{multiple-choice}\\\text{converted score}}} + \frac{}{\substack{\text{essay}\\\text{converted score}}} = \frac{}{\substack{\text{final}\\\text{converted score}}} \text{(of possible 150)}$$

### *Probable Final AP Score*

| *Final Converted Score* | *Probable AP Score* |
|---|---|
| 150–104 | 5 |
| 103– 92 | 4 |
| 91– 76 | 3 |
| 75– 50 | 2 |
| 49–  0 | 1 |

# ANSWERS AND EXPLANATIONS FOR PRACTICE TEST 1

## SECTION I: MULTIPLE-CHOICE QUESTIONS

*First Passage*

From *The Writing Life* by Annie Dillard.

1. (D) The figure is a metaphor, not a simile. Synesthetic imagery moves from the stimulation of one sense to a response by another sense, as a certain odor induces the visualization of a certain color. Here, the act of reading, a visual stimulus, produces sounds.

2. (B) The paragraph describes a cause (the large cardboard butterfly) and its effect ("He jumps the piece of cardboard"). The paragraph does not contain any metaphors, similes, extended definitions, or concessions to an opposing view. The paragraph is used to compare the butterfly's and the human response to size, but the comparison is not made in this paragraph.

3. (C) The first sentence of the third paragraph makes clear the relevance of the second. As the butterfly automatically responds to size, so humans respond to the larger stimuli of films. The last sentence makes the comparison explicit with its simile. The third paragraph doesn't qualify the second (A) and (D). The second paragraph doesn't ask why butterflies behave as they do (B).

4. (D) The nine-foot handsome face with its three-foot-wide smile is an image on the movie screen to which we cannot help responding. Since the point of the paragraph is the irresistible appeal of size, the reference is to the larger-than-life film rather than to the television set.

5. (B) Although the author claims she can recognize and will dislike a book written with an eye on film adaptation, she makes no comment on the quality of the films these books may become. The first four sentences of the paragraph assert the superiority of films in depicting spectacle and scenes of action. Her dissatisfaction with novels written for film adaptation is expressed twice in terms of smell: "a faint but unmistakable, and ruinous, odor" and "I smelled a rat."

6. (A) The figure here is personification. The metaphor compares books to people (who can be "uneasy," "eager," and wear "disguises"). The figure is neither understated nor ironic. It is a metaphor, not a simile or a syllogism.

7. (A) The question uses the phrase "according to the passage," and although the writer uses colloquial language ("smell a rat"), she doesn't call it a characteristic of literature. These qualities are cited in the first paragraph ("the imagination's vision . . . the moral sense . . . the intellect") and the last ("the more purely verbal, crafted sentence by sentence, the more imaginative").

8. (B) The phrase means something like "a greater waste of time." The best of the five choices here is "poorer occupation." "Sorry" here means "sad" or "pathetic" ("a sorry excuse"), and "pursuit" means "occupation," not "chase."

9. (B) Choice (A) can't be right, since "our" is the first person plural possessive pronoun. The phrase, like most of the passage, makes only modest claims for literature, based upon the greater subtlety of the verbal appeal. The move from the first person singular ("I") of the fourth paragraph to the plural here seems intended to assert a solidarity with the people "who like literature." Choice (E) explains the phrase "a poor thing," but the question asks about the plural "our." Choice (D) is untrue and (C) most unlikely. Many readers won't notice the allusion at all, and if they do, they won't see that it is an oblique form of self-promotion.

10. (A) Throughout the passage, the author frankly admits the limitations of the written word and concedes to the film advantages in certain areas. All three of these sentences admit that writing is not powerful, or not immediately so, or not so effective in some areas as other forms of expression. The first two don't deal with film (B). Choices (C), (D), and (E) are all untrue. The passage is genuine and doesn't employ overstatement or irony.

11. (C) The first paragaraph supports the idea that life is more exciting than writing. The whole passage suggests that reading is a special taste which some people have acquired, but it makes no case for forcing literature upon those who prefer film or television. In fact, the last sentence contends that the attempt to win over nonreaders is foolish (E). The third paragraph calls film "irresistible." The passage makes no claim of universal appeal for even the best books (C). Literature, it calmly argues, will appeal to those who like literature.

12. (C) The focus of the passage is on the nature of writing and film and their differences. The only mention of the novel is of the book written to be made into film (E). The passage ignores the difficulties of being a writer (B). Although the author may agree with the ideas of (A) and (C), neither is the central concern of this passage.

13. (D) The first and last paragraphs are primarily about writing. The second paragraph, about the butterfly, is an analogy for the appeal of the big, the film as opposed to literature, and the third and fourth paragraphs are about films and novels written to become films. Choice (E) misrepresents the first, second, and final paragraphs. Choice (A) misrepresents the entire passage.

14. (E) The passage doesn't employ irony. There is a personal anecdote in the description of the author's reading novels written for film (paragraph four), an extended analogy in paragraphs two (the butterfly) and three (the film), short sentences throughout the passage, and colloquialism in a phrase like "I smelled a rat."

*Second Passage*

From *The American Crisis* by Thomas Paine.

15. (C) It is the author's intent that American citizens will read this essay and thus become inspired to support the revolution. There is no indication that he is speaking to the government of either Great Britain or America, choices (A) and (D). British citizens, choice (B), is an unreasonable answer, unsupported by the essay. Choice (E) is far too general; the author is speaking only to the oppressed people of America, not of all the world.

16. (D) The "summer soldier" and the "sunshine patriot" serve their country only when conditions are favorable to themselves, a behavior akin to that of the proverbial "fair-weather friend." These conditionally patriotic citizens, who want to get involved only on their own terms, are the target of the author's criticism in this sentence. Choices (A) and (E) are unreasonable; neither army reserves nor special forces existed at this time. Choice (B) also makes no sense; while the word "infidel" is used in the second paragraph, it has nothing to do with the quotation given. Choice (C) is contradictory to the meaning of the quotation given; if the professional British soldiers were instead "summer soldiers," the revolution would be easier to accomplish.

17. (B) The essay is filled with aphorisms—brief, witty sayings—and emotional appeals. Examples of aphorisms here are "the harder the conflict, the more glorious the triumph" (lines 6–7) and "What we obtain too cheap, we esteem too lightly" (lines 7–8). The author appeals to emotions in his claim that a man's children will curse his cowardice if he fails to act now. Answer (A) is inaccurate because, although it can be argued that parts of the essay are allegorical, it does not use didactic rhetoric. The author's purpose is clearly to persuade, not to teach, and the rhetoric is too highly charged with emotion to be described as didactic. Choice (C) is only partially correct. An argument can be made that the essay uses symbolism; for example, the man who runs the tavern at Amboy may be a symbol for all that the author considers to be wrong with American citizens. But

this lone example does not constitute "heavy use." Although "God" is mentioned in three of the four paragraphs, those mentions are not technically biblical allusion. The author does not use paradox and invective (D) or historical background and illustration (E).

18. (E) The author groups the King of Britain with murderers, highwaymen, and housebreakers (lines 28–29) but not with cowards. The line "the blood of his children will curse his cowardice" (lines 52–53) refers to Americans who fail to support the revolution, not to the king.

19. (A) God, as characterized here, is a just and principled deity who will not let a people perish through military destruction because they have "earnestly and so repeatedly sought to avoid the calamities of war" (lines 21–22). Nor, the author suggests, will this God abandon humans, giving them up "to the care of devils" (line 26). None of the references to God are negative, so "vexed" (angry), "indifferent," and "pernicious" (extremely destructive) are inappropriate answers. Choice (D), "contemplative," implies merely that God meditates, but the author suggests a more acitve God.

20. (D) The author's forceful language is nearly the opposite of understatement. He does use anecdote (the story of the tavern owner), simile (for example, "clear as a ray of light"—line 60), aphorisms (for example, "What we obtain too cheap, we esteem too lightly"—lines 7–8), and symbolism (for example, the story of the tavern owner).

21. (B) In lines 9–11,the author claims that "Heaven knows how to put a proper price upon its goods; and it would be strange indeed if so celestial an article as freedom should not be highly rated." Choice (A) is inaccurate because the author never addresses the relationship between freedom and cowardice. (C) contradicts the essay. The author states strongly that freedom does not come easily. (D) also contradicts the essay; the author hopes that one day Americans will know true freedom. (E) is not addressed in the essay.

22. (C) The picture of the tavern owner holding the hand of his child is likely designed to increase the emotional appeal of this essay, appealing to every man's desire to protect his family, even if he has to fight in order to save them. As the author says, it is "sufficient to awaken every man to duty." Choice (A) is too simplistic. True, the mention of the child shows that this man has a family, but introducing that fact is not the purpose of the reference. Answer (B) is incorrect because it isn't the image of the *child* that provokes the author's anger, but the image of the child's complacent *father*. The author *may* feel that the tavern owner is "evil," but the child's image doesn't symbolically increase the evil (D). Choice (E) contradicts the passage. The author appeals to the traditional values of family and freedom.

23. (D) Since aphorisms are short, proverbial sayings of general truth, choice (D) doesn't fit the definition but rather may be more accurately considered a cliché.

24. (A) The author states that America's "situation is remote from all the wrangling world, and she has nothing to do but to trade with them" (lines 43–45). The author does picture America as the "conqueror" but only with regard to winning its freedom from Britain, which makes choice (B) too strong a statement to be correct. The author never implies that America should be greater than Britain (C) or sanctified by God (D). Choice (E) contradicts the passage; if a country conducts trade, its stance is not one of "complete isolationism."

25. (E) The author hopes to encourage his readers to take action, and he writes persuasively to achieve that aim.

26. (E) There is a strong emotional appeal as the author warns men that their children will think them cowards and as he claims that the heart of a reader who does not feel as he does is "dead." Choice (A) has no support in the essay. Choice (B) isn't his *purpose,* the outcome he desires. He wants men to join the revolution, to take action, not simply to be afraid. (C) is inaccurate because the sentence quoted in this question is not directed to the king, but to American citizens. There is no

mention of the superiority of either American or British forces and no mention of the advisability of retreat (D).

27. (C) The author demonstrates no ambivalence in this paragraph. He takes a strong stand without vacillation. The paragraph does include the other devices listed. For example, aphorism—"'Tis the business of little minds to shrink" (line 57), simile—"My own line of reasoning is . . . as straight and clear as a ray of light" (lines 59–60), parallel construction—"What signifies it to me . . . an army of them?" (lines 66–69), and analogy—the comparison of the king to common theives (line 63 to end).

28. (D) Clearly, this author hopes his readers will feel that it is their patriotic duty toward America to join in supporting the revolution. While the author might value "peace and rational thinking," he also clearly suggests that revolution now is necessary to produce later peace. The negative 'overemotional" and "unwarranted" in choices (B) and (C) should alert you to the fact that these are not likely answers. The essay contradicts choice (E). The author suggests that "Tyranny, like hell, is not easily conquered," that is, freedom will *not* come immediately. In addition, the essay's primary purpose is to persuade Americans to join in the struggle to win their liberty, not simply to demand that the British government grant it to them.

### Third Passage

From *Tess of the D'Urbervilles* by Thomas Hardy.

29. (B) The author uses personification several times as he describes the sun. For example, the sun had a "curious sentient, personal look," demands a "masculine pronoun," and is a "golden-haired, beaming, mild-eyed, God-like creature."

30. (E) The passage begins at dawn and moves toward midmorning. Choice (E) best shows this progression. The other choices occur early in the morning and don't suggest the passage of time.

31. (C) The key phrase of the question, "steady movement," reinforces "restless momentum" in choice (C). Choice (A) is incorrect because the author implies no "positive aspects" of progress; in fact, the destruction of the animals' environment suggests a negative attitude. "Alacrity" (D), which means cheerful readiness or promptness, is not suggested in the passage.

32. (E) The reaping-machine is responsible for the destruction of the animals' homes in the field. It mows down the wheat ("corn" here is a general term for grain of any kind), leaving the homeless animals to await death at the hands of the field crews. Choices (A), (B), (C), and (D) are not addressed in the passage. While the machine may *possibly* be an improvement for humans, an inevitable aspect of the future, or a benevolent companion, the author doesn't address these possibilities.

33. (D) The sun is described in powerful terms, with its "vigour and intentness of youth" and light that "broke . . . like red-hot pokers." Because the machine's description immediately follows that of the sun, it is also seen as powerful, with phrases that subtly compare the machine to the sun, such as "brightest . . . intensified . . . by the sunlight" and "having been dipped in liquid fire." Choice (B) is incorrect; while the passage suggests a connection between the sun and the machine, the machine is not human. Choice (C) is incorrect because, even though the sun is personified, the machine is not. Choice (E) is also incorrect. Although there is negativity here concerning the reaping-machine, there is none concerning the sun.

34. (A) Industrialization, exemplified by the reaping-machine, is shown to have a strong effect on nature. The author doesn't characterize the humans who must kill the animals as "ruthless" (B), but rather comments on the occurrence matter-of-factly. There is no evidence of satire in the passage (C) or comment about the senselessness of the animals' death (D).

35. (E) "Ephemeral" means transitory or temporary, and "refuge" means shelter (the field of wheat).

36. (B) Visually, the description of the buttons on the men's trousers is humorous. One pictures these hard-working field men whose buttons on their backsides "twinkled . . . at every movement . . . as if they were a pair of eyes." There is no metaphor (A) or evidence of self-consciousness around women (C). Although some readers might feel that the detail is superfluous (D), that is not the *effect* of the description. And although some exaggeration (hyperbole) may exist here, there is no irony (E).

37. (D) The author claims that a woman becomes a "portion of the field" (a component of it), that she has "assimilated herself with it."

38. (C) The "eye returns involuntarily" to the girl, and although she "seduces casual attention," she "never courts it." It is obvious, then, that she doesn't "flaunt" her beauty (A), and there is no evidence that she is "aristocratic" (D). Choice (B) is incorrect because the girl's beauty *is* possible to detect: she is a "handsome young woman with deep dark eyes." While choice (E) is an inference one could possibly draw, it is not a certain one.

39. (A) The author's tone is engrossed, occupied with his subject. The fine attention to detail—from the sun, to the machine, to the girl—demonstrates the author's interest.

40. (D) The girl in the pink jacket doesn't talk to the other workers and keeps her head down as she works, supporting the idea that she is reserved, quiet. It can be inferred that the others are less reserved because, while the girl "never courts [attention], the other women often gaze around them." There is no evidence in the passage to support choices (A) or (E), and choice (B) contradicts the passage as you've seen. Choice (C) is incorrect because, although the girl is obviously attractive, "overwhelmingly" is an exaggeration.

41. (B) The girl in the pink jacket has paler cheeks, more regular teeth, and thinner lips than do the other country-bred girls. The author sets this girl apart from the other villagers. In the

passage, no kinship to others (A) or sophistication (D) is suggested. The author does not concentrate on her dignity (C), but on her appearance and behavior as she works in the field. The word "nonconformist" (E) implies an intentional failure to conform, and there is no evidence of such intent in the passage.

42. (B) The passage is not allegorical; the characters are literal country villagers, not representative of abstract qualities. The passage does use hyperbole (in the description of the sun, the machine, and the buttons on men's trousers), personification (also in the description of the sun), allusion (in the comparison of the machine's arms to a Maltese cross), and simile (in phrases such as "like red-hot pokers").

43. (E) The passage begins in the sky, with the sun, moves down to earth, into the village, and finally to specific villagers as they wake and begin their day.

**Fourth Passage**

From "Of Studies" by Francis Bacon.

44. (B) Most of these comments explain the benefits of studies (for pleasure, discussion, business, and so forth). Thus, the audience that would most benefit from this essay's message is likely to be those who think they don't need studies. Choices (A), (D), and (E) name audiences who are probably already aware of the benefits of studies. Poor readers (C) don't necessarily need to be convinced of the benefits of studies but rather may need to improve their reading skills.

45. (E) The author explains how students may focus on their studies incorrectly. One may spend too much time in studies and thus be guilty of sloth, or one may use them only to impress others (displaying affectation). Also, one may make judgments based solely upon studies, failing to consider real-life experience. The author uses the term "humor," while modern writers might label the scholars' tendency temperament, or disposition.

46. (C) The author claims, in lines 10–11, that studies "are perfected by <u>experience</u>" and in lines 13–14, that they are "bounded in by <u>experience</u>."

47. (D) Parallel construction is evident—"to contradict and confute," "to believe and take," " to find talk and discourse," "to weigh and consider."

48. (E) The author, in this sentence, discusses how people need to "prune" their natural abilities by study. At the same time, however, studies need to be "bounded in by experience." The message is one of moderation and inclusion—neither studies nor experiences should be relied on exclusively or predominantly.

49. (A) The wisdom "won by observation" is analogous to that "perfected by experience" (lines 10–11). In both instances, the author recommends reading to gain knowledge but also incorporating life's observations and experiences to obtain wisdom.

50. (E) The author suggests all three of these uses in the second sentence. Personal reading brings "delight" (enjoyment), contributes to "discourse" (intelligent conversation), and aids in the "disposition of business" (sound judgment).

51. (B) "To spend too much time in studies is sloth" (lines 7–8) paradoxically suggests that too much work on studies can lead to laziness and lack of work. In other words, overemphasis on studies avoids work in the outside world. Choices (A), (D), and (E) are not paradoxes. While choice (C) might have paradoxical elements, it is not mentioned in the essay.

52. (D) In lines 17–19, the author claims that one should read "not to contradict and confute, nor to believe and take for granted, nor to find talk and discourse, but to <u>weigh and consider</u>." A reader should think. Reading voraciously or only for pleasure, choices (A) and (E), are not necessarily "errors." Choices (B) and (C) are perhaps reading mistakes, but the nonthinking reader is presented as the greater problem.

53. (D) The sentence in this question uses analogy, comparing reading to eating. In choice I, reading is compared to pruning a plant. In choice III, a third analogy compares "impediments" in understanding to physical diseases of the body. There is no analogy in choice II.

54. (C) This sentence discusses how readers might adapt their reading style to the subject matter and and their purpose. By reading "not curiously," the author means reading without great care or scrutiny, reading cursorily. Choices (A), (B), and (E) directly contradict the idea of reading without considerable scrutiny.

55. (A) The sentence in the question contains parallel construction in which three ideas make up the sentence. Choice (A) uses the same structure, presenting three similarly phrased ideas which make up the sentence.

56. (B) By "wit," the author means one's mind, one's intelligence, which can be focused through specific types of reading. Choice (A) may appear to be correct, but the author never addresses intuition. In addition, if a person has already attained wisdom, his or her mind is not likely to need the remedies proposed by the author.

57. (D) The eating analogy in lines 19–21 suggests that books should be consumed in different manners and for different purposes.

# SECTION II: ESSAY QUESTIONS

## Question 1

### *Scoring Guide for Question 1 (Virginia Woolf)*

8–9  In a well-written essay, this writer clearly demonstrates an understanding of Woolf's attitude about women in society, while also analyzing how the author's structure, diction, tone, and detail convey that attitude. The writer presents a clear, relevant thesis supported by strong evidence from the passage. Analysis of the evidence and how it reflects the author's attitude about women in society is insightful. Not necessarily without flaws, the essay still shows maturity in its use of language and sentence structure.

6–7  Well presented, this essay accurately describes Woolf's attitude about women in society, but perhaps less explicitly than does the high-scoring essay. Discussion of the author's techniques may be less thorough, or evidence presented may be less specific. Connection between the evidence and the thesis may be less insightful. Although some errors may be present, the essay, overall, shows satisfactory control of format and language.

5  The writer of the average paper may recognize the author's attitude about women in society but may be less precise in discussing that attitude. Attempts to analyze the author's language may be simplistic, or evidence offered may be insufficient to prove the thesis adequately. Organization may be clear but not as effective as that of the better-written paper. Inconsistencies in the command of language may be present.

3–4  This essay attempts to address the essay question but may fail to accurately address the author's attitude. It may not complete all of the tasks of the question. Inadequate evidence for the writer's ideas may be a problem. Insights may be inaccurate or superficial. The essay may convey ideas, but weak control over language may distract the reader's attention. Frequent errors in mechanics may be present.

1–2 This essay fails to respond sufficiently to the question or the passage. It may fail to recognize the author's attitude or may misread the passage so as to distort it. With little or no evidence offered, the essay may fail to persuade the reader, and the connection between the evidence and the thesis may be shallow or nonexistent. Persistent weaknesses may be evident in the basic elements of composition or writing skills.

*High-Scoring Essay*

The difference between men's and women's colleges were considerable in Virginia Woolf's day. Rather than assert this in a pedestrian, expository way, Woolf uses the respective meals served at each college to illustrate the discrepancies between the schools. The meals are a metaphorical device, akin to a poetic conceit; Woolf makes a far more forceful, profound distinction between the male and female schools through such juxtaposition than if she had merely enumerated their inconsistencies. Woolf details the relative poverty of the women's school, and therefore women's position in society, through varied sentence structure, diction and imagery between the descriptions of the meals.

Fundamentally different premises underlie each meal. The men's meal is a luxury to be enjoyed, the women's a metabolic necessity to be endured. Woolf, in describing the men's meal, dismisses the notion that ". . . soup and salmon and ducklings were of no importance whatsoever, as if nobody ever smoked a cigar or drank a glass of wine." She offers a breathless explanation of the sensual joy the meal affords. Diction and sensory detail showcase the piquant pleasure to be taken in foods "spread . . . of the whitest cream," "Sharp and sweet . . . succulent." The men's meal is a catalyst for the "profound, subtle and subterranean glow . . . of rational intercourse." Of course, no similar premium is put on rational intercourse among women, judging by the amenities of the women's meal. They drink not wine "flushed crimson," but rather eat "transparent . . . plain gravy soup." Dry biscuits and water replace partridges, and such victuals provide no stimulus for enlightened conversation; when the eating is done, the women rise and that is all.

Woolf describes the women's meal in plain language, in blunt, staccato, repetitive bursts: "Here was my soup . . . Dinner was ready. Here was the soup. It was a plain gravy soup . . . The plate was plain." All the eloquent wordiness has vanished. The images are those of poverty and ugliness, and the meal is only justified as being superior to that of a coal miner. The prunes are ". . . stringy as a miser's heart and exuding a fluid such as might run in misers' veins. . . ." In contrast, the other meal's imagery is that of opulence. The potatoes are like coins, the sprouts "foliated as rosebuds."

This is a meal fit for kings, and the diction is suggestive of royalty: "The partridges . . . came with all their retinue. . . ." The men are reassured by the meal that they are all going to heaven; the women's meal is a hurried "homely trinity."

As a metaphor for the chasm separating male and female education, and society as a whole, Woolf's piece is mordantly effective. Her point is made with more economy and vivacity through anecdote than it would be through explanation or a propounding of evidence about the inferiority of female schools. By painting the male university as lavish and its female counterpart as lowly, Woolf succeeds in crystalizing her attitude for readers.

### Analysis of the High-Scoring Essay

This writer addresses the question; he or she also demonstrates a deep understanding of the subtle differences between the two passages. This writer's thesis is relevant and on topic. The body paragraphs provide ample evidence for ideas, and the quotations are used effectively to prove this writer's points. This paper does not merely dwell on the obvious aspects of the passage, but probes more deeply into the ramifications of the two meals. Especially effective is the section in which the writer demonstrates how Woolf's diction suggests the meaning of each meal. For example, reread the end of the fourth paragraph as this writer connects the word "retinue" with royalty and goes on to suggest what that royal meal does for the men; it reassures them that they are going to heaven. This type of thinking demonstrates the level of analysis necessary for a high score; the writer understands *how* the language of the essay helps to create an effect.

The vocabulary and sentence structure are also very sophisticated, as they should be in all top-scoring essays. The phrasing is creative and pleasing. Wording such as "akin to a poetic conceit," "a metabolic necessity," "piquant pleasure," and "mordantly effective" are just a few of the phrases that sing to the reader's ear. In addition, this writer demonstrates a keen sense of sentence structure and thus adds sufficient variety in both sentence pattern and length.

Although very well written, this essay could be improved by providing a stronger connection between ideas, evidence, and thesis. Also, a more profound point could be made about the deeper issues involved in the "chasm separating male and female education." In addition, the writer could concentrate more on Woolf's attitude *as* he or she presents the evidence.

### Medium-Scoring Essay

Meals are important, but they are often ignored or not thought of much. People often eat in a hurry, and often they don't pay much attention to the details of what they are actually eating.

Virginia Woolf calls readers' attention to this in the selection about two meals which she had when she was at the university. She had one of these at the men's college and the other at the women's college. They were very different in the food but also in the whole atmosphere of the place where she ate.

Woolf says that though people don't often notice it, the food we eat tells us important things about where we are. She compares the two parts of the university with the different meals. She uses narrative structure, details and tone to present her attitude about the two meals and inform readers of which one she likes better, and why.

The first meal she describes, which is at the men's college, is the one which Woolf likes better. The reasons become obvious for this, because the food is far more appetizing and the atmosphere is just nicer generally. Woolf uses lots of details and metaphors to describe this meal, and often her descriptions are full of imagery. It is all very fancy, with a uniformed waiter serving roast, and Woolf drinks a lot of wine, which sends a glow down her spine. She comments that all the other eaters were very friendly and everything seemed nice and happy after the meal. "We are all going to heaven" she says after the meal. It is almost a religious experience for them.

The second meal is at the women's college, and Woolf's attitude toward it is not as positive. That is understandable, but the food is not even close to as good. Woolf uses lots of metaphors to make the food seem gross and very repulsive. The beef is like "the rumps of cattle in a muddy market, and sprouts curled and yellowed at the edge" she says. The prunes are stringy and miserly, and instead of the good pudding that she ate at the men's college, she has to eat custard that is not nearly so good. The biscuits are dry and unappetizing, which makes for a meal that is not very appealing. She doesn't talk about friends or smoking at this meal, which makes it far less homely than the men's meal.

Thus, through her metaphors and affective descriptions of the food at the two meals, Woolf compares them and strongly shows her attitude to the readers. She makes one realize that even though we don't often think about meals, they are important. The differences are something to realize, and Woolf's excellent description helps you do just that.

### Analysis of the Medium-Scoring Essay

This essay earns a medium score because it recognizes some of the differences between the two meals. However, it doesn't merit a higher score because it fails to address Woolf's attitudes as displayed through her descriptions of the meals. The introductory remarks go on far too long (for three paragraphs). When the thesis is finally stated, it's bland and obvious, as is the entire essay. This writer mentions that Woolf presents her attitudes but never clarifies what he or she thinks these attitudes are; basically, the thesis merely restates portions of the question.

This writer has chosen to discuss the two meals separately, in two paragraphs, a technique which doesn't allow for strong comparison. This writer does accurately present some evidence, but in many cases, it is not sufficient. For example, where are the metaphors referred to? Since they aren't included in the essay, the reader is left guessing. The writer does see some interesting description in the passages but fails to make an intelligent point about it, and the analysis offered is shallow and obvious. Also, no connection is made between the evidence presented and the major topic of Woolf's attitude.

In addition, this essay demonstrates some stylistic and grammatical problems and is not helped by the use of unsophisticated words and phrases such as "things," "a lot," and "not as good." Some awkward sentences tend to distract the reader's attention from this writer's ideas. Incorrect word choices, such as "affective" instead of "effective," show that this writer doesn't have a strong command of the language. This difficulty is further demonstrated by pronoun problems, such as the use of "you" in the last sentence and "them" at the end of the fourth paragraph.

The positive aspects of this essay are few; it does try to make a point, and it follows many of the conventions of proper writing style. However, the numerous errors and its uninteresting, obvious ideas keep it from achieving a higher score.

## Question 2

*Scoring Guide for Question 2 (Ralph Waldo Emerson)*

8–9 This well-written essay clearly takes a stand concerning Emerson's ideas about the usefulness of books and substantially supports it. The thesis is well thought out and relevant to the topic. The paper provides ample evidence to prove the writer's ideas and clearly connects the evidence to the thesis. Thoroughly convincing, the paper demonstrates a significant understanding of the needs of the essay. Although it need not be without errors, the paper shows a mature command of style and language.

6–7 This essay demonstrates understanding of Emerson's ideas but produces a less explicit thesis than that of higher-scoring essays. Perhaps less relevant evidence is offered, making the essay less persuasive. Still, it is fairly convincing and shows clear thinking. The connection between the evidence and the thesis may not be as articulate as in top-scoring essays. Although well written, this essay may demonstrate some errors while still showing satisfactory control over diction and the essay requirements.

5 This adequately written essay shows some understanding of Emerson's ideas but produces a thesis that may be weak or predictable. The opinions may be too hastily conceived after a cursory reading of Emerson's concepts. Overall, the argument, although acceptable, may not be persuasive or thought provoking. It may appear opinionated without sufficient evidence to support the opinions. Acceptable organization may be evident, but the style may not be as sophisticated as that of higher-scoring essays.

3–4 This low-scoring essay fails to convince the reader. The weak presentation may show an unsubstantiated thesis or no thesis at all, weak paragraph development and/or weak organization, insufficient evidence for points made, or superficial thinking.

Confusion about Emerson's ideas may be evident, and frequent mechanical errors may be present.

1–2 This poorly written essay lacks coherence and clarity. The thesis may be overly obvious or absent. Little or no evidence may be offered for the thesis, and connection between the evidence and the thesis may be shallow or nonexistent. The paper may be unusually short and exhibit poor fundamental essay skills. Weak sentence construction may persist, and persistent weaknesses in command of the language may be present.

### *High-Scoring Essay*

Ralph Waldo Emerson is perhaps overly strident in his speech, "The American Scholar." But such zeal serves to make a trenchant point about the tendency toward rigid reverence of "Great Works," as if each were the Holy Grail itself. He asserts: "Books are the best of things, well used; abused, among the worst." Emerson delivers a stinging indictment of "bookworms." He argues that even the greatest thinkers were once humble students. The danger, Emerson claims, is that of transferring our respect from the venerable acts of creation, of thought, to that endeavor's imperfect product. He believes scholars must not so prostrate themselves before the majesty of profound works, that they forget their creators, whom they should emulate in creative thought. They should not idolize the books themselves in a sort of cult of inferiority, Emerson says, but rather write their own books, their own truths, undertake their own sacred acts of creation.

In a strict sense, these points are valid. But Emerson goes beyond these points; he overstates his case. He is treading the ground between the good scholar and the singular genius. Perhaps, given his own stature, it is only fitting that he should hold us to such lofty standards. Nevertheless, his warnings against showing too much respect for books, are not altogether true. Such arguments, about the paramount importance of individual thought, can readily be misused to justify a dismissal of the past. Often such self-indulgent, arrogant, arguments are used by those less gifted than Emerson as an excuse to disregard the wisdom that has come before them.

A social critic recently said, "It's fine to learn how to think, but what's the point if you have nothing to think about?" The modern education system has sought to shoulder the burden of "teaching students how to think," often elevating such a subjective goal to status superior to teaching facts and sharing insights about past generations. In short, they focus more on method and process than what students actually learn.

Some students graduate from American high schools ignorant of when the Civil War occurred or the difference between the Preamble to the Constitution and Das Kapital. Reading and digesting the thoughts of the past is as essential as learning the rules of grammar so as to intelligently violate them. In light of today's high illiteracy rate, society's problems hardly include too many people being "bookworms" or attempting to follow the doctrines of Plato or John Locke or Mahatma Gandhi.

We as Americans share a heritage of ideas. Common assumptions must be examined so that we understand where such "conventional wisdom" came from, for it is only then that we may change the portions of it which may be unjust or clouded by bias. Certainly great books should not be locked away, immune from criticism. Neither, however, should they be lambasted out of visceral ignorance, in the name of "individuality."

Studying and learning from the works of the past, and creating new original writing and thought in the present are not mutually exclusive propositions. Most scholars lack Emerson's genius, but they will be hard-pressed to find a spark of creativity by meditating in the dark.

Emerson implies that ideas are not great <u>in and of themselves.</u> But ideas <u>can</u> be great. Proof positive resides in the overwhelming numbers of anonymous poems that fill anthology books. How many aphorisms are repeated daily by speakers who know not whether they generated from the tongue of Winston Churchill or Will Rogers? This is not to suggest that great ideas cannot be proved wrong. That Emerson denies perfection to any ideas is hardly a danger. Since no writer, however brilliant, is perfect, it is perfectly safe to acknowledge certain ideas as great, without granting them perfection and immunity.

When people do not know the past, they face the peril of perpetually re-inventing the wheel—blissfully ignorant of their tendency toward trite alliteration or insipid cliches.

### Analysis of the High-Scoring Essay

This thorough, thoughtful, and well-written essay deserves a high score. It begins with the topic and promptly takes a relevant position on the issue of studying from books and ideas of the past. The student shows a clear understanding of Emerson's ideas by restating and elaborating on the major points.

The student then points out a major dilemma inherent in a facile acceptance of Emerson's ideas—that of dismissing the past and wisdom that has come before.

The student's essay proceeds with a two-paragraph discussion of the state of education today, pointing out the dual needs of teaching both facts and the thinking process. These paragraphs are particularly relevant to the topic, and the student's examples are presented with insight.

The student also acknowledges our American heritage and the necessity of using books to understand that heritage so that the country's great ideas are not hidden away.

The next paragraph counters Emerson's position with optimism—the student claims that we can have it all; we can learn from the past and still become clear, independent thinkers who create new ideas.

The essay points out that great new ideas do exist and cites contemporary, anonymous poems as examples of these new ideas. The student also acknowledges that ideas can be great while being imperfect and that such imperfection is no reason to dismiss them entirely.

The student completes the essay with a brief conclusion reminding the reader that humans may be doomed to repeat their mistakes and to reinvent the wheel unless they learn from the great ideas of the past. Overall, this essay's points are valid, and without dismissing Emerson lightly, the student intelligently discusses his concepts.

### Medium-Scoring Essay

The process of finding meaningful things in life is not always clear. It is not simple to discover what is true and what is just fancy rhetoric or skirting of the issues. Ralph Waldo Emerson, considered one of our best writers and speakers, gave a speech in Cambridge in 1837, where he talked about books and how they can help us to find the truth which we are seeking in our life.

Emerson said in his speech that books are noble and age old scholars gave arrangement to the life they saw and organized it. Then they put it into the books that they wrote, and produced a new truth for people to refer to. But he also says that each new generation of Americans has to write their own books. They have to discover their own versions of the truth, and what that truth actually means to them.

He was right. He was also right when he said that we can't just go by what was said then, because the ones who wrote the books that fill our libraries were just young and naive when they authored those books. How can we be sure they are right, just because they are old? Why are they elevated to the status of classics as if they are perfect?

He says you shouldn't spend all your time in the library, however, I know some people who do just this. The result is that instead of having their own ideas, they just listen to all the old ones, and their creativity is stifled. I agree that it is more important to be a thinking man than one who just accepts everything. You need to have the freedom to have your own ideas, to let them flow without being influenced by principles and underlying ideas already presented in books. These ideas might be right, but if everyone only reads them without thinking for themselves, the country will be full of brainwashed people. They might be well educated, but what will be the price of that education?

He said that books can be best if they are used well, but among the worst of things if they are abused. What this actually encourages is for one to be intelligent about reading and not to believe everything that you read. Also, he says that we should not be bookworms so caught up in the details of what people said in the past that we don't bother to think our own thoughts about the present or concerning the issues of the future that are important to our society. This is the centerpiece of his speech. He means that books have a noble "theory." He also means that in practice we must live up to that theory. We must live up to that theory by not being blind or gullible. Instead we must be <u>Thinking Men</u> and not <u>thinkers only</u>. He talked about how what we observe has to be filtered in to the truth by our own original ideas. We have to use books wisely, Emerson believed, and I agree wholeheartedly.

## Analysis of the Medium-Scoring Essay

This essay would score at the low end of the medium range. It begins with a vague introduction that essentially restates a few points from Emerson's speech. The student does not yet state a thesis or take a position.

The second paragraph continues this trend, merely paraphrasing Emerson's speech without critical thinking about those ideas. An essay that *only* paraphrases the passage will score no higher than a three.

Eventually, in the third paragraph, the student presents an opinion and takes a position, although it is repetitively worded. The student seems to have finally started thinking as he or she questions the validity of older books and the pedestal upon which the classics have been placed.

The fourth paragraph is probably the best in this student's essay and saves the score from sinking even lower. The student uses personal experience as an example, citing other students who have become "stifled" in their creativity by spending too much time in the library, consuming old books and old ideas without thinking while they read. The writer apparently understands the need for every student to become an individual thinker, an analyzer of ideas.

However, the next paragraph reverts to simple paraphrasing. It offers no additional commentary from the student.

The essay reaches an adequate conclusion, explaining the need to read wisely and not be gullible. Ultimately, the student writer manages to insert enough of his or her own commentary about Emerson's concepts to salvage the score. However, this essay could be greatly improved by reducing the paraphrasing and including much more analysis and evidence. Remember that this topic specifically directs students to "use evidence from your own experience, reading, or observation to develop your essay." This writer has barely accomplished that goal, and thus, the score suffers.

## Question 3

*Scoring Guide for Question 3 (Samuel Johnson)*

8–9 This well-written essay clearly takes a stand concerning Johnson's ideas on possessions and substantially supports it. The thesis is articulate and relevant to the topic. The paper provides strong and relevant evidence intelligently connected to the thesis and demonstrates an understanding of the needs of the essay. Although it need not be without errors, the paper shows a mature command of style and language.

6–7 This essay contemplates Johnson's ideas on possessions but produces a less explicit thesis. Perhaps less relevant or insufficient evidence is offered, and the reader may not be as thoroughly convinced as with a top-scoring paper. Although well written, the essay may demonstrate some errors while still showing satisfactory control over diction and the essay requirements.

5 The adequate presentation in this essay includes a thesis but one that is perhaps not as well thought out as in higher-scoring essays. The ideas may be too hastily conceived. Overall, the argument may not be as strong or convincing as in a higher-scoring paper. It may appear more opinionated without sufficient evidence to support the opinions. Acceptable organization may be evident, but the style may not be as sophisticated as that in higher-scoring essays.

3–4 This low-scoring essay fails to convince the reader. The weak presentation may include an unsupported or unsubstantiated thesis, weak paragraph development, and/or poor organization. Confusion may be present in the paper's ideas. Superficial thinking and evidence may be present. Frequent mechanical errors may persist.

1–2 This poorly written essay lacks clarity and coherence. It may have an overly obvious thesis or no thesis at all. Little or no evidence may be a problem, and the connection between the evidence and the thesis may be shallow or nonexistent. The paper may be unusually short and exhibit poor fundamental essay skills. Weak sentence construction may persist, and persistent weaknesses in command of the language may be present.

*High-Scoring Essay*

There are as many different motivations and convictions which serve to "make people tick" as there are people to experience such impulses. Beyond the broad abstractions, each of us may have a unique force driving us toward happiness—toward the degree of success or self-fulfillment we desire. Nevertheless, the American Dream of financial security and independence, of building a comfortable life, is widespread if not universal.

The poor must struggle for the rudimentary elements of sustenance. The rich are at times perceived as avaricious, striving continually like Philistines for material rewards. Yet such characteristics tend to oversimplify the issues. The truth of the inverse relation Samuel Johnson describes—"Our desires increase with our possessions"—depends closely on his wording.

Desires may increase with our possessions, in the sense that they will numerically increase. Desire, however, the drive and will to succeed, tends to stay constant with each individual, whether poor or wealthy. A person who has worked relentlessly from humble beginnings will likely not abandon that work ethic simply because he has reached some nebulous, ill-defined level of attainment that others term "success." Conversely, Johnson's statement may not apply to the stereotypical "happy-go-lucky" person who desires nothing more than an average home and job, and who may be completely satisfied with his life, once having attained these possessions. Some people simply do not want to improve their place in society, nor do they want to increase their possessions.

Johnson's second statement is more unequivocally true. He writes, "The knowledge that something remains yet unenjoyed impairs our enjoyment of the good before us." Consistent with many a common aphorism–a bird in the hand is worth two in the bush, the grass is always greener on the other side, ad infinitum— Johnson is correctly attesting that many possessions and concrete rewards tend to numb and dull our perceptions, to make us less cognizant of the simple things which enrich our lives more than any amount of gold or stock certificates ever can.

The trick to correctly evaluating the veracity of Johnson's assertion is to avoid blanket generalizations, i.e. "all rich are greedy" or "all poor people are easily pleased." Discerning readers will be able to point to instances in which Johnson is proved correct, and others which contradict his thesis. Nevertheless, it would not be unfair to say that he makes a reasonable statement.

### Analysis of the High-Scoring Essay

The first paragraph, although it doesn't directly address Samuel Johnson's concepts, indirectly qualifies them. The student seems to feel that Johnson's remarks don't universally apply, that people have "different motivations."

The second paragraph deals with Johnson's ideas more overtly and states the student's opinion more clearly—that to accept Johnson's generalities is to "oversimplify" the issues.

The third paragraph offers a more philosophical discussion of Johnson's notion regarding desire. The student makes a distinction between "desires" and "desire," defining "desire" as the "drive and will to succeed" and asserting that people possess this quality in varying degrees. The writer provides hypothetical examples: the person who has a diligent work ethic and doesn't abandon it, even after achieving success, and one who has earned some possessions, such as a home, and desires no more. These examples provide support to the student's opinion that the first half of Johnson's statement should be qualified.

The fourth paragraph examines Johnson's second assertion and agrees that humans are not always happy with what they have (an idea the student supports by citing two aphorisms, although the first incorrectly suggests a point of view opposite to that of Johnson and the student writer). The writer asserts that we are "less cognizant" of the simple pleasures of life which "enrich our lives more" than material objects ever can.

The student's conclusion restates his or her opinion that Johnson's statement, although partially true, cannot be universally applied. The essay, on the whole, is well written and insightful.

### Medium-Scoring Essay

Most people want to have money and attain success. But then what happens when you achieve that goal, and move from poor to rich? Many Americans just become greedy. They already have alot, but they just want more. Their thirst for money cannot be satisfied, like a man in the desert.

Samuel Johnson addressed this problem. He wrote, "Our desires increase with our possessions. The knowledge that something remains yet unenjoyed impairs our enjoyment of the good before us." I agree that this is usually true, and it can be seen in all classes of society. Even poor people prove this point, because they need to first get a house and food for their family. Once they do that, they can feel that the house is no longer good enough and they want to move up. So this family works harder to get a newer house and more possessions, but they forget to appreciate what they have at the time, always thinking that they need more. It's like the unsatisfied family in D.H. Lawrence's "Rocking Horse Winner" that knows "there must be more money!"

This is also the usual attitude that rich people have about money. They are usually less humble about money because they are rich. It is like a game to these rich people, to see how much more money they can get. They are usually more likely to be greedy than the poor or middle class people who just want food, a place to live, and maybe an entertaining evening on occasion; these people think like the lead actor in the movie "Wall Street" who said that "Greed is good."

Rich people are greedier. They usually want to have yachts and fly all over the world to visit ancient ruins or walk the streets of Paris. But poor and middle class people, whether they admit it or not, would probably like the same things, or at least they would like the opportunity for the same things. People just forget to enjoy what they have and always think of what else they need, what else they can buy. Samuel Johnson was correct years ago; his ideas are even more true in modern times.

*Analysis of the Medium-Scoring Essay*

This essay would likely receive a score near the lower end of the medium range. The introductory paragraph seems to agree with Johnson but is not clear on the agreement.

The second paragraph states the student's opinion—that he or she does agree with Johnson—and continues with the theoretical example of a poor family that wants more possessions even after basic needs have been met. The student includes a pertinent quotation from D. H. Lawrence, but the presentation is not sophisticated, with the quotation seeming to be appended as an afterthought.

The third paragraph addresses the rich and their attitudes toward money. As previously, the student doesn't substantiate opinions with convincing discussion or specific evidence. The quotation from the movie *Wall Street,* while superficially related to the subject, provides no strong evidence.

The conclusion restates the student's opinion once again and continues to make generalities about human nature that need additional support in order to convince a reader. The student *is* to be commended for integrating Johnson's ideas throughout the essay and for good organization. However, these positive points are offset by the negative: an overly opinionated tone, a lack of both adequate discussion and convincing examples, and faults in style and command of language, both of which are simplistic.

# PRACTICE TEST 2

## SECTION I: MULTIPLE-CHOICE QUESTIONS

**Time: 60 Minutes**
**56 Questions**

This section consists of selections from prose works and questions on their content, form, and style. Read each selection carefully. Choose the best answer of the five choices.

*Questions 1–14.* Read the following passage carefully before you begin to answer the questions.

Here then was I (call me Mary Beton, Mary Seton, Mary Carmichael or by any name you please—it is not a matter of any importance) sitting on the banks of a river a week or two ago in fine October weather, lost in thought. That collar I
(5) have spoken of, women and fiction, the need of coming to some conclusion on a subject that raises all sorts of prejudices and passions, bowed my head to the ground. To the right and left bushes of some sort, golden and crimson, glowed with the colour, even it seemed burnt with the heat,
(10) of fire. On the further bank the willows wept in perpetual lamentation, their hair about their shoulders. The river reflected whatever it chose of sky and bridge and burning tree, and when the undergraduate had oared his boat through the reflections they closed again, completely, as if
(15) he had never been. There one might have sat the clock round lost in thought. Thought—to call it by a prouder name than it deserved—had let its line down into the stream. It swayed, minute after minute, hither and thither among the reflections and the weeds, letting the water lift it
(20) and sink it, until—you know the little tug—the sudden conglomeration of an idea at the end of one's line: and then the cautious hauling of it in, and the careful laying of it out? Alas, laid on the grass how small, how insignificant this

thought of mine looked; the sort of fish that a good
(25) fisherman puts back into the water so that it may grow fatter
and be one day worth cooking and eating. I will not trouble
you with that thought now, though if you look carefully you
may find it for yourselves. . . .

But however small it was, it had, nevertheless, the
(30) mysterious property of its kind—put back into the mind, it
became at once very exciting, and important; and as it
darted and sank, and flashed hither and thither, set up such
a wash and tumult of ideas that it was impossible to sit still.
It was thus that I found myself walking with extreme rapidity
(35) across a grass plot. Instantly a man's figure rose to intercept
me. Nor did I at first understand that the gesticulations of a
curious-looking object, in a cut-away coat and evening shirt,
were aimed at me. His face expressed horror and indigna-
tion. Instinct rather than reason came to my help; he was a
(40) Beadle; I was a woman. This was the turf; there was the
path. Only the Fellows and Scholars are allowed here; the
gravel is the place for me. Such thoughts were the work of a
moment. As I regained the path the arms of the Beadle
sank, his face assumed its usual repose, and though turf is
(45) better walking than gravel, no very great harm was done.
The only charge I could bring against the Fellows and
Scholars of whatever the college might happen to be was
that in protection of their turf, which has been rolled for 300
years in succession, they had sent my little fish into hiding.
(50)    What idea it had been that had sent me so audaciously
trespassing I could not now remember. The spirit of peace
descended like a cloud from heaven, for if the spirit of peace
dwells anywhere, it is in the courts and quadrangles of
Oxbridge on a fine October morning. Strolling through
(55) those colleges past those ancient halls the roughness of the
present seemed smoothed away; the body seemed contained
in a miraculous glass cabinet through which no sound could
penetrate, and the mind, freed from any contact with facts
(unless one trespassed on the turf again), was at liberty to
(60) settle down upon whatever meditation was in harmony with
the moment. As chance would have it, some stray memory
of some old essay about revisiting Oxbridge in the long

vacation brought Charles Lamb to mind. . . . Indeed, among all the dead, . . . Lamb is one of the most congenial. . . . For
(65) his essays are superior . . . because of that wild flash of imagination, that lightning crack of genius in the middle of them which leaves them flawed and imperfect, but starred with poetry. . . . It then occurred to me that the very manuscript itself which Lamb had looked at was only a few
(70) hundred yards away, so that one could follow Lamb's footsteps across the quadrangle to that famous library where the treasure is kept. Moreover, I recollected, as I put this plan into execution, it is in this famous library that the manuscript of Thackeray's *Esmond* is also preserved . . . but
(75) here I was actually at the door which leads to the library itself. I must have opened it, for instantly there issued, like a guardian angel barring the way with a flutter of black gown instead of white wings, a deprecating, silvery, kindly gentleman, who regretted in a low voice as he waved me back that
(80) ladies are only admitted to the library if accompanied by a Fellow of the College or furnished with a letter of introduction.

That a famous library has been cursed by a woman is a matter of complete indifference to a famous library. Vener-
(85) able and calm, with all its treasures safe locked within its breast, it sleeps complacently and will, so far as I am concerned, so sleep forever. Never will I wake those echoes, never will I ask for that hospitality again.

1. According to the passage, the narrator uses several names (lines 1–2) in order to
   (A) make a universal statement about all humankind
   (B) deemphasize her personal identity
   (C) introduce her many pseudonyms as an author
   (D) attempt to impress the reader with her literacy
   (E) mask her true identity from the reader

2. The literary device used to describe the speaker's thought ("Thought . . . eating"—lines 16–26) is
   (A)  a simile
   (B)  a metaphor
   (C)  personification
   (D)  an apostrophe
   (E)  hyperbole

3. In the phrase "you know the little tug" (line 20), the speaker abstractly refers to
   (A)  a fish's pull on a fishing line
   (B)  the Beadle's insisting she move off the lawn
   (C)  the annoying loss of a thought
   (D)  the sudden awareness of an idea
   (E)  the pull of her guilty conscience

4. The effect that the Beadle has on the narrator is to
   (A)  encourage her pursuit of knowledge
   (B)  cause her thoughts to retreat
   (C)  assure her of correct directions
   (D)  condemn the women's movement
   (E)  inquire if she needs additional assistance

5. It can be inferred that the narrator realizes that she cannot remember her thought because
   (A)  it passes so quickly
   (B)  the student rowing by interrupts it
   (C)  it is not important enough
   (D)  it does not compare to great authors' ideas
   (E)  it is so carefully and slowly thought out

6. The lawn and library serve the purpose of
   (A)  symbolizing the obstacles that women face
   (B)  reminding readers of the rigors of university study
   (C)  contrasting relaxation with research
   (D)  introducing the existence of equality for women
   (E)  minimizing the author's point about women's roles

7. The passage contains all of the following rhetorical devices EXCEPT
   (A) personification
   (B) metaphor
   (C) simile
   (D) literary allusion
   (E) allegory

8. The author's purpose in the passage is to
   (A) explain her anger at the Beadle
   (B) personify nature's splendor
   (C) illustrate how men can inhibit women's intellectual pursuits
   (D) recall the enticing glory of university study
   (E) preach her beliefs about women's roles in society

9. The organization of the passage could best be characterized as
   (A) stream of consciousness mixed with narration of specific events
   (B) comparison and contrast of two incidents
   (C) exposition of the women's movement and the author's opinions
   (D) description of both external reality and the author's thoughts
   (E) flowing smoothly from general ideas to specific statements

10. The pacing of the sentence "But however small it was . . . it was impossible to sit still" (lines 29–33)
    (A) reflects the acceleration of her thoughts
    (B) represents a continuation of the pace of the description of the river
    (C) contrasts with the fish metaphor
    (D) suggests a sluggishness before the Beadle's interruption
    (E) parallels that of the description of the library doorman

11. The speaker's description of the Beadle and the library door-man serves to
    (A) confirm the horror of what she has done
    (B) frighten women away from universities
    (C) encourage women to rebel against men
    (D) contrast the men's manners
    (E) satirize the petty men who enforce the rules

12. The phrase "for instantly there issued . . . waved me back"(lines 76–79) can best be characterized as containing
    (A) obvious confusion from the doorman
    (B) metaphorical reference to a jailer
    (C) awed wonder at the man's position
    (D) humorous yet realistic description
    (E) matter-of-fact narration

13. At the time of the occurrences she describes, the speaker probably felt all of the following EXCEPT
    (A) indignation
    (B) bewilderment
    (C) delight
    (D) exasperation
    (E) repression

14. The pattern of the passage can best be described as
    (A) alternating between a description of external reality and internal commentary
    (B) the presentation of a social problem followed by its resolution
    (C) general statements followed by illustrative detail
    (D) presentation of theory followed by exceptions to that theory
    (E) comparison and contrast of great authors' ideas

*Questions 15–26.* Read the following passage carefully before you begin to answer the questions.

[Alexander Pope] professed to have learned his poetry from Dryden, whom, whenever an opportunity was presented, he praised through his whole life with unvaried liberality; and perhaps his character may receive some
(5) illustration if he be compared with his master.

Integrity of understanding and nicety of discernment were not allotted in a less proportion to Dryden than to Pope. The rectitude of Dryden's mind was sufficiently shown by the dismission of his poetical prejudices, and the
(10) rejection of unnatural thoughts and rugged numbers. But Dryden never desired to apply all the judgment that he had. He wrote, and professed to write, merely for the people, and when he pleased others, he contented himself. He spent no time in struggles to rouse latent powers; he never attempted
(15) to make that better which was already good, nor often to mend what he must have known to be faulty. He wrote, as he tells us, with very little consideration; when occasion or necessity called upon him, he poured out what the present moment happened to supply, and, when once it had passed
(20) the press, ejected it from his mind: for when he had no pecuniary interest, he had no further solicitude.

Pope was not content to satisfy; he desired to excel, and therefore always endeavored to do his best: he did not court the candor, but dared the judgment of his reader, and,
(25) expecting no indulgence from others, he showed none to himself. He examined lines and words with minute and punctilious observation, and retouched every part with indefatigable diligence, till he had left nothing to be forgiven. . . .

(30) His declaration that his care for his works ceased at their publication was not strictly true. His parental attention never abandoned them; what he found amiss in the first edition, he silently corrected in those that followed. He appears to have revised the *Iliad*, and freed it from some of
(35) its imperfections, and the *Essay on Criticism* received many improvements after its first appearance. It will seldom be

found that he altered without adding clearness, elegance, or vigor. Pope had perhaps the judgment of Dryden; but Dryden certainly wanted the diligence of Pope.

(40)    In acquired knowledge, the superiority must be allowed to Dryden, whose education was more scholastic, and who before he became an author had been allowed more time for study, with better means of information. His mind has a larger range, and he collects his images and illustrations

(45) from a more extensive circumference of science. Dryden knew more of man in his general nature, and Pope in his local manners. The notions of Dryden were formed by comprehensive speculation, and those of Pope by minute attention. There is more dignity in the knowledge of

(50) Dryden, and more certainty in that of Pope.

Poetry was not the sole praise of either; for both excelled likewise in prose; but Pope did not borrow his prose from his predecessor. The style of Dryden is capricious and varied; that of Pope is cautious and uniform. Dryden obeys

(55) the motions of his own mind; Pope constrains his mind to his own rules of composition. Dryden is sometimes vehement and rapid; Pope is always smooth, uniform, and gentle. Dryden's page is a natural field, rising into inequalities, and diversified by the varied exuberance of abundant vegeta-

(60) tion; Pope's is a velvet lawn, shaven by the scythe, and leveled by the roller.

Of genius, that power which constitutes a poet; that quality without which judgment is cold, and knowledge is inert, that energy which collects, combines, amplifies, and

(65) animates; the superiority must, with some hesitation, be allowed to Dryden. It is not to be inferred that of this poetical vigor Pope had only a little, because Dryden had more; for every other writer since Milton must give place to Pope; and even of Dryden it must be said, that, if he has

(70) brighter paragraphs, he has not better poems. Dryden's performances were always hasty, either excited by some external occasion, or extorted by domestic necessity; he composed without consideration, and published without correction. What his mind could supply at call, or gather in

(75) one excursion, was all that he sought, and all that he gave.

The dilatory caution of Pope enabled him to condense his sentiments, to multiply his images, and to accumulate all that study might produce or chance might supply. If the flights of Dryden therefore are higher, Pope continues

(80) longer on the wing. If of Dryden's fire the blaze is brighter, of Pope's the heat is more regular and constant. Dryden often surpasses expectation, and Pope never falls below it. Dryden is read with frequent astonishment, and Pope with perpetual delight.

15. The essay's organization could best be described as
   (A) exposition of a thesis followed by illustrations
   (B) chronological presentation of each author's works
   (C) presenting ideas based on their order of importance
   (D) basing each paragraph on a different argument
   (E) comparison of and contrast between the two writers

16. In context, "candor" (line 24) can be interpreted to mean
   (A) kindness
   (B) criticism
   (C) excellence
   (D) sincerity
   (E) indifference

17. In each of the following pairs of words, the first refers to Dryden, the second to Pope. Which pair best describes their prose style?
   (A) Dignified vs. simplistic
   (B) Passionate vs. lyrical
   (C) Unsystematic vs. harmonious
   (D) Punctilious vs. careless
   (E) Pedantic vs. impetuous

18. Which of the following best describes Pope's attitude toward his own writing?
    (A) "[he] dared the judgment of his reader" (line 24)
    (B) "His parental attention never abandoned them" (lines 31–32)
    (C) "It will seldom be found that he altered without adding clearness" (lines 36–37)
    (D) "Pope is cautious and uniform" (line 54)
    (E) "Pope continues longer on the wing" (lines 79–80)

19. The passage's points could be more convincing if the writer were to offer
    (A) less emphasis on Pope's writing and editing diligence
    (B) more direct language to present his ideas about the authors
    (C) more discussion of Dryden's editing theories
    (D) more point-by-point comparisons of each author's prose
    (E) specific examples from each poet's work to support his opinions

20. Which of the following ideas is NOT found in the essay?
    (A) For Pope, good writing meant rewriting.
    (B) Both authors were productive.
    (C) Dryden is the superior prose writer.
    (D) Dryden follows his own mind more than Pope does.
    (E) Pope's writing is like a manicured lawn.

21. Which of the following best characterizes Dryden's method of writing?
    (A) "he never attempted to make better that which was already good" (lines 14–15)
    (B) "he poured out what the present moment happened to supply" (lines 18–19)
    (C) "when he had no pecuniary interest, he had no further solicitude" (lines 20–21)
    (D) "His mind has a larger range" (lines 43–44)
    (E) "the superiority must, with some hesitation, be allowed to Dryden" (lines 65–66)

22. Although Pope did not have as strong a scholastic background as did Dryden, the writer implies that Pope
    (A) chose subjects unrelated to Dryden's
    (B) had great familiarity with his subject matter
    (C) feigned completing university study
    (D) compensated by emulating Dryden
    (E) undermined any effort in his behalf

23. According to the passage, genius can invigorate which of the following in an author?

    I. Judgment
    II. Knowledge
    III. Power

    (A) I only
    (B) III only
    (C) I and II only
    (D) II and III only
    (E) I, II, and III

24. What does the writer suggest as the main reason that Dryden's writing style labels him a genius?
    (A) The apparent effortlessness of his writing
    (B) He "continues longer on the wing" (lines 79–80)
    (C) That his prose is a "natural field"
    (D) That his academic studies prepared him so well
    (E) That the age he lived in was noted for intelligence

25. In lines 58–61 ("Dryden's page . . . roller"), which of the following literary devices is used to summarize the differences between Dryden's and Pope's prose?
    (A) Syllogism
    (B) Personification
    (C) Understatement
    (D) Metaphor
    (E) Simile

26. Of the following, which is NOT a major distinction the writer draws between Dryden and Pope?
   (A)  Their educational foundation
   (B)  Their prose style
   (C)  Their skill in writing
   (D)  Their vigor in writing
   (E)  Their editing practices

*Questions 27–41.* Read the following passage carefully before you begin to answer the questions.

It is remarkable that there is little or nothing to be remembered written on the subject of getting a living; how to make getting a living not merely honest and honorable, but altogether inviting and glorious; for if *getting* a living is
(5) not so, then living is not. One would think, from looking at literature, that this question had never disturbed a solitary individual's musings. Is it that men are too much disgusted with their experience to speak of it? The lesson of value which money teaches, which the Author of the Universe has
(10) taken so much pains to teach us, we are inclined to skip altogether. As for the means of living, it is wonderful how indifferent men of all classes are about it, even reformers, so called,—whether they inherit, or earn, or steal it. I think that Society has done nothing for us in this respect, or at
(15) least has undone what she has done. Cold and hunger seem more friendly to my nature than those methods which men have adopted and advise to ward them off.

The title *wise* is, for the most part, falsely applied. How can one be a wise man, if he does not know any better how
(20) to live than other men?—if he is only more cunning and intellectually subtle? Does Wisdom work in a tread-mill? or does she teach how to succeed *by her example*? Is there any such thing as wisdom not applied to life? Is she merely the miller who grinds the finest logic? Is it pertinent to ask if
(25) Plato got his *living* in a better way or more successfully than his contemporaries,—or did he succumb to the difficulties of life like other men? Did he seem to prevail over some of

them merely by indifference, or by assuming grand airs? or find it easier to live, because his aunt remembered him in
(30) her will? The ways in which most men get their living, that is, live, are mere makeshifts, and a shirking of the real business of life,—chiefly because they do not know, but partly because they do not mean, any better.

The rush to California, for instance, and the attitude, not
(35) merely of merchants, but of philosophers and prophets, so called, in relation to it, reflect the greatest disgrace on mankind. That so many are ready to live by luck, and so get the means of commanding the labor of others less lucky, without contributing any value to society! And that is called
(40) enterprise! I know of no more startling development of the immorality of trade, and all the common modes of getting a living. The philosophy and poetry and religion of such a mankind are not worth the dust of a puffball. The hog that gets his living by rooting, stirring up the soil so, would be
(45) ashamed of such company. If I could command the wealth of all the world by lifting my finger, I would not pay *such* a price for it. Even Mahomet knew that God did not make this world in jest. It makes God to be a moneyed gentleman who scatters a handful of pennies in order to see mankind
(50) scramble for them. The world's raffle! A subsistence in the domains of Nature a thing to be raffled for! What a comment, what a satire, on our institutions! The conclusion will be, that mankind will hang itself upon a tree. And have all the precepts in all the Bibles taught men only this? and is
(55) the last and most admirable invention of the human race only an improved muck-rake? Is this the ground on which Orientals and Occidentals meet? Did God direct us so to get our living, digging where we never planted,—and He would, perchance, reward us with lumps of gold?
(60)    God gave the righteous man a certificate entitling him to food and raiment, but the unrighteous man found a facsimile of the same in God's coffers, and appropriated it, and obtained food and raiment like the former. It is one of the most extensive systems of counterfeiting that the world has
(65) ever seen. I did not know that mankind was suffering for want of gold. I have seen a little of it. I know that it is very

malleable, but not so malleable as wit. A grain of gold will gild a great surface, but not so much as a grain of wisdom.

(70) The gold-digger in the ravines of the mountains is as much a gambler as his fellow in the saloons of San Francisco. What difference does it make whether you shake dirt or shake dice? If you win, society is the loser. The gold-digger is the enemy of the honest laborer, whatever checks and compensations there may be. It is not enough to

(75) tell me that you worked hard to get your gold. So does the Devil work hard. The way of transgressors may be hard in many respects. The humblest observer who goes to the mines sees and says that gold-digging is of the character of a lottery; the gold thus obtained is not the same thing with the

(80) wages of honest toil. But, practically, he forgets what he has seen, for he sees only the fact, not the principle, and goes into trade there, that is, buys a ticket in what commonly proves another lottery, where the fact is not so obvious.

27. The author believes that "getting a living" must be both
   (A) moral and pious
   (B) ethical and admirable
   (C) accessible and sensible
   (D) desirable and attainable
   (E) humble and profitable

28. According to the author, although man must earn money, he is indifferent to
   (A) religion
   (B) society
   (C) cold and hunger
   (D) lessons of value
   (E) laborers

29. The author asserts that
   (A) we have forgotten the proper value of money
   (B) good, hard work will save mankind
   (C) the world operates solely on luck
   (D) religion fails to address the merit of labor
   (E) gold-digging is acceptable under certain conditions

30. The "Author of the Universe" (line 9) can be interpreted as a
    (A) symbol for cosmic consciousness
    (B) metaphor for a contemporary writer
    (C) symbol for judgment
    (D) metaphor for all artists
    (E) metaphor for God

31. The author's purpose in referring to Plato seems to be to
    (A) make the point about gold-digging more universal and timeless
    (B) qualify the assertions about gold-diggers and their luck
    (C) question whether ancient philosophers faced the same dilemmas that others do
    (D) consider the ancient philosophers' premises about morality in society
    (E) create an authoritative tone to lend credence to the argument

32. What is the antecedent for "it" (line 47)?
    (A) "immorality" (line 41)
    (B) "philosophy" (line 42)
    (C) "hog" (line 43)
    (D) "wealth" (line 45)
    (E) "world" (line 46)

33. Which of the following is the best example of aphorism?
    (A) "The ways in which most men . . . any better." (lines 30–33)
    (B) "Nature a thing to be raffled for!" (line 51)
    (C) "A grain of gold . . . a grain of wisdom." (lines 67–68)
    (D) "What difference does it make . . . shake dice?" (lines 71–72)
    (E) "So does the Devil work hard." (lines 75–76)

34. An unstated assumption of the author is that
    (A) philosophers should work harder to apply their teachings
    (B) a pig would be mortified by some men
    (C) society is gradually improving
    (D) true wisdom comes only through hard work
    (E) what appears honest to one can be harmful to society

35. The author's comments about the California gold rush serve the purpose of
    (A) comparing gold-diggers to the ancient Greeks
    (B) illustrating how immorally men are earning a living
    (C) explaining the relationship of Orientals to Occidentals
    (D) sensationalizing a topical and popular occupation
    (E) criticizing those who think gold-digging romantic

36. Which of the following negative phrases is, in context, a qualified negative?
    (A) "men are . . . disgusted with their experience" (lines 7–8)
    (B) "Cold and hunger" (line 15)
    (C) "the greatest disgrace on mankind" (lines 36–37)
    (D) "the unrighteous man" (line 61)
    (E) "society is the loser" (line 72)

37. The essay contains all of the following devices EXCEPT
    (A) simile
    (B) historical allusion
    (C) rhetorical question
    (D) syllogistic reasoning
    (E) religious reference

38. The sentence "A grain of gold . . . a grain of wisdom" (lines 67–68) can best be restated as
    (A) knowledge is more valuable than gold
    (B) gold-diggers must work harder than philosophers
    (C) gold will last longer than knowledge
    (D) erudition takes longer to achieve than money
    (E) money has no practical purpose

39. The tone of the essay can best be described as
    (A) condescending
    (B) skeptical
    (C) worrisome
    (D) indignant
    (E) pedestrian

40. Which of the following is NOT part of the author's argument against gold-digging?
    (A) "The hog . . . would be ashamed of such company." (lines 43–45)
    (B) "digging where we never planted" (line 58)
    (C) "I know that it is very malleable" (lines 66–67)
    (D) "the enemy of the honest laborer" (line 73)
    (E) "of the character of a lottery" (lines 78–79)

41. Which of the following is NOT discussed in the passage?
    (A) Man can learn to improve his lot in life.
    (B) Authors have not addressed "getting a living."
    (C) Gamblers have damaged society.
    (D) The title "wise" may be misapplied.
    (E) Men are easily lured by monetary rewards.

*Questions 42–56.* Read the following passage carefully before you begin to answer the questions.

The object of this essay is to assert one very simple principle, as entitled to govern absolutely the dealings of society with the individual in the way of compulsion and control, whether the means used be physical force in the
(5) form of legal penalties or the moral coercion of public opinion. That principal is that the sole end for which mankind are warranted, individually or collectively, in interfering with the liberty of action of any of their number is self-protection. That the only purpose for which power
(10) can be rightfully exercised over any member of a civilized community, against his will, is to prevent harm to others. His own good, either physical or moral, is not a sufficient warrant. He cannot rightfully be compelled to do or forbear because it will be better for him to do so, because it will
(15) make him happier, because, in the opinions of others, to do so would be wise or even right. These are good reasons for remonstrating with him, or reasoning with him, or persuading him, or entreating him, but not for compelling him or visiting him with any evil in case he do otherwise. To justify

(20) that, the conduct from which it is desired to deter him must be calculated to produce evil to someone else. The only part of the conduct of anyone for which he is amenable to society is that which concerns others. In the part which merely concerns himself, his independence is, of right, absolute.
(25) Over himself, over his own body and mind, the individual is sovereign.

It is, perhaps, hardly necessary to say that this doctrine is meant to apply only to human beings in the maturity of their faculties. We are not speaking of children or of young
(30) persons below the age which the law may fix as that of manhood or womanhood. Those who are still in a state to require being taken care of by others must be protected against their own actions as well as against external injury. For the same reason we may leave out of consideration
(35) those backward states of society in which the race itself may be considered as in its nonage. The early difficulties in the way of spontaneous progress are so great that there is seldom any choice of means for overcoming them; and a ruler full of the spirit of improvement is warranted in the
(40) use of any expedients that will attain an end perhaps otherwise unattainable. Despotism is a legitimate mode of government in dealing with barbarians, provided the end be their improvement and the means justified by actually effecting that end. Liberty, as a principle, has no application
(45) to any state of things anterior to the time when mankind have become capable of being improved by free and equal discussion. Until then, there is nothing for them but implicit obedience to an Akbar or a Charlemagne, if they are so fortunate as to find one. But as soon as mankind have
(50) attained the capacity of being guided to their own improvement by conviction or persuasion (a period long since reached in all nations with whom we need here concern ourselves), compulsion, either in the direct form or in that of pains and penalties for noncompliance, is no longer
(55) admissible as a means to their own good, and justifiable only for the security of others.

42. The "one very simple principle" (lines 1–2) is that
   (A) the individual should comply with the government's princi-
       ples under all conditions
   (B) a domineering government is an effective government
   (C) the government should coerce an individual only when that
       individual's actions will harm others
   (D) individuals have the right to ignore the government's
       wishes
   (E) children do not have sovereignty

43. The predicate nominative that complements "That principal,"
   the subject of the second sentence (lines 6–9), is
   (A) "sole end"
   (B) "warranted"
   (C) "liberty of action"
   (D) "self-protection"
   (E) "that the sole end . . . self-protection"

44. According to the passage, which of the following may society
   compel to act correctly?
   (A) Those who act selfishly
   (B) Those who harm only themselves
   (C) Those who demonstrate personal corruption
   (D) Those who harm others
   (E) Those who protest against despotism

45. The sentence "These are good reasons . . . otherwise" (lines
   16–19) is effective because of its
   (A) abstract meaning
   (B) parallel syntax
   (C) metaphorical references
   (D) ironic understatement
   (E) personification of government

46. The principle embodied in the phrase "the individual is sovereign" (lines 25–26) is limited to actions that
    (A) adversely affect all society
    (B) are legal
    (C) affect only the individual
    (D) society generally ignores
    (E) are directed at political enemies

47. According to the passage, which of the following groups may be forced to act in a particular way?

    I. Children
    II. Adults
    III. Immature societies

    (A) I only
    (B) II only
    (C) I and II only
    (D) I and III only
    (E) I, II, and III

48. It can be inferred from the passage that despotism is NOT acceptable when
    (A) the government's actions do not produce the necessary improvement in its citizens
    (B) barbarians are allowed to do as they wish
    (C) the government's actions harm children
    (D) society in general is insecure and unsafe
    (E) the people voice opinions against the despot

49. Which of the following are given as allowable methods for preventing members of a society from harming other individuals?

    I. Physical force
   II. Moral coercion of public opinion
 III. Legal penalties

  (A) I only
  (B) II only
  (C) I and II only
  (D) II and III only
  (E) I, II, and III

50. Which of the following does the passage imply the author values most highly?
  (A) Unlimited individual freedom
  (B) Protection of the members of society
  (C) Law and order in society
  (D) Despotism by the leaders
  (E) The sovereignty of children

51. The second paragraph relates to the first paragraph in that it
  (A) gives exceptions to the principle of individual sovereignty discussed in the first paragraph
  (B) illustrates the actions a government can take in controlling its citizens
  (C) lists evidence supporting the assertions made in the first paragraph
  (D) gives concrete examples of effective governments
  (E) provides anecdotal evidence of individuals acting in self-protection

52. With which of the following would the author most likely agree?
    (A) Children should be allowed sovereignty.
    (B) Charlemagne would make a good ruler in a society able to be "guided" to its "own improvement."
    (C) Forced obedience will always be necessary for mankind.
    (D) The only appropriate reason to inhibit a citizen having mature faculties is to prevent harm to others.
    (E) Despots will always exist.

53. Which term best describes the tone of the essay?
    (A) Sarcastic
    (B) Cynical
    (C) Optimistic
    (D) Matter of fact
    (E) Pessimistic

54. Which of the following would the author be LEAST likely to encourage?
    (A) Despotism for barbarians
    (B) Control over children
    (C) Absolute freedom of action
    (D) Reasoning and persuasion
    (E) Self-destructive actions

55. Which of the following rhetorical devices can be found in the essay?
    (A) Metaphor
    (B) Personification
    (C) Syllogistic reasoning
    (D) Simile
    (E) Historical allusion

56. A major purpose of the passage is to
    (A) preach against despotism
    (B) clarify the conditions under which a government may coerce citizens to act a certain way
    (C) alert society to the potential harm of individual rights
    (D) explain why a government should allow individual freedoms
    (E) assert the sovereign rights of every individual

**STOP.** IF YOU FINISH BEFORE TIME IS CALLED, CHECK YOUR WORK ON THIS SECTION ONLY. DO NOT WORK ON SECTION II.

# SECTION II: ESSAY QUESTIONS

**Time: 2 Hours**
**3 Questions**

## Question 1

(Suggested time—40 minutes. This question counts one-third of the total essay section score.)

The following passages are comments on two places, M. F. K. Fisher on the French port of Marseille and Maya Angelou on the small town of Stamps, Arkansas. Read both carefully and write an essay on how the two passages are similar and different in their effect and in their authors' handling of the resources of language.

1

One of the many tantalizing things about Marseille is that most people who describe it, whether or not they know much about either the place or the languages they are supposedly using, write the same things. For centuries this
(5) has been so, and a typically modern opinion could have been given in 1550 as well as 1977.

Not long ago I read one, mercifully unsigned, in a San Francisco paper. It was full of logistical errors, faulty syntax, misspelled French words, but it hewed true to the familiar
(10) line that Marseille is doing its best to live up to a legendary reputation as world capital for "dope, whores, and street violence." It then went on to discuss, often erroneously, the essential ingredients of a true bouillabaisse! The familiar pitch had been made, and idle readers dreaming of a great
(15) seaport dedicated to heroin, prostitution, and rioting could easily skip the clumsy details of marketing for fresh fish. . . .

"Feature articles" like this one make it seem probable that many big newspapers, especially in English-reading countries, keep a few such mild shockers on hand in a back
(20) drawer, in case a few columns need filling on a rainy Sunday. Apparently people like to glance one more time at the same old words: evil, filthy, dangerous.

Sometimes such journalese is almost worth reading for its precociously obsolete views of a society too easy to forget. In (25) 1929, for instance, shortly before the Wall Street Crash, a popular travel writer named Basil Woon published *A Guide to the Gay World of France: From Deauville to Monte Carlo* (Horace Liveright, New York). (By now even his use of the word "gay" is quaintly naïve enough for a small chuckle. . . .)

(30)    Of course Mr. Woon was most interested in the Côte d'Azur, in those far days teeming and staggering with rich English and even richer Americans, but while he could not actively recommend staying in Marseille, he did remain true to his journalistic background with an expectedly titillating (35) mention of it:

If you are interested in how the other side of the world lives, a trip through old Marseilles—by daylight—cannot fail to thrill, but it is not wise to venture into this district at night unless dressed like a stevedore and well armed. (40) Thieves, cutthroats, and other undesirables throng the narrow alleys, and sisters of scarlet sit in the doorways of their places of business, catching you by the sleeve as you pass by. The dregs of the world are here, unsifted. It is Port Said, Shanghai, Barcelona, and Sidney combined. Now that (45) San Francisco has reformed, Marseilles is the world's wickedest port.

2

There is a much-loved region in the American fantasy where pale white women float eternally under black magnolia trees, and white men with soft hands brush wisps of wisteria from the creamy shoulders of their lady loves. (5) Harmonious black music drifts like perfume through this precious air, and nothing of a threatening nature intrudes.

The South I returned to, however, was flesh-real and swollen-belly poor. Stamps, Arkansas, a small hamlet, had subsisted for hundreds of years on the returns from cotton (10) plantations, and until World War I, a creaking lumbermill. The town was halved by railroad tracks, the swift Red River and racial prejudice. Whites lived on the town's small rise (it

couldn't be called a hill), while blacks lived in what had been
known since slavery as "the Quarters." . . .

(15)     In my memory, Stamps is a place of light, shadow, sounds
and entrancing odors. The earth smell was pungent, spiced
with the odor of cattle manure, the yellowish acid of the
ponds and rivers, the deep pots of greens and beans cooking
for hours with smoked or cured pork. Flowers added their
(20) heavy aroma. And above all, the atmosphere was pressed
down with the smell of old fears, and hates, and guilt.

On this hot and moist landscape, passions clanged with
the ferocity of armored knights colliding. Until I moved to
California at thirteen I had known the town, and there had
(25) been no need to examine it. I took its being for granted and
now, five years later, I was returning, expecting to find the
shield of anonymity I had known as a child.

## Question 2

(Suggested time—40 minutes. This question counts one-third of the total essay section score.)

Read the following excerpt from William Hazlitt's *Lectures on the English Comic Writers* (1819). Then write a well-developed essay analyzing the author's purpose by examining tone, point of view, and stylistic devices.

Man is the only animal that laughs and weeps; for he is the only animal that is struck with the difference between what things are, and what they ought to be. We weep at what thwarts or exceeds our desires in serious matters: we laugh
(5) at what only disappoints our expectations in trifles. We shed tears from sympathy with real and necessary distress; as we burst into laughter from want of sympathy with that which is unreasonable and unnecessary, the absurdity of which provokes our spleen or mirth, rather than any serious
(10) reflections on it.

To explain the nature of laughter and tears, is to account for the condition of human life; for it is in a manner compounded of these two! It is a tragedy or a comedy—sad or merry, as it happens. The crimes and misfortunes that are
(15) inseparable from it, shock and wound the mind when they once seize upon it, and when the pressure can no longer be borne, seek relief in tears: the follies and absurdities that men commit, or the odd accidents that befall them, afford us amusement from the very rejection of these false claims
(20) upon our sympathy, and end in laughter. If every thing that went wrong, if every vanity or weakness in another gave us a sensible pang, it would be hard indeed: but as long as the disagreeableness of the consequences of a sudden disaster is kept out of sight by the immediate oddity of the circum-
(25) stances, and the absurdity or unaccountableness of a foolish action is the most striking thing in it, the ludicrous prevails over the pathetic, and we receive pleasure instead of pain from the farce of life which is played before us, and which discomposes our gravity as often as it fails to move our anger
(30) or our pity!

## Question 3

(Suggested time—40 minutes. This question counts one-third of the total essay section score.)

The following excerpt is taken from Benjamin Franklin's *Autobiography*. Read the passage carefully and develop an essay that evaluates the validity of Franklin's assertions about the ability to justify one's actions through reasoning. Use evidence from your reading or experience to make your argument convincing.

> I believe I have omitted mentioning that in my first voyage from Boston, being becalmed off Block Island, our people set about catching cod and hauled up a great many. Hitherto I had stuck to my resolution of not eating animal food; and
> (5) on this occasion I considered with my Master Tryon, the taking of every fish as a kind of unprovoked murder, since none of them had or ever could do us any injury that might justify the slaughter. All this seemed very reasonable. But I had formerly been a great lover of fish, and when this came
> (10) hot out of the frying pan, it smelled admirably well. I balanced some time between principle and inclination: till I recollected, that when the fish were opened, I saw smaller fish taken out of their stomachs: Then, thought I, if you eat one another, I don't see why we mayn't eat you. So I dined
> (15) upon cod very heartily and continued to eat with other people, returning only now and then occasionally to a vegetable diet. So convenient a thing it is to be a *reasonable creature,* since it enables one to find or make a reason for everything one has a mind to do.

### END OF EXAMINATION

## ANSWER KEY FOR PRACTICE TEST 2

### Section I: Multiple-Choice Questions

*First Passage*

| | | |
|---|---|---|
| 1. B | 6. A | 11. E |
| 2. B | 7. E | 12. D |
| 3. D | 8. C | 13. C |
| 4. B | 9. D | 14. A |
| 5. C | 10. A | |

*Second Passage*

| | | |
|---|---|---|
| 15. E | 19. E | 23. C |
| 16. A | 20. C | 24. A |
| 17. C | 21. B | 25. D |
| 18. B | 22. B | 26. C |

*Third Passage*

| | | |
|---|---|---|
| 27. B | 32. D | 37. D |
| 28. D | 33. C | 38. A |
| 29. A | 34. E | 39. D |
| 30. E | 35. B | 40. C |
| 31. C | 36. B | 41. A |

*Fourth Passage*

| | | |
|---|---|---|
| 42. C | 47. D | 52. D |
| 43. E | 48. A | 53. D |
| 44. D | 49. E | 54. C |
| 45. B | 50. B | 55. E |
| 46. C | 51. A | 56. B |

### Section II: Essay Questions

Essay scoring guides, student essays, and analysis appear beginning on page 207.

## PRACTICE TEST 2 SCORING WORKSHEET

Use the following worksheet to arrive at a probable final AP grade on Practice Test 2. While it is sometimes difficult to be objective enough to score one's own essay, you can use the sample essay answers that follow to approximate an essay score for yourself. You might also give your essays (along with the sample essays) to a friend or relative to score if you feel confident that the individual has the knowledge necessary to make such a judgment and that he or she will feel comfortable in doing so.

### Section I: Multiple-Choice Questions

$$\frac{\phantom{xxxx}}{\substack{\text{right} \\ \text{answers}}} - (\tfrac{1}{4} \text{ or } .25 \times \frac{\phantom{xxxx}}{\substack{\text{wrong} \\ \text{answers}}}) = \frac{\phantom{xxxx}}{\substack{\text{multiple-choice} \\ \text{raw score}}}$$

$$\frac{\phantom{xxxx}}{\substack{\text{multiple-choice} \\ \text{raw score}}} \times 1.20 = \frac{\phantom{xxxx}}{\substack{\text{multiple-choice} \\ \text{converted score}}} \text{ (of possible 67.5)}$$

### Section II: Essay Questions

$$\frac{\phantom{xxx}}{\substack{\text{question 1} \\ \text{raw score}}} + \frac{\phantom{xxx}}{\substack{\text{question 2} \\ \text{raw score}}} + \frac{\phantom{xxx}}{\substack{\text{question 3} \\ \text{raw score}}} = \frac{\phantom{xxx}}{\substack{\text{essay} \\ \text{raw score}}}$$

$$\frac{\phantom{xxxx}}{\substack{\text{essay} \\ \text{raw score}}} \times 3.055 = \frac{\phantom{xxxx}}{\substack{\text{essay} \\ \text{converted score}}} \text{ (of possible 82.5)}$$

### Final Score

$$\frac{\phantom{xxxx}}{\substack{\text{multiple-choice} \\ \text{converted score}}} + \frac{\phantom{xxxx}}{\substack{\text{essay} \\ \text{converted score}}} = \frac{\phantom{xxxx}}{\substack{\text{final} \\ \text{converted score}}} \text{ (of possible 150)}$$

### Probable Final AP Score

| Final Converted Score | Probable AP Score |
|:---:|:---:|
| 150–104 | 5 |
| 103– 92 | 4 |
| 91– 76 | 3 |
| 75– 50 | 2 |
| 49–  0 | 1 |

# ANSWERS AND EXPLANATIONS FOR PRACTICE TEST 2

## SECTION I: MULTIPLE-CHOICE QUESTIONS

### First Passage

From Virginia Woolf's *A Room of One's Own.*

1. (B) The phrase that follows the list of names explains this answer: "call me . . . by any name you please—it is <u>not a matter of any importance.</u>"

2. (B) The speaker uses a metaphor as she describes her thought, imagining it to be on a fishing line that "swayed . . . among the reflections." The thought becomes a metaphorical fish that she hauls to shore on the line. The device is not personification (C) because here an abstract is given animal characteristics rather than human (her thought is compared to a *fish* caught on a line). The remaining choices are not used in this part of the passage.

3. (D) The phrase that follows the quotation clearly identifies the answer: "the sudden conglomeration of an idea at the end of one's line." Choice (A) names not the abstract meaning but the literal meaning on which the metaphor is based. Choices (B) and (C) mention later occurrences unrelated to this "tug." There is no suggestion that the author has a guilty conscience (E).

4. (B) Being made aware that she is in an area in which only "Fellows and Scholars" are allowed to walk sends her metaphorical "fish into hiding." The Beadle doesn't encourage, direct, or ask her questions—(A), (C), and (E). The women's movement (D) is not addressed in the passage.

5. (C) In the fish metaphor, the author points out "how small, how insignificant" her thought is when examined. There is no evidence that the thought passes very quickly (A) or is carefully

197

thought out (E) or that either has to do with her forgetting. Notice of the rower (B) occurs before mention of the thought and does not cause her to forget.

6. (A) The lawn that the author may not walk on and the library that she may not enter are symbols of the obstructions all women face. Choice (D) contradicts the purpose of the passage—to point out *inequality*. Choice (E) is incorrect because these two symbols reinforce, not distract from, the author's point.

7. (E) There is no allegory, the use of characters to symbolize truths about humanity, in this passage. The passage does use personification ("willows wept in perpetual lamentation"), metaphor (the "fish" sequence), simile ("like a guardian angel"), and literary allusion (to *Esmond*).

8. (C) The vignettes demonstrate how men have told women where they may and may not go; on a deeper level, they suggest that men's attitudes inhibit women in their intellectual pursuits. The author *is* angry (A) and touches on nature (B), but neither fact names the purpose of the essay. Choice (D) contradicts the passage; women have been *kept away* from university study. Choice (E) overstates. The author neither preaches nor discusses society and women's roles in general.

9. (D) The passage presents external reality, such as the descriptions of the environs of the university and the actions of the Beadle and the doorman, while interspersing the author's thoughts about the events. The passage is too logical and grammatical to be classified as stream of consciousness (A) (which is a narrative technique not a structural element). The passage doesn't compare or contrast the two events (B) or address the women's movement (C). While choice (E) might be a method of organization, it is not used here.

10. (A) The sentence accelerates as do her thoughts—"it became at once very exciting, and important; . . . it darted and sank . . . flashed hither and thither . . . tumult of ideas . . . impossible to sit still."

11. (E) The description of the men, of their pompous behavior and dress, satirically emphasizes how trifling are the author's supposed crimes, walking on the grass and attempting to enter the library, and how foolish is the men's self-important enforcement of discriminatory rules. Choices (A) and (B) contradict the passage. The author doesn't consider what she's done a "horror" nor would she intend to frighten women away from universities. Choice (C) is not addressed. Choice (D) is incorrect because the men's manners are similar, not contrasting.

12. (D) The description of the gentleman is realistic but also takes a humorous turn in describing a simple doorman as "like a guardian angel barring the way with a flutter of black gown instead of white wings . . . deprecating" as he bars the author from entering the library. The doorman is not confused (A), and the reference is not to a jailer (B), but to a guardian angel.

13. (C) It is highly unlikely that the events described produced a feeling of delight.

14. (A) The author blends a presentation of her thoughts as she walks with description of external reality, such as the Beadle and the library doorman. Choice (B) is incorrect because there is no resolution to her problem. Choices (C), (D), and (E) are not accurate descriptions of the passage's pattern.

**Second Passage**

From *The Lives of the English Poets* by Samuel Johnson.

15. (E) The essay compares and contrasts the two authors, Dryden and Pope. Johnson begins by explaining that Dryden was a strong influence on Pope. Hence, Johnson sets out to "compare [Pope] with his master." The second paragraph explains Dryden's method of writing; the two following paragraphs discuss the care Pope took in writing and editing. The fifth paragraph explains the differences in the authors' educational backgrounds, and the sixth compares their prose skills. The

essay's concluding paragraph continues to draw comparisons and contrasts, ultimately calling Dryden the better poet, while acknowledging both men's strengths. The essay is primarily one of opinion. There is no thesis given and no extensive use of illustrations (A) (other than mention of the *Iliad* and the *Essay on Criticism*). Both choices (B) and (C) are inaccurate. Johnson does not present a different argument in each paragaraph (D) or strictly present *arguments* at all. The passage is an *analysis* of their styles.

16. (A) In the eighteenth century, the word "candor" meant kindness, a meaning that fits in context here. Pope did not court his readers' kindness, but "dared [their] judgment." Because the sentence sets up an opposition, "criticism," "excellence," "sincerity" (the modern meaning of "candor"), and "indifference" make little sense, as they are not good opposites of "judgment."

17. (C) In the sixth paragraph (lines 51–61), Dryden's prose style is described as "capricious," obeying the "motions of his own mind," sometimes "vehement and rapid," producing prose that is a "natural field, rising into inequalities . . . diversified"—that is, unsystematic, written quickly and without a preconceived order. Pope's prose, on the other hand, is described as "uniform," while he "constrains his mind to . . . rules of composition." Pope's prose is "smooth, uniform, and gentle," a "velvet lawn." If you check the first word of each answer pair, you will see that choices (A), (D), and (E) can be quickly eliminated as either not suggested or inappropriate to refer to Dryden's prose. Finally, you can eliminate choice (B). While Dryden might be considered passionate, there is no suggestion that Pope is lyrical. (Note: In answering questions of this sort, you can also begin by checking the second term of each pair.)

18. (B) Pope's *attitude* toward his own writing is best seen in "His parental attention never abandoned them," which suggests a nurturing attitude toward his work. Choice (A) shows not so much an attitude toward his writing as it does an attitude toward his audience. While a possible answer, choice (C) deals

with the outcome of Pope's editing and is not as clearly an *attitude* as is choice (B). Choices (D) and (E) are primarily Johnson's opinions of Pope's work.

19. (E) A reader might be more convinced that Johnson's opinions are valid if presented with some evidence, some examples. He mentions Pope's editing of the *Iliad* but never explains exactly what was changed. He calls Dryden's prose "vehement and rapid" but, again, offers no proof. A reader might be left to wonder what Johnson had read of Pope's and Dryden's works that led him to reach these conclusions, and some examples would help. Choice (A) is incorrect because *less* emphasis would hardly provide a *more* convincing argument. The language of the passage is direct (B), and point-by-point comparisons (D) are made; more of the same is unlikely to more thoroughly convince the reader. Dryden, it seems, did little editing (C), so additional discussion here would not be helpful either.

20. (C) Johnson makes no definitive claim about the superiority of either author's prose. In the sixth paragraph, they are presented as different in style but not necessarily in quality. It is Dryden's poetry that Johnson says is superior (although with some hesitation).

21. (B) Johnson explains how quickly Dryden wrote: "He spent no time in struggles to rouse latent powers," and "He wrote, as he tells us, with very little consideration." Choice (A) deals with Dryden's *lack* of rewriting, not his method of writing—what he did not do rather than what he did.

22. (B) Johnson claims that even though Pope did not have the same educational opportunities that Dryden enjoyed, Pope gave his subjects his "minute attention"; he had "more certainty" than Dryden, suggesting that Pope knew his subjects well.

23. (C) Genius invigorates judgment (without which it is cold) and knowledge (without which it is inert). Genius is not said to invigorate power, rather it *is* a power.

24. (A) The author suggests Dryden's ease in writing as a component of his genius. The fact that Dryden could produce great poetry and admirable prose so quickly and without laborious rewriting and editing attests to Dryden's genius. The quotation given in choice (B) refers to Pope, not to Dryden. Choice (C) may be an apt description of Dryden's prose, but Johnson claims Dryden is a genius in his *poetry*. Although Dryden had a strong educational foundation (D), Johnson does not address Dryden's education in relation to his genius.

25. (D) Johnson uses an effective pair of metaphors to summarize his opinion of the two authors' prose: Dryden's is a "natural field," while Pope's is a "velvet lawn." The remaining choices are not used in this sentence.

26. (C) Johnson clearly acknowledges that both authors are gifted, skillful, and talented and levels little criticism of either writer. All other distinctions given are addressed in the essay.

### Third Passage

From Henry David Thoreau's "Life Without Principle."

27. (B) Thoreau insists that "getting a living" should be "not merely honest and honorable" (ethical), "but altogether inviting and glorious" (admirable).

28. (D) Thoreau explains that "the lesson of value which money teaches . . . we are inclined to skip altogether" (lines 8–11).

29. (A) A major assertion of the essay is that people no longer understand the proper value of money. The author claims that people get money in the wrong way and use it based on the wrong principles. Thoreau never addresses what will "save mankind" (B). And while he acknowledges that gold-digging may be "hard work," "the gold thus obtained is not the same thing with the wages of honest toil" and "society is the loser." Although Thoreau believes that gold-diggers rely on luck to find

gold, he doesn't believe that the entire world operates this way (C). Neither (D) nor (E) is suggested in the essay.

30. (E) The "Author of the Universe" to this author is God. None of the other choices is a reasonable answer.

31. (C) The author wonders if Plato had to face the same dilemmas that others do, if Plato lived his life more admirably than did his contemporaries. The author's points about gold-digging—(A) and (B)—are not addressed in the discussion of Plato. Thoreau doesn't mention Plato's premises about morality (D). Mentioning Plato does nothing to change the tone of the essay (E), and it is highly unlikely that the author uses Plato merely to impress his readers.

32. (D) Thoreau claims that he would not raise a finger for all the wealth of the world.

33. (C) An aphorism, a brief, pointed statement of fundamental truth, is similar to a proverb. Choice (C) fits this definition.

34. (E) Thoreau suggests that, although gold-digging may appear to be an honest way to earn "food and raiment" to some, it harms society in the same way that gambling does; it "is not the same thing with the wages of honest toil." The author never implies that philosophers should work harder (A), that society is improving (C), or that hard work produces wisdom (D). In fact, he suggests the opposite: hard work can be the "enemy." Choice (B) is not an unstated assumption, but a paraphrase of an explicit statement.

35. (B) The California gold rush, which some saw as an example of hard-working men diligently trying to get ahead, is used by this author as an example of immorality, of gambling in life. Thoreau doesn't compare gold-diggers to Greeks (A), explore relations of Orientals and Occidentals (C) (that relationship is only touched on), sensationalize (D), or criticize those who saw the gold rush as romantic (E) (he directly criticizes those who participate in the gold-digging).

36. (B) Thoreau states that "cold and hunger seem more <u>friendly</u> to my nature." Cold and hunger, generally undesirable states, are here seen as better than man's methods of warding them off.

37. (D) There is no syllogistic reasoning in this essay. The author does use simile ("The gold-digger . . . is as much a gambler as his fellow in the saloons"—lines 69–70), historical allusion (to Plato and to the gold rush), rhetorical question (for example, "Does Wisdom work in a tread-mill?"), and religious reference (for example, mention of Mahomet and God).

38. (A) Knowledge is more valuable than gold; wisdom will gild more surface than gold will.

39. (D) The author is angry, indignant at mankind's unseemly pursuit of money.

40. (C) This quotation is not part of the argument against gold-digging. It simply states a fact about gold.

41. (A) Thoreau doesn't directly address man's improving his lot in life, although one can infer that he probably believes man should do so.

### Fourth Passage

From "On Liberty" by John Stuart Mill.

42. (C) The author makes this clear distinction in lines 9–11: the "only purpose for which power can be rightfully exercised over any member . . . is to prevent harm to others." Choices (A) and (B) are innacurate statements of Mill's ideas, and choice (D) is not addressed. Mill does contend that children do not have sovereignty (E), but that contention is not the "one very simple principle."

43. (E) The predicate nominative is the entire clause "that the sole end . . . self-protection." The clause states precisely what "That principle" is.

44. (D) Mill insists that the only justification for controlling the acts of an individual is to prevent harm to others. No other answer choice names such individuals.

45. (B) Parallel syntax is evident in the repetition of "or" plus a gerund: "or reasoning . . . or persuading . . . or entreating." None of the other answer choices can be found in this sentence.

46. (C) Individuals have complete freedom in actions that affect only themselves—as Mill puts it, "Over himself, over his own body and mind." Choice (A) contradicts the passage, and (B), (D), and (E) are not addressed.

47. (D) Children and "those backward states of society in which the race itself may be considered as in its nonage" (immaturity) may be forced to behave in a particular way by parent or government. Competent adults may be coerced only if their actions cause harm to others.

48. (A) Despotism *is* acceptable "when dealing with barbarians" and when that form of government produces the improvement of its citizens. If this end is *not* achieved, despotism is unacceptable.

49. (E) All of the choices, according to Mill, are allowable.

50. (B) It can be inferred that, of the choices given, the author values the protection of society most highly. The essay deals primarily with the sovereignty of the individual except in matters of self-protection. But sovereignty of the individual is not among the answer choices. Choice (A) is incorrect because of the word "unlimited." Mill places restrictions on individual freedom; it is not absolute.

51. (A) The second paragraph gives exceptions to the general principle of individual sovereignty—in the case of children and of "backward states of society." The second paragraph does none of the things listed in choices (B) through (E).

52. (D) This is the major thrust of the essay. Choice (A) contradicts the passage. We have no way to determine Mill's opinion on whether Charlemagne would rule a mature society well (B); he is mentioned only as ruling a "backward society." Choices (C) and (E) can be eliminated because of the word "always."

53. (D) The passage is presented in a matter-of-fact, analytical tone, without emotional wording. There is no evidence of sarcasm, cynicism, or pessimism. Nor is there evidence of optimism; by acknowledging that it is at times necessary for a government to interfere in citizens' lives, Mill is more realistic than optimistic.

54. (C) As we've seen, Mill does not encourage "absolute" freedom of action. He does not encourage behavior that harms others. While it is unlikely that Mill would strongly encourage people to indulge in "self-destructive" actions, he does assert that an individual should be free to do so, leaving (C) as the best answer.

55. (E) Historical allusions are made to the governments of Akbar and Charlemagne. None of the other rhetorical devices is present in the essay.

56. (B) The first paragraph is devoted to the assertion that a government may control individuals only to keep others from harm; the second paragraph gives exceptions to this general principle and lists children and barbarians as those who must be kept from harming themselves. Therefore, the purpose of the passage is one of explanation, of clarification. Mill does not preach against despotism (A), mention the harm of individual rights (C), or assert the sovereign rights of *every* individual (E). Choice (D) is incorrect. Mill suggests circumstances in which individual freedoms should be allowed, but he does not discuss "why" that is so.

## SECTION II: ESSAY QUESTIONS

### Question 1

*Scoring Guide for Question 1 (M. F. K. Fisher and Maya Angelou)*

8–9   This well-written essay clearly demonstrates understanding of the similarities of and differences between the effects of the two passages and the authors' handling of the resources of language in producing these effects. The paper supports its points with specific and cogently presented evidence from the passage. While the paper may contain a few minor errors, it demonstrates the ability to communicate effectively and precisely.

6–7   This essay, also well written, accurately identifies the effects of the two passages but perhaps in a less convincing manner than do top-scoring essays. The discussion of the handling of resources of language may be less thorough and specific. Connection between the thesis and the evidence may not be as clear as that in top-scoring papers. Some errors in mechanics may occur, but overall, this essay shows satisfactory control over organization, development, and use of language.

5   This average essay shows a general understanding of the effects of the passages but may not present as clear a thesis concerning those effects. Its attempts to analyze the handling of resources of language may be simplistic, or evidence offered to support the essay's points may be insufficient and may not be clearly related to the authors' use of the resources of language. The essay may be coherently organized but may show inconsistent control of diction.

3–4   This essay attempts to identify and discuss the effects of the passages but does so based on an inaccurate reading or with presentation of inadequate evidence. It may fail to complete all of the tasks given. This paper may simply catalog the devices, the resources of language, without analysis or comment on the connection between effect and language use. Weak control of the essay format and/or language may be evident, and mechanical errors may be frequent.

1–2 This essay fails to sufficiently respond to the question or the passage. It may fail to understand the effects of the passages, misreading them in a way that distorts those effects. Little or no attention may be given to resources of language used in the passages. This essay fails to convince the reader of its points, and its thesis may be shallow or nonexistent. Persistent weaknesses in grammar and organization may be evident.

*High-Scoring Essay*

Although M. F. K. Fisher's description of Marseille and Maya Angelou's description of Stamps both seek to dispell illusions of their places, they differ in the use of technique, tone, and diction. In the first passage, Fisher uses a satiric style to poke fun of Marseilles' misconceived reputation as "the world's wickedest port." In the other passage, Maya Angelou uses fantastic imagery to also reveal a faulty reputation, this time, of the South. Both authors are attempting to reform mistaken opinions of their places, but they both use extremely different techniques.

In his passage, M. F. K. Fisher seeks only to quell Marseilles' misrepresentation. By wryly examining articles describing Marseilles, Fisher never directly gives his impression of this French port, but instead he reveals the spurious nature of these descriptions. Throughout the passage, a satiric tone is employed. Before introducing Basil Woon's piece on Marseilles, Fisher writes "Sometimes such journalese is almost worth reading for its precociously obsolete views." This statement ridicules Woon's work even before it is introduced. Contributing to the tone of his piece, Fisher not only derides the descriptions of Marseille, but also the backgrounds of their writers. Although Woon did not recommend visiting Marseilles, "he did remain true to his journalistic background with an expectedly titillating mention of it." Fisher masks an otherwise intense diatribe with the light-hearted, humorous use of satire.

The use of precise and informal diction also contributes to the effects of the first passage. In describing newspaper descriptions of Marseilles, the words "mild shockers" are used. The concise image formed by these words contributes to the informal mood of the passage. Also, instead of employing the more conservative and respected word "journalism," Fisher chose to use the word "journalese." This simple substitution embodies the essence of the passage. Like the word journalese, the passage continually ridicules writers' misrepresentations of Marseilles.

Using an opposite style of attack, Maya Angelou does not mock the faulty representation of the South. Instead she contrasts both a discription of the "American fantasy" of the South with her own vivid impressions. The dream-like tone of the first paragraph is aided by the rich choice of diction. "Women float eternally" among "wisps of wisteria." Like paradise, the word eternally allows this scene of gentle alliteration to last forever.

This fantasy is contrasted in the remaining paragraphs with an intense, passionate tone of life. The descriptions, like smells "spiced with the odor of cattle manure, the yellowish acid of the ponds and rivers, the deep pots of greens and beans," are all concrete. These concrete images sharply contrast the ethereal images of women floating eternally. The misrepresentation of the South is easily dispelled by the reality of Maya Angelou's observations. Furthermore, the choice of diction is superb. Angelou's South was "flesh-real and swollen-belly poor." These words easily bring to mind the harshness of black life in the South. Towards the end of the passage, a metaphor is used to change the direction of the passage from concreteness into memories. " . . . passions clanged with the ferocity of armored knights colliding." After erasing the erroneous images of the South, the passage prepares to tell Angelou's story.

Though these passages are similar in their goals, their distinct uses of diction and tone drastically differ their methods of dispelling illusions.

## Analysis of the High-Scoring Essay

The paper begins by directly addressing the topic with a relevant comparison of the essays, pointing out that each "seek[s] to dispel illusions" of the perception of a location. This student recognizes that, although the essays have the same purpose, their differences lie in their stylistic choices. Such interesting ideas as these engage the reader.

The next two paragraphs analyze the Fisher passage on Marseille and together demonstrate a clear understanding of Fisher's use of humor and satire to ridicule those who have painted Marseille as the world's "wickedest port." The student supports the point with appropriate quotations from the passage. The second paragraph specifically analyzes and gives evidence for Fisher's purpose—to dispell the myths about Marseille—while the third paragraph explores how the language of the passage contributes to the effect. The student here uses effective organization and sophisticated diction, making this a strong section.

The fourth and fifth paragraphs deal with the Angelou passage, again analyzing the author's effect and the language used to create it. The analysis begins with Angelou's first paragraph, noting its differences from the Fisher passage—specifically, that she "does not mock the faulty representation" as Fisher does and noting that Angelou creates a "dream-like tone" contrasting with her own impressions. The analysis continues with a discussion of diction, noting how effectively Angelou dispels the misrepresentation of the South with her use of concrete images, an exploration of Angelou's use of metaphor, and an explanation of the metaphor's effect in introducing the realistic treatment which would follow in the work.

The paper concludes with a brief summary of its point—that the authors have similar goals but differing technique. Although the statement is not itself thought provoking, it is an adequate end to the essay. Overall, this student makes points clearly while demonstrating a competent command of language. The essay prompt asks specifically for a comparison and contrast of the "effect" of the two pieces, and this essay can be faulted because it, to some degree, confuses effect with purpose. The essay also misreads the tone of the Fisher passage as an "intense diatribe" and could benefit from additional evidence from the passages. On the whole, however, the paper is intelligent, articulate, and substantiated with enough evidence to make it an upper-half paper.

### Medium-Scoring Essay

Although both passages describe places, their styles are very different. The first passage illustrates how most descriptions of Marseilles treat this city unfairly. This is accomplished through the author's humiliation of these articles. The second passage shows how most people's description of the South is wrong. But rather than through satire, this is accomplished through the use of imagery. Thus both pieces are similar in their effect, but are different in their author's handling of the resources of language.

The first piece by M. F. K. Fisher about the French port of Marseille succeeds in showing that writers about this place only tell the wrong side of the story. Although Marseille like all cities has its attractions and its good points, these writers unfairly give it "A legendary reputation as a world capital for 'dope, whores, and street violence.'" Thus this piece humiliates and satirizes those writers. The tone of this piece is very light and humorous, but it hides the meaning of the author's words. For instance, "The familiar pitch had been made, and idle readers dreaming of a great seaport dedicated to heroin, prostitution, and rioting could easily skip the clumsy details of marketing for fresh fish." By including the talk of fresh fish in the sentence, this passage is making a parody of the article where dope, whores, and street violence are combined with how to make a true boullabaisse. The other article that this passage also talks about says "Marseilles is the world's wickedest port." The passage ridicules this piece with the satiric sentence "Sometimes such journalese is almost worth reading for its precociously obsolete views of a society too easy to forget." This piece is sarcasticaly saying that readers should read this article because it is a great example of something bad. Therefore, this passage is able to use sarcasm, satire, and humiliation to show how Marseille is improperly represented by writers.

The second piece by Maya Angelou about the small town of Stamps, Arkansas tries to show how this place is also improperly represented. This is done by using imagery. First, that passage describes the South as "a much-loved region in the American fantasy where pale white women float eternally under black magnolia trees." These images show that the American fantasy is a peaceful, relaxed South where white people linger around. In fact, this image is wrong. In the next part of the passage, the south is shown in the harsh light of reality. "The South I returned to, however, was flesh-real and swollen-belly poor." These images succeed in showing the harshness of the life the African Americans led in the South. This sentence also shows this point. "And above all, the atmosphere was pressed down with the smell of old fears, and hates, and guilt." The use of atmosphere adds to the depressingly real tone created by these images. Also a metaphor is used "passions clanged with the ferocity of armored knights colliding." This adds to the electrical atmosphere of the passage. By using such strong images to create the electrical atmosphere of the passage, the illussion of the first paragraph is shown for what it truly is. Therefore, this passage is able to use images, words, and atmosphere to show how Stamps, Arkansas is improperly represented by the American Fantasy of the South. The style of this passage is different from the other which humiliates the improper representation. Therefore, both passages use their author's handling of the resources of language in a different way to talk about the same effect.

*Analysis of the Medium-Scoring Essay*

The essay's introduction accurately addresses the topic. However, the student's writing style and depth of thought do not demonstrate the sophistication needed for a high-scoring essay. To claim merely that the two passages are "similar in effect, but . . . different" in their use of language only touches on the topic.

The second paragraph concentrates on Fisher's article and points out that Fisher humiliates (an inaccurate word in this context) and satirizes the authors who had presented Marseille as the "wickedest port." The student seems to recognize Fisher's effect but doesn't extend the observation, merely stating that Fisher is "making a parody" through use of sarcasm. Some examples from the passage are included but are treated perfunctorily and obviously, without depth or strong analysis.

The last paragraph also is accurate in its discussion but presents its points simplistically and uninterestingly. For example, "This sentence also shows the point" fails to connect the two examples effectively, and the claim that the use of methphor creates an "electrical atmosphere" doesn't explain in what way "armored knights colliding" does so. This paragraph, as do those preceding, makes valid points but doesn't explore them in enough depth to engage or convince the reader. This essay could be greatly improved with the use of deeper analysis and more sophisticated presentation.

## Question 2

*Scoring Guide for Question 2 (William Hazlitt)*

8–9  This well-written essay clearly demonstrates an understanding of Hazlitt's purpose in his discussion of comedy and its nature. In addition, it demonstrates a thorough comprehension of how Hazlitt's tone, point of view, and use of stylistic devices reflect that purpose. The thesis is thoughtful and articulate. Strong and relevant evidence from Hazlitt's essay supports intelligent insights concerning Hazlitt's purpose. Thoroughly convincing, this essay shows a clear command of essay writing skills. Although it need not be without errors, the paper shows a mature style and use of language.

6–7  This essay comprehends Hazlitt's purpose, but its thesis may be less explicit than that of the top-scoring essay. The evidence offered may be less convincing, but the paper still demonstrates clear thinking. The connection between the evidence and Hazlitt's purpose may not be as clear as in the top-scoring essays. Although well written, the essay may show some errors while maintaining satisfactory control over diction and the essay's requirements.

5  This adequately written essay shows some understanding of Hazlitt's purpose but may not clearly comprehend the relationship between his language and that purpose. The writer may merely list the devices Hazlitt uses without relating them to his purpose. The thesis may be simplistic and the evidence insufficient to prove the writer's assertions. Acceptable organization and development may be evident, but the style may not be as sophisticated as that of higher-scoring essays.

3–4  This low-scoring essay fails to convince the reader. The weak presentation may not demonstrate a clear understanding of Hazlitt's purpose. Comprehension of how Hazlitt's manipulation of language reflects his purpose may be lacking. The thesis may be unsubstantiated, paragraph development may be weak, and superficial thinking may be evident. Frequent errors in composition that distract the reader may be present.

1–2 This poorly written essay lacks coherence and clarity. It may attempt to state Hazlitt's purpose without any mention of how his language reflects his purpose. The thesis may be overly obvious or absent. Little or no evidence may be offered, and any connection between the evidence and the thesis may be shallow or nonexistent. The paper may be unusually short, and persistent grammatical problems may exist.

### High-Scoring Essay

Two masks symbolize the theater, the one merry, joyful, the other weeping and forlorn. In its turn, the theater acts as a microcosm of life, its twin emblems representative of life's paramount elements: comedy coupled with tragedy.

William Hazlitt explores the relationship of comedy and tragedy, tears and laughter, in <u>Lectures on the English Comic Writers</u>. Hazlitt proposes that, like love and hate, mirth and sadness are not really the opposites that some assume them to be. Apathy is perhaps the true opposite of all four emotions. Both comedy and tragedy are intensely concerned with the human condition. Responses to comedy and tragedy are perhaps our most profound reflexive reactions to the world around us, so it is instructive to examine, as Hazlitt does, the similar foundations of the two.

Hazlitt's enthusiastic tone fits his purpose of persuasion. He writes as if he has just made an amazing discovery, and cannot wait to tell readers about his find. Exploring the nature of the two responses, comedy and tragedy, to the world, Hazlitt writes that both are spurred by man's perception of possibilities, and disappointment or joy results when these are not met, depending on the gravity or ludicrousness of the situation. Indeed comedy often issues from the wellsprings of tragedy and hurt. Laughter can be a defense mechanism, a protective response to the realities of the world and an opportunity to mock the frightening rather than cower before it.

Hazlitt's point of view has arguably become a part of the conventional wisdom these days. Comedy and tragedy are two sides of the same coin, he asserts. Comedy is made up of trifling tragedies. Not serious enough to wound, they instead inspire ridicule and heckling. Confusion can exist between the emotions: People often cry tears of joy on happy occasions or laugh inappropriately in the face of despair. Hazlitt successfully persuades readers of the inexorable relationship between the emotions.

Hazlitt's prose is brisk, almost breathless. Even though compounded with prepositional phrases and the like, the first paragraph of his essay speeds along with emphasized repetition: "We weep . . . we laugh . . . we shed tears . . . we burst into laughter." Hazlitt keeps the reader to a relentless pace with a series of phrases and clauses separated by commas and semicolons, filling long complex sentences. His last sentence in the essay effectively uses this technique as it builds to a crescendo. The <u>eureka</u> tone of amazed discovery is in part achieved by a liberal smattering of exclamation points throughout the essay, such as "it is in a manner compounded of these two!" and "it fails to move our anger or our pity!" The <u>gee whiz!</u> tone which these literary techniques help to create does aid in persuading the reader that Hazlitt's conclusions are valid.

Hazlitt's skillful, rhythmic writing seems capable of lulling readers into believing anything he asserts. He accomplishes his purpose with an enthusiastic passage that clearly demonstrates the inseparable connection between laughter and tears. Understand that, and we are well on our way to understanding life.

*Analysis of the High-Scoring Essay*

This well-written essay begins with two paragraphs that immediately spark the reader's interest, mentioning the comic and tragic masks of the theater and then effectively relating the theater, as a "microcosm of life," to the essay's content and to the topic question. There is no thesis statement, but that isn't an absolute requirement. This student is definitely on the right track, addressing the issue of Hazlitt's purpose and his means of achieving it.

The next two paragraphs explore Hazlitt's point of view and his success in achieving his purpose. It's clear that the student comprehends both Hazlitt's purpose and his perception of comedy and tragedy, relating that perception to contemporary society's. No strong evidence is presented in these paragraphs, but none is required in paragraphs that serve primarily to discuss Hazlitt's ideas.

The fifth paragraph presents an analysis of Hazlitt's technique and style, noting the use of repetition and aptly describing the essay's pace as "breathless . . . relentless." The student also notes that Hazlitt's use of exclamation points produces a "tone of amazed discovery." This writer demonstrates an accurate understanding of how a writer's technique can produce a specific effect on the reader.

The concluding paragraph reiterates the relationship of Hazlitt's "rhythmic writing" to his purpose but doesn't stop at mere summary. It points to the essay's wider implication—that through understanding laughter and tears, we can broaden our understanding of life. This student, like Hazlitt, demonstrates both lively style and discriminating diction.

### Medium-Scoring Essay

William Hazlitt begins by describing the differences between humans and animals. He writes that man has the emotions of humor and sadness that animals don't because men see that things aren't always as good as they could be.

Sometimes people laugh, and sometimes people cry about life, depending on the situation. Through Hazlitt's use of tone and stylistic devices he achieves his purpose—to convince the reader that comedy and tragedy spring from the same well of emotion and essentially help mankind to cope with the vicissitudes of life. People just react to life in different ways.

Depending on people and situations, this can be true. "It is a tragedy or a comedy—sad or merry, as it happens," Hazlitt wrote, showing that people can and do react in a different way to the same event. One of Hazlitt's reasons for writing is to prove that mankind needs different reactions; it is part of man's defense mechanism.

Hazlitt's tone tries to educate people about laughing and crying. Perhaps this is so people can feel less self conscious and work together better in the future without worrying whether their response is right or not, since there isn't a lot of difference between comedy and tragedy. So where one person might see one thing as tragic, the other person may not.

Hazlitt uses many literary devices so readers can picture the differing details of comedy and sadness he discusses. He says tragedy can "shock and wound the mind." He describes tears of relief about comedy or happy times without tragedy. He also uses repetition and exclamation to achieve his purpose. Readers now understand the relationship of comedy and tragedy, and agree with his conclusions.

### Analysis of the Medium-Scoring Essay

This essay clearly demonstrates areas in which a student writing under time pressure can make mistakes. This paper has a variety of problems in coherence, organization, diction, and proof.

The first paragraph fails to elicit much excitement. A good AP essay doesn't necessarily have to grab attention, but this one is particularly uninteresting, merely paraphrasing Hazlitt's opening comment on humans and animals. The second paragraph improves. The student attempts to identify Hazlitt's purpose. But while the statement is well worded, it does not yet deal with one of the assigned tasks, a discussion of Hazlitt's technique.

The third and fourth paragraphs discuss Hazlitt's contentions, but perfunctorily and without great insight. Although Hazlitt's tone is mentioned at the beginning of the fourth paragraph, no analysis or examples follow. Weaknesses of this sort usually arise from inadequacies in planning and organization.

The last paragraph finally addresses literary devices and lists "repetition and exclamation," but once again, no evidence follows proving the connection between literary devices and purpose. Here, the student seems to be grasping for ideas and unsure of his or her point.

While this essay shows some understanding of Hazlitt's purpose, which is to be commended, attempts at proof, analysis, and discussion produce confused sentences with murky ideas. In addition, the student's language, while occasionally sophisticated, is more often than not simplistic. Cumulatively, the essay fails to convince the reader.

## Question 3

*Scoring Guide for Question 3 (Benjamin Franklin)*

8–9   This well-written essay demonstrates clear ideas substantially supported by thoughtful, relevant evidence. It illustrates a sound awareness of the logical requirements of an argumentative essay. Stylistically, this essay is mature, using sophisticated sentence structure and diction. The writing need not be error free, but it clearly shows the writer's ability to construct an effective essay through a combined command of language and logic.

7–6   This essay advances a thesis but may provide weaker evidence for it, although the writer's assertions are clear and well presented. The essay's style is appropriate to the task, but perhaps with less maturity than that of the top-scoring papers. Some errors in diction or syntax may be present, but the writer demonstrates satisfactory control over the conventions of writing and presents his or her ideas distinctly.

5   This essay may be tentative in its assertion of a thesis and may not provide sufficient evidence or discussion to thoroughly convince the reader. It may be adequately written but without control of the full range of elements of composition. Organization may be evident but not entirely effective.

3–4   This essay takes the initial steps toward a thesis but falls short in the details necessary to convince a reader. It attempts to convey a point of view but demonstrates weak control over diction, syntax, development, or organization. This essay may have frequent grammatical or spelling errors.

1–2   This essay lacks the clarity and persuasive force required for effective presentation of an argument. Some attempt may be made to address the issue, but with little or no evidence, the paper fails to satisfy the reader. It may be exceptionally short and poorly written on several counts. Organization and paragraph development may be particularly weak. Persistent weaknesses in grammar and spelling may distract the reader.

*High-Scoring Essay*

It is his reason that separates man from the creatures of the wild. Reason also fathers conscience, to act as a counterweight to the volatile animal passions of which his sentience has suddenly made him aware. If this were the only function of reason, to launch conscience, the world could theoretically be a better place. Imagine a society where a criminal, about to rob a hapless victim, stops as his mind reasons out the consequences. Reaching the reasonable conclusion that any punishment would be longer lasting and worse than the immediate benefits of his crime, the robber stops. Unfortunately, in reality, the human mind just does not work this way. Reason is not entirely an agent of good, of conscience. Reason can enter Promethean combat with the conscience it creates and shrewdly invent a means for its owner to justify some of his baser impulses.

Ben Franklin addresses man's propensity to justify and explain away his actions through reasoning, to allow caprices and animal impulses to persist. His Autobiography makes the valid point that once someone has his mind set on doing something, reason frequently acts as a tool to circumvent conscience rather than as an agent of that conscience.

Indeed, virtually any action can be justified through some semblance of reason, no matter how faulty the logic, how heinous the crime. For every violence, for every deceit, a dozen specious premises rise to the task of denying any wrongdoing by the criminal. For example, study the logic which convinced looters during any recent riots in American inner cities that they were justified in robbing innocent storekeepers. This kind of reasoning, sadly, occurs daily in the minds of humanity.

Empirical approaches to life, from the Socratic method to Hegelian philosophy, have relied on reason to explain both the natural world and the human response to that world. Moral relativism and "situational ethics" depend on reason of a sort. Proponents of such philosophies insist that man must abandon preconceptions, that he must judge each situation as it happens, and use reason to determine what is morally correct under each set of specific circumstances which arise. But it is not only relativists who look to reason as a means of understanding and reacting to the world. Strict, Draconian moral codes find their justification in reason as well. Man's actions, whether representing the "rule of law," or the most liberal definitions of right and wrong, are always defended with arguments paying homage to Reason. This holds as true for the Supreme Court justice as for the urban pickpocket . . . whether the subject feels he is doing the will of God and country, or knows he is shrewdly evading responsibility. Reason is the tool of man's shell game with his conscience.

Franklin, then, is essentially correct. After a moment of balancing "between principle and inclination," man seizes upon the "convenience" of being a "reasonable creature, since it enables one to find or make a reason for everything one has a mind to do." What one has a mind to do may be quixotic or craven, vainglorious or altruistic, but whatever the case man can use reason to nullify the conscience that is its offspring.

*Analysis of the High-Scoring Essay*

This high-scoring essay begins with a relevant discussion of reason and its function. Initiating the idea that "reason fathers conscience," the student provides a hypothetical example of a robber who stops in midcrime because his reason has convinced him the punishment would exceed the gain. The student's thesis follows, with the interesting concept that reason can engage in "Promethean combat" with the conscience to justify any human action.

The next paragraph acknowledges Ben Franklin as the inspiration for this topic and capsulizes Franklin's remarks about reason. This paragraph serves as direct tie to the essay question.

The third paragraph suggests that humans use reason to justify any kind of action, even immoral ones, and provides another relevant example, looters during recent riots who feel justified in their unlawful actions.

The fourth paragraph includes an intelligent review of several philosophies and "empirical approaches" that use reason as a way of determining one's actions. This paragaraph notes that all those taking positions, from Supreme Court justices to common thieves, use reason to justify actions. The paragraph ends with a somewhat mixed but still effective metaphor—"reason is the tool of man's shell game with his conscience."

The concluding paragraph mentions again Franklin's insight, that humans will always find a reasonable way to explain any action. The student once more uses sophisticated style and diction with phrasing like "quixotic or craven, vainglorious or altruistic." This writer posses the command of language evidenced only in top-scoring essays. This essay might be improved if it recognized Franklin's obviously playful tone and responded in kind, at least to some extent. But, overall, the paper is on topic, philosophically insightful, and intelligently presented and provides sufficient convincing examples from real-life situations.

### Medium-Scoring Essay

Ben Franklin is one of our most important Founding Fourfathers. Like Alexander Hamilton and others who never achieved the presidency, he still had a profound impact on the U.S. His importance is shown in his autobiography, where he discusses vegetarianism and the morality of eating fish among other topics.

Ben Franklin contemplates how people can change their mind about things, such as whether it's O.K. to eat animals that have been alive (like fish). He acknowledges that sometimes people are tempted to do something they might think wrong, just as he was tempted by the delightful smell of the fish cooking when he was on a boat trip. Franklin also explains that people use reason to approve their actions. His ideas about reason are right. Man frequently employs reason to back up his deeds, whether they are right or wrong. It seems that everyone can find a way to defend their actions. I have personally seen this trait at work, both in myself and my friends.

By using reason, Franklin proved that eating the fish, even though he believed in vegetarianism before, wasn't wrong after all. In the end, Ben Franklin says that it is a good thing that he is a reasonable creature. He means that he was reasonable enough to be open-minded about eating fish; he changed his mind accordingly after listening to his reason. I think Franklin was correct in this point too. It's important to be open-minded about things and not to eliminate what you're willing to try. Like Franklin, we shouldn't be scared to try something new if our reason can explain it to us.

Thus, Ben Franklin shows that reason is a valid tool in helping man to defend his actions, because without reason his actions might be stuck in the same old ways. He would never try some thing new. And Benjamin Franklin, as he was a great man of our country, is someone to whom that was important.

### Analysis of the Medium-Scoring Essay

This poorly written essay would score at the bottom of the medium range. The first paragraph is ineffective. It fails to address the question of the validity of Franklin's assertions on justifying one's actions through reasoning. The paragraph lacks a thesis and includes such irrelevant information as the reference to Alexander Hamilton. The student also demonstrates weak command of language, misusing words such as "Founding Fourfathers."

The second paragraph improves a bit and approaches the topic. Beginning with a paraphrase of Franklin's fish-eating experience, the student gives an opinion on the validity of using reason. But this thesis is especially weak, merely claiming that Franklin was "right." The writer offers no evidence to convince the reader, but rather claims only to have personally seen some examples.

The next paragraph discusses the need for one to be reasonable in order to try new things. The writer is on shaky ground once again, exhibiting simplistic ideas with no support.

The conclusion merely summarizes the essay and still avoids the topic. This essay deserves a low score because it offers no proof for its assertions, its treatment of the topic is superficial, and its presentation is riddled with errors and unsophisticated diction.

# PRACTICE TEST 3

## SECTION I: MULTIPLE-CHOICE QUESTIONS

**Time: 60 Minutes**
**56 Questions**

This section consists of selections from prose works and questions on their content, form, and style. Read each selection carefully. Choose the best answer of the five choices.

*Questions 1–15.* Read the following passage carefully before you begin to answer the questions.

　　At Oxford in 1850 the contemporaries of young Robert Cecil agreed that he would end as Prime Minister either because or in spite of his remorselessly uncompromising opinions. Throughout life he never bothered to restrain
(5)　them. His youthful speeches were remarkable for their virulence and insolence; he was not, said Disraeli, "a man who measures his phrases." A "salisbury" became a synonym for a political imprudence. He once compared the Irish in their incapacity for self-government to Hottentots
(10)　and spoke of an Indian candidate for Parliament as "that black man." In the opinion of Lord Morley his speeches were always a pleasure to read because "they were sure to contain one blazing indiscretion which it is a delight to remember." Whether these were altogether accidental is
(15)　open to question, for though Lord Salisbury delivered his speeches without notes, they were worked out in his head beforehand and emerged clear and perfect in sentence structure. In that time the art of oratory was considered part of the equipment of a statesman and anyone reading from a
(20)　written speech would have been regarded as pitiable. When Lord Salisbury spoke, "every sentence," said a fellow member, "seemed as essential, as articulate, as vital to the argument as the members of his body to an athlete."

Appearing in public before an audience about whom he
(25) cared nothing, Salisbury was awkward; but in the Upper
House, where he addressed his equals, he was perfectly and
strikingly at home. He spoke sonorously, with an occasional
change of tone to icy mockery or withering sarcasm. When a
recently ennobled Whig took the floor to lecture the House
(30) of Lords in high-flown and solemn Whig sentiments, Salisbury asked a neighbor who the speaker was and on hearing
the whispered identification, replied perfectly audibly, "I
thought he was dead." When he listened to others he could
become easily bored, revealed by a telltale wagging of his leg
(35) which seemed to one observer to be saying, "When will all
this be over?" Or sometimes, raising his heels off the floor,
he would set up a sustained quivering of his knees and legs
which could last for half an hour at a time. At home, when
made restless by visitors, it shook the floor and made the
(40) furniture rattle, and in the House his colleagues on the front
bench complained it made them seasick. If his legs were at
rest his long fingers would be in motion, incessantly twisting
and turning a paper knife or beating a tattoo on his knee or
on the arm of his chair. . . .
(45)    Mr. Gladstone, though in political philosophy his bitter-
est antagonist, acknowledged him "a great gentleman in
private society." In private life he was delightful and
sympathetic and a complete contrast to his public self. In
public acclaim, Salisbury was uninterested, for—since the
(50) populace was uninstructed—its opinions, as far as he was
concerned, were worthless. He ignored the public and
neither possessed nor tried to cultivate the personal touch
that makes a political leader a recognizable personality to
the man in the street and earns him a nickname like "Pam"
(55) or "Dizzy" or the "Grand Old Man." Not in the press, not
even in *Punch,* was Lord Salisbury ever called anything but
Lord Salisbury. He made no attempt to conceal his dislike
for mobs of all kinds, "not excluding the House of
Commons." After moving to the Lords, he never returned to
(60) the Commons to listen to its debates from the Peers' Gallery
or chat with members in the Lobby, and if compelled to
allude to them in his own House, would use a tone of airy

contempt, to the amusement of visitors from the Commons
who came to hear him. But this was merely an outward pose
(65) designed to underline his deep inner sense of the patrician.
He was not rank-conscious; he was indifferent to honors or
any other form of recognition. It was simply that as a Cecil,
and a superior one, he was born with a consciousness in his
bones and brain cells of ability to rule and saw no reason to
(70) make any concessions of this prescriptive right to anyone
whatever.

Having entered the House of Commons in the customary
manner for peers' sons, from a family-controlled borough in
an uncontested election at the age of twenty-three, and,
(75) during his fifteen years in the House of Commons, having
been returned unopposed five times from the same borough, and having for the last twenty-seven years sat in the
House of Lords, he had little personal experience of
vote-getting. He regarded himself not as responsible *to* the
(80) people but as responsible *for* them. They were in his care.
What reverence he felt for anyone was directed not down
but up—to the monarchy. He revered Queen Victoria, who
was some ten years his senior, both as her subject and, with
chivalry toward her womanhood, as a man. For her he
(85) softened his brusqueness even if at Balmoral he could not
conceal his boredom.

1. In relation to the passage as a whole, the first sentence of the
first paragraph presents
   (A) a paradox that reveals a dominant characteristic of Lord
   Salisbury's character
   (B) a criticism of Lord Salisbury that the rest of the passage
   will withdraw
   (C) a definition of the principles upon which Lord Salisbury
   was to base his life
   (D) an exception to the ideas that make up the rest of the
   passage
   (E) an amusing comment with no important relevance to the
   development of the rest of the passage

2. Disraeli's description of Lord Salisbury as not "a man who measures his phrases" (lines 6–7) is an example of
   (A) simile
   (B) understatement
   (C) indirect discourse
   (D) *ad hominem* argument
   (E) diatribe

3. Compared to the second, third, and fourth paragraphs, the first paragraph makes more extensive use of
   (A) direct quotations from Lord Salisbury himself
   (B) direct quotations from Lord Salisbury's contemporaries
   (C) cause and effect reasoning
   (D) *ad hominem* argument
   (E) abstract generalizations

4. Which of the following best describes the function of the second paragraph of the passage?
   (A) It makes an assertion that is proven in the third paragraph.
   (B) It defines more clearly the flaws of Lord Salisbury's character.
   (C) It develops the idea of Lord Salisbury's "political imprudence."
   (D) It enlarges the characterization begun in the first paragraph.
   (E) It refutes a common misconception about Lord Salisbury.

5. We can infer that Salisbury was awkward before an audience he cared little about (paragraph two) because he
   (A) was speaking without notes
   (B) lacked public-speaking skills
   (C) had not bothered to prepare
   (D) was nervous about appearing before an audience that he feared was unsympathetic to his ideas
   (E) feared he would betray his real feelings of contempt

6. In line 43, the word "tattoo" can be best defined as a
   (A) rhythm
   (B) continuous drumming
   (C) picture on the skin
   (D) forbidden activity
   (E) percussion instrument

7. In the first sentence of the third paragraph, the author cites Gladstone's words about Lord Salisbury because
   I. they have the special authority of words of praise from a political opponent
   II. they introduce a favorable presentation of Lord Salisbury's private life
   III. it would especially embarrass Lord Salisbury to be praised by a political enemy

   (A) II only
   (B) I and II only
   (C) I and III only
   (D) II and III only
   (E) I, II, and III

8. From the phrase in the third paragraph "not in the press, not even in *Punch,* was Lord Salisbury ever called anything but Lord Salisbury," we can infer that *Punch* was probably a
   (A) contemporary novel
   (B) political report
   (C) conservative magazine
   (D) satirical publication
   (E) daily newspaper

9. In the last sentence of the third paragraph, all of the following words or phrases function as intensifiers and could be omitted EXCEPT
   (A) "simply"
   (B) "and brain cells"
   (C) "no reason"
   (D) "any"
   (E) "whatever"

10. Which of the following accurately describe(s) the long sentence which begins the last paragraph of the passage ("Having entered . . . vote-getting")?

    I. It is a sentence containing more than ten prepositional phrases.
    II. It is a sentence using parallel participial phrases.
    III. It is a periodic sentence.

    (A) I only
    (B) I and II only
    (C) I and III only
    (D) II and III only
    (E) I, II, and III

11. To which of the following would Lord Salisbury have been most likely to have shown deference?
    (A) the Prince of Wales
    (B) the President of the United States
    (C) an elderly female newspaper-seller
    (D) the British Prime Minister
    (E) a Scottish knight

12. The speaker of the passage may be best described as
    (A) a skeptical biographer
    (B) a political supporter
    (C) a sympathetic observer
    (D) a mordant satirist
    (E) an objective commentator

13. In its presentation of the character of Lord Salisbury, the passage overtly employs all of the following sources EXCEPT the
    (A) words of contemporary politicians
    (B) author's interpretation of Lord Salisbury's actions
    (C) words of Lord Salisbury himself
    (D) judgments of other modern historians
    (E) words of unnamed contemporaries of Lord Salisbury

14. Which of the following does the passage present as central to an understanding of Lord Salisbury?
    (A) His deep-seated fear of the possibility of major social change
    (B) His intense consciousness of his social rank
    (C) His hypocrisy
    (D) His genuine respect for men and women of all classes
    (E) His firm belief in the native superiority of his family

15. The passage reveals all of the following biographical facts about Lord Salisbury EXCEPT that he
    (A) served in the House of Commons
    (B) was a contemporary of Queen Victoria and of Gladstone
    (C) disapproved of home rule for Ireland
    (D) served in the House of Lords
    (E) became Prime Minister late in the nineteenth century

*Questions 16–28.* Read the following passage carefully before you begin to answer the questions.

### *Of Democracy*

The power that makes the laws knows better than any other person how they ought to be executed and how interpreted. It seems from this that the best constitution would be that where the legislative and executive powers are
(5)   united: but that very union is the thing which renders this government so unsatisfactory in certain respects, because those things which ought to be distinguished are not, and because the prince and the Sovereign, then the same, form in a manner a government without a government.
(10)   It is not good for the power that makes the laws to execute them; neither would it be proper that the body of the people should turn their eyes from general views to fix them on particular objects. Nothing is more dangerous than private interest having any influence on public affairs, and the abuse
(15) of the laws by the government is a lesser evil than the corruption of the legislator, which is an infallible consequence of such private views. In such a case, the very

substance of the State is changed, and all reformation becomes impossible. A people who never abused the powers
(20) of government would never abuse independence; a people who always governed well would have no need to be governed.

Taking the word "democracy" in its strict sense, perhaps there never did, and never will, exist such a government. It is
(25) against the natural order that the greater number should govern, and the smaller number be governed. It cannot be imagined that the chief part of the people should be always assembled for the discharge of public affairs, and it is evident that commissioners cannot be appointed to govern
(30) without the form of administration changing.

In fact, I believe it may be laid down as a principle that, when the functions of government are divided among a number of tribunals, the fewer in number will sooner or later acquire the greatest authority, if it were for no other
(35) reason than because affairs will be transacted with greatest ease and expedition in fewest hands, which naturally brings them control of affairs.

Besides, how many circumstances must conspire to make such a government possible! First, the State must be a very
(40) small one, where the people can easily assemble, and where each citizen can easily know all the others; there must, in the second place, be great simplicity of manners to prevent a multiplicity of affairs and those tedious discussions which are the consequence of them; and there must also be much
(45) equality in the rank and fortunes of all the citizens, or there will not be equality of rights and authority for long; finally there must be little or no luxury, for whether luxury be considered as the effect of riches, or as the incitement to covet them, it corrupts at once both the wealthy and the
(50) poor, the one by its possession, the other by the desire of possessing; it betrays a nation into effeminate softness, and debases it by vanity; and it takes away all the citizens from the State by making them subservient to each other, and all the slaves of opinion.
(55)    This is the reason why a celebrated author[1] has made virtue the principle on which a republic must be founded;

because all these circumstances could never subsist without her ruling influence. But this fine genius has not only omitted making the necessary distinctions, but he is not
(60) always exact, and sometimes obscure, and he did not perceive that, the sovereign authority being everywhere the same, the same principle must prevail in every well-formed State, though in a greater or less degree, according to its form of government.

(65)    I must yet add that there is no government so subject to civil wars and internal agitations as the democratic or popular one, because there is not one which has so strong and so continual a tendency to change its form, or which needs more vigilance and courage to maintain it. This is the
(70) constitution which, more than any other, requires the citizen to arm himself with strength and constancy, and to repeat every day of his life what a virtuous Palatine[2] said in the Diet of Poland: *Mal Pericolosam Libertatem Quam Quietum Servitum.*[3]

(75)    If there were a nation of gods they might be governed by a democracy. So perfect a government will not agree with men.

[1]Montesquieu, from *The Spirit of Laws,* Book III, chapter 3.
[2]The Palatine of Posen, father of the King of Poland.
[3]"Better liberty with danger than peace with slavery."

16. Which of the following does the author cite as possibly a major danger to democracy?
    (A) Overcrowded courts
    (B) Ineffective committees
    (C) Power-hungry leaders
    (D) Organized religion
    (E) Private enterprise

17. According to the author, which of the following tribunals would be most efficient?
    (A) One that represents all socioeconomic levels
    (B) One with the fewest members
    (C) One of all legislators
    (D) One with an equal number of legislators and private-interest groups
    (E) One made up of experts on the issue

18. Adding to the coherency of the second sentence in the fifth paragraph (lines 39–54) is
    (A) heavy use of extended metaphor
    (B) persuasive and argumentative tone
    (C) complex use of parallel structure
    (D) biting condemnation of democracy
    (E) use of ironic hyperbole

19. The fifth paragraph (lines 38–54) differs from the other paragraphs in that it
    (A) defines how a democracy could be possible
    (B) criticizes present democracies
    (C) ridicules those who believe in democracy
    (D) suggests the ease of implementing a democracy
    (E) hypothesizes the traits of a good leader

20. According to the passage, which of the following groups is most likely to function smoothly under a democracy?
    (A) Perfect, godlike people
    (B) Lawmakers
    (C) Minorities
    (D) Political leaders
    (E) Private business owners

21. It can be inferred from the passage that the foremost obstacle to democracy is
    (A) civil war
    (B) seditious legislators
    (C) avaricious capitalists
    (D) the natural order
    (E) inequality among citizens

22. According to the author, which of the following conditions is/are necessary for an efficient democracy?

    I. Financial equality
   II. Enthusiastic obedience
  III. Simple, uncomplicated lifestyle

   (A) I only
   (B) I and II only
   (C) I and III only
   (D) II and III only
   (E) I, II, and III

23. The organization of each of the essay's body paragraphs can best be described as presenting
   (A) a further discussion of previous tangents
   (B) an aspect of democracy and discussion of the aspect
   (C) comparison and contrast
   (D) strong, persuasive arguments
   (E) specific examples illustrating suppositions

24. Which of the following best represents the paradox the author sees in democracy?
   (A) "the best constitution . . . so unsatisfactory" (lines 3–6)
   (B) "the prince and the Sovereign . . . government without a government" (lines 8–9)
   (C) "Nothing is more dangerous than . . . public affairs" (lines 13–14)
   (D) "a people who always . . . no need to be governed" (lines 20–22)
   (E) "Taking the word . . . such a government." (lines 23–24)

25. The essay may best be characterized as
   (A) exposition
   (B) argumentation
   (C) description
   (D) narration
   (E) demonstration

26. Of the following phrases, which demonstrates the most condescending attitude?
    (A) "a government without a government" (line 9)
    (B) "infallible consequence" (lines 16–17)
    (C) "those tedious discussions" (line 43)
    (D) "needs more vigilance and courage" (line 69)
    (E) "will not agree with men" (lines 76–77)

27. Which of the following, if present, would best strengthen the
author's argument?
    (A) A comparison of democracy with monarchy
    (B) Other expert opinions
    (C) A historical background of democracies
    (D) Examples of more efficient forms of government
    (E) Examples of incompetent laws

28. The author's overall attitude toward democracy may best be
described as
    (A) aggressive
    (B) vituperative
    (C) moderate
    (D) skeptical
    (E) sanguine

*Questions 29–42.* Read the following passage carefully before you
begin to answer the questions.

    This single stick, which you now behold ingloriously lying
in that neglected corner, I once knew in a flourishing state in
a forest; it was full of sap, full of leaves, and full of boughs;
but now, in vain, does the busy art of man pretend to vie
(5) with nature, by tying that withered bundle of twigs to its
sapless trunk; 'tis now, at best, but the reverse of what it was,
a tree turned upside down, the branches on the earth, and
the root in the air; 'tis now handled by every dirty wench,
condemned to do her drudgery, and, by a capricious kind of
(10) fate, destined to make other things clean, and be nasty itself;
at length, worn to the stumps in the service of the maids,

either thrown out of doors, or condemned to the last use, of
kindling a fire. When I beheld this, I sighed, and said within
myself: *Surely Man is a Broomstick!* Nature sent him into the
(15) world strong and lusty, in a thriving condition, wearing his
own hair on his head, the proper branches of this reasoning
vegetable, until the axe of intemperance has lopped off his
green boughs, and left him a withered trunk; he then flies to
art, and puts on a periwig, valuing himself upon an unnatu-
(20) ral bundle of hairs (all covered with powder) that never
grew on his head; but now should this our broomstick
pretend to enter the scene, proud of all those birchen spoils
it never bore, and all covered with dust, though the
sweepings of the finest lady's chamber, we should be apt to
(25) ridicule and despise its vanity. Partial judges that we are of
our own excellences, and other men's defaults!

But a broomstick, perhaps you will say, is an emblem of a
tree standing on its head; and pray, what is a man but a
topsy-turvy creature, his animal faculties perpetually
(30) mounted on his rational, his head where his heels should be,
groveling on the earth! And yet, with all his faults, he sets up
to be a universal reformer and corrector of abuses, a
remover of grievances, rakes into every slut's corner of
nature, bringing hidden corruption to the light, and raises a
(35) mighty dust where there was none before; sharing deeply all
the while in the very same pollutions he pretends to sweep
away; his last days are spent in slavery to women, and
generally the least deserving; till, worn out to the stumps,
like his brother broom, he is either kicked out of doors, or
(40) made use of to kindle flames for others to warm themselves
by.

29. All of the following are present in the opening sentence of the
passage EXCEPT
(A) syntactically complex structure
(B) parallel construction
(C) a pedantic tone
(D) the narrative of a broomstick's life
(E) subordinate clauses

30. According to the author, both a broomstick and a man
    (A) cleanse the world
    (B) become corrupted by the evil in society
    (C) can be proud of their humble accomplishments
    (D) symbolize integrity in the world
    (E) were untainted in their natural state

31. Which of the following does the author imply?

    I. Man has the ability to return to a better state.
   II. Man in his youthful, natural state is closer to perfection
       than when he is older.
  III. Man misuses nature for his own needs.

    (A) I only
    (B) II only
    (C) I and II only
    (D) II and III only
    (E) I, II, and III

32. According to the passage, the broomstick symbolizes
    (A) society's corruption of the youth
    (B) the goodness in nature that man uses and discards
    (C) the triumph of nature over man's evil tendencies
    (D) the evil inherent in man's soul
    (E) the tremendous power of nature that man fears

33. The "axe of intemperance" (line 17) can be interpreted as
    (A) an understatement of man's dominance over nature
    (B) a metaphor for nature's nourishing elements
    (C) a simile comparing man and tree
    (D) a hyperbole describing man's destruction
    (E) a metaphor for man's excesses

34. The author's attitude toward mankind can best be described as
    (A) disillusionment at man's deeds
    (B) perplexed concern for man's future
    (C) guarded optimism for man's soul
    (D) anger at the society man has created
    (E) sincere praise for man's use of nature

35. Which of the following does NOT demonstrate a negative attitude by this author?
    (A) "a flourishing state in a forest" (lines 2–3)
    (B) "the axe of intemperance" (line 17)
    (C) "an unnatural bundle of hairs" (lines 19–20)
    (D) "sweepings of the finest lady's chamber" (line 24)
    (E) "sharing . . . the very same pollutions he pretends to sweep away" (lines 35–37)

36. According to the author, which of the following is NOT a similarity between man and the broomstick?
    (A) Both endure the same fate.
    (B) Both began life in a healthy state.
    (C) Both are turned "topsy-turvy."
    (D) Both accomplish magnificent achievements.
    (E) Both attempt to cleanse while being dirty.

37. The word referred to by the phrase "this reasoning vegetable" (lines 16–17) is
    (A) "*Man*" (line 14)
    (B) "hair" (line 16)
    (C) "head" (line 16)
    (D) "branches" (line 16)
    (E) "green boughs" (line 18)

38. In the essay, the author uses all of the following literary devices EXCEPT
    (A) metaphor
    (B) parallel syntax
    (C) oxymoron
    (D) analogy
    (E) symbolism

39. In context, "this our broomstick" (line 21) is a
    (A) symbol for the thriving forest
    (B) metaphor for man's pretentious character
    (C) link between nature and society
    (D) demonstration of nature's control
    (E) representation of man's intelligence

40. What does the author imply about man's ability to be a "corrector of abuses" (line 32)?
    (A) Man easily solves his own problems.
    (B) Man effectively improves society.
    (C) Man can act as a fair arbitrator in disputes.
    (D) Man readily accepts his role as a social reformer.
    (E) Man causes problems where none previously existed.

41. The tone of the passage can best be described as
    (A) neutral toward society
    (B) condescending toward nature
    (C) cynical toward mankind
    (D) bellicose toward mankind
    (E) dogmatic toward society

42. Which of the following represents the strongest statement of the author's theme?
    (A) "condemned to do her drudgery" (line 9)
    (B) "destined to make other things clean" (line 10)
    (C) "the axe of intemperance has lopped off his green boughs" (lines 17–18)
    (D) "Partial judges that we are of our own excellences" (lines 25–26)
    (E) "his last days are spent in slavery" (line 37)

*Questions 43–56.* Read the following passage carefully before you begin to answer the questions.

The time is coming, I hope, when each new author, each new artist, will be considered, not in his proportion to any other author or artist, but in his relation to the human nature, known to us all, which it is his privilege, his high
(5) duty, to interpret. "The true standard of the artist is in every man's power" already, as [Edmund] Burke says; Michelangelo's "light of the piazza," the glance of the common eye, is and always was the best light on a statue; . . . but hitherto the mass of common men have been afraid to apply their own
(10) simplicity, naturalness, and honesty to the appreciation of

the beautiful. They have always cast about for the instruction of some one who professed to know better, and who browbeat wholesome common-sense into the self-distrust that ends in sophistication. . . . They have been taught to
(15) compare what they see and what they read, not with the things that they have observed and known, but with the things that some other artist or writer has done. Especially if they have themselves the artistic impulse in any direction they are taught to form themselves, not upon life, but upon
(20) the masters who became masters only by forming themselves upon life. The seeds of death are planted in them, and they can only produce the still-born, the academic. They are not told to take their work into the public square and see if it seems true to the chance passer, but to test it by the work of
(25) the very men who refused and decried any other test of their own work. The young writer who attempts to report the phrase and carriage of every-day life, who tries to tell just how he has heard men talk and seen them look, is made to feel guilty of something low and unworthy by the stupid
(30) people who would like to have him show how Shakespeare's men talked and looked, or Scott's, or Thackeray's, or Balzac's, or Hawthorne's, or Dickens's; he is instructed to idealize his personages, that is, to take the life-likeness out of them, and put the book-likeness into them. He is
(35) approached in the spirit of the wretched pedantry into which learning . . . always decays when it withdraws itself and stands apart from experience in an attitude of imagined superiority, and which would say with the same confidence to the scientist: "I see that you are looking at a grasshopper
(40) there which you have found in the grass, and I suppose you intend to describe it. Now don't waste your time and sin against culture in that way. I've got a grasshopper here, which has been evolved at considerable pains and expense out of the grasshopper in general; in fact, it's a type. It's
(45) made up of wire and cardboard, very prettily painted in a conventional tint, and it's perfectly indestructible. It isn't very much like a real grasshopper, but it's a great deal nicer, and it's served to represent the notion of a grasshopper ever since man emerged from barbarism. You may say that it's

(50) artificial. Well, it is artificial; but then it's ideal too; and what you want to do is to cultivate the ideal. You'll find the books full of my kind of grasshopper, and scarcely a trace of yours in any of them. The thing that you are proposing to do is commonplace; but if you say that it isn't commonplace, for
(55) the very reason that it hasn't been done before, you'll have to admit that it's photographic."

... I hope the time is coming when not only the artist, but the common, average man, who always "has the standard of the arts in his power," will have also the courage to apply it,
(60) and will reject the ideal grasshopper wherever he finds it, in science, in literature, in art, because it is not "simple, natural, and honest," because it is not like a real grasshopper. But ... I think the time is yet far off, and that the people who have been brought up on the ideal grasshopper, the
(65) heroic grasshopper, the impassioned grasshopper, the self-devoted, adventureful, good old romantic cardboard grasshopper, must die out before the simple, honest, and natural grasshopper can have a fair field. I am in no haste to compass the end of these good people, whom I find in the
(70) meantime very amusing. It is delightful to meet one of them, either in print or out of it—some sweet elderly lady or excellent gentleman whose youth was pastured on the literature of thirty or forty years ago—and to witness the confidence with which they preach their favorite authors as
(75) all the law and the prophets. They have commonly read little or nothing since or, if they have, they have judged it by a standard taken from these authors, and never dreamed of judging it by nature; they are destitute of the documents in the case of the later writers; they suppose that Balzac was
(80) the beginning of realism, and that Zola is its wicked end; they are quite ignorant, but they are ready to talk you down, if you differ from them, with an assumption of knowledge sufficient for any occasion. The horror, the resentment, with which they receive any question of their literary saints is
(85) genuine; you descend at once very far in the moral and social scale, and anything short of offensive personality is too good for you; it is expressed to you that you are one to be avoided, and put down even a little lower than you have naturally fallen.

43. The tone of the passage could best be described as
    (A) somber
    (B) ornate
    (C) didactic
    (D) critical
    (E) formal

44. The author feels common people make which of the following mistakes?
    (A) Judging a work of art too quickly
    (B) Letting their own interpretations interfere with their reading
    (C) Letting authorities tell them how to interpret literature
    (D) Basing their judgments on appearances only
    (E) Not modeling their tastes after their neighbors'

45. The phrase "The seeds of death" (line 21) is a
    (A) metaphor for imitative art
    (B) symbol for the destruction of art
    (C) metaphor for the art of an older age
    (D) reference to Michelangelo's art
    (E) symbol of artistic immaturity

46. In context, which of the following does NOT represent an object of the author's criticism?
    (A) "some one . . . who browbeat wholesome common-sense" (lines 12–13)
    (B) "are taught to form themselves, not upon life" (line 19)
    (C) "he is instructed to idealize his personages" (lines 32–33)
    (D) "put the book-likeness into them" (line 34)
    (E) "will reject the ideal grasshopper" (line 60)

47. The author's criticism of those who read only older literature is tempered by the fact that he
    (A) is certain their ideas will die out quickly
    (B) finds them entertaining and delightful
    (C) dismisses them as unimportant
    (D) alleges they do little harm to the average reader
    (E) acknowledges that they have great knowledge

48. The idealized grasshopper is a symbol for
    (A) the quest to merge art and science
    (B) the human search for perfection
    (C) art that lasts through the ages
    (D) artificial rather than realistic art
    (E) the scientist's folly in trying to describe nature

49. According to the author, the irony of the idealized grasshopper is that
    (A) it ceases to be realistic
    (B) scientists will find it useful
    (C) it blends science and art into one
    (D) it cannot be distinguished from a real grasshopper
    (E) it has not been created

50. Which of the following types of grasshopper does the author feel will be the slowest to become integrated into mainstream literature?
    (A) The heroic grasshopper
    (B) The ideal grasshopper
    (C) The simple, honest, natural grasshopper
    (D) The impassioned grasshopper
    (E) The good old romantic cardboard grasshopper

51. Which of the following would the author recommend for modern readers?

    I. Read only classical literature.
    II. Read literature from all ages.
    III. Read with your own interpretation.

    (A) I only
    (B) II only
    (C) III only
    (D) I and II only
    (E) II and III only

52. The story of the grasshopper contains
    (A) hidden hyperbole
    (B) satiric humor
    (C) overstated oxymoron
    (D) ruthless criticism
    (E) remarkable realism

53. In context, which of the following best represents the author's main idea about art appreciation?
    (A) "simplicity, naturalness, and honesty" (line 10)
    (B) "people who would like to have him show how Shakespeare's men talked" (lines 30–31)
    (C) "an attitude of imagined superiority" (lines 37–38)
    (D) "it is artificial; but then it's ideal too" (line 50)
    (E) "witness the confidence with which they preach their favorite authors" (lines 73–74)

54. What similarity is suggested between the scientist and artist who discuss the grasshopper?
    (A) The models of their studies will both be artificial.
    (B) They both love to observe nature.
    (C) They both look to old masters for inspiration.
    (D) Both of their methods will become obsolete.
    (E) They both spend too much time on research.

55. Which of the following devices is NOT used in the passage?
    (A) Irony
    (B) Metaphor
    (C) Motif
    (D) Allusion
    (E) Analogy

56. The "sweet elderly lady or excellent gentleman" (lines 71–72) represents a stereotype of
    (A)  current literary critics
    (B)  the well-rounded literary audience
    (C)  those who reject new artistic representations
    (D)  those who read carelessly
    (E)  middle-class readers

**STOP.** IF YOU FINISH BEFORE TIME IS CALLED, CHECK YOUR WORK ON THIS SECTION ONLY. DO NOT WORK ON SECTION II.

# SECTION II: ESSAY QUESTIONS

**Time: 2 Hours**
**3 Questions**

## Question 1

(Suggested time—40 minutes. This question counts one-third of the total essay section score.)

The following excerpt is from Henry James's short story "The Jolly Corner," in which the author tells of a man who returns to his native New York City after living in Europe for thirty-three years. As the passage begins, the main character has reintroduced himself to an old friend, Alice Staverton. Read the passage carefully; then write an essay in which you analyze how the author's style effectively implies his attitude toward the past and present. Examine how such elements as narrative structure, manipulation of language, sentence complexity, selection of detail, and overall tone reflect this attitude.

> . . . nothing was now likely, he knew, ever to make [Alice Staverton] better-off than she found herself, in the after-noon of life, as the delicately frugal possessor and tenant of the small house in Irving Place to which she had subtly
> (5) managed to cling through her almost unbroken New York career. If he knew the way to it now better than to any other address among the dreadful multiplied numberings which seemed to him to reduce the whole place to some vast ledger-page, overgrown, fantastic, of ruled and criss-crossed
> (10) lines and figures—if he had formed, for his consolation, that habit, it was really not a little because of the charm of his having encountered and recognised, in the vast wilderness of the wholesale, breaking through the mere gross generali-sation of wealth and force and success, a small still scene
> (15) where items and shades, all delicate things, kept the sharpness of the notes of a high voice perfectly trained, and where economy hung about like the scent of a garden. His old friend lived with one maid and herself dusted her relics and trimmed her lamps and polished her silver; she stood

(20) off, in the awful modern crush, when she could, but she sallied forth and did battle when the challenge was really to "spirit," the spirit she after all confessed to, proudly and a little shyly, as to that of the better time, that of *their* common, their quite far-away and antediluvian social period

(25) and order. She made use of the street-cars when need be, the terrible things that people scrambled for as the panic-stricken at sea scramble for the boats; she affronted, inscrutably, under stress, all the public concussions and ordeals; and yet, with that slim mystifying grace of her

(30) appearance, which defied you to say if she were a fair young woman who looked older through trouble, or a fine smooth older one who looked young through successful indifference; with her precious reference, above all, to memories and histories into which he could enter, she was as exquisite

(35) for him as some pale pressed flower (a rarity to begin with), and, failing other sweetnesses, she was a sufficient reward of his effort. They had communities of knowledge, "their" knowledge (this discriminating possessive was always on her lips) of presences of the other age, presences all overlaid, in

(40) his case, by the experience of a man and the freedom of a wanderer, overlaid by pleasure, by infidelity, by passages of life that were strange and dim to her, just by "Europe" in short, but still unobscured, still exposed and cherished, under the pious visitation of the spirit from which she had

(45) never been diverted.

## Question 2

(Suggested time—40 minutes. This question counts one-third of the total essay section score.)

The following passage is the opening of Susan Sontag's book *Illness as Metaphor*. Read the passage carefully, and write a cohesive essay in which you discuss Sontag's attitudes toward and use of metaphor in this excerpt.

     Illness is the night-side of life, a more onerous citizenship. Everyone who is born holds dual citizenship, in the kingdom of the well and in the kingdom of the sick. Although we all prefer to use only the good passport, sooner or later each of
(5)  us is obliged, at least for a spell, to identify ourselves as citizens of that other place.
     I want to describe, not what it is really like to emigrate to the kingdom of the ill and live there, but the punitive or sentimental fantasies concocted about that situation: not
(10)  real geography, but stereotypes of national character. My subject is not physical illness itself but the uses of illness as a figure or metaphor. My point is that illness is *not* a metaphor, and that the most truthful way of regarding illness—and the healthiest way of being ill—is one most
(15)  purified of, most resistant to, metaphoric thinking. Yet it is hardly possible to take up one's residence in the kingdom of the ill unprejudiced by the lurid metaphors with which it has been landscaped. It is toward an elucidation of those metaphors, and a liberation from them, that I dedicate this
(20)  enquiry.

## Question 3

(Suggested time—40 minutes. This question counts one-third of the total essay section score.)

Henry David Thoreau wrote, "Many men go fishing all of their lives without knowing that it is not fish they are after."

In a well thought out essay, examine the accuracy of this aphorism in modern society. Concentrate on examples from your observations, reading, and experiences to develop your ideas.

### END OF EXAMINATION

ANSWER KEY FOR PRACTICE TEST 3

## Section I: Multiple-Choice Questions

### First Passage

| | | |
|---|---|---|
| 1. A | 6. B | 11. A |
| 2. B | 7. B | 12. E |
| 3. B | 8. D | 13. D |
| 4. D | 9. C | 14. E |
| 5. C | 10. E | 15. E |

### Second Passage

| | | |
|---|---|---|
| 16. E | 21. D | 25. B |
| 17. B | 22. C | 26. C |
| 18. C | 23. B | 27. C |
| 19. A | 24. D | 28. D |
| 20. A | | |

### Third Passage

| | | |
|---|---|---|
| 29. C | 34. A | 39. B |
| 30. E | 35. A | 40. E |
| 31. D | 36. D | 41. C |
| 32. B | 37. A | 42. D |
| 33. E | 38. C | |

### Fourth Passage

| | | |
|---|---|---|
| 43. D | 48. D | 53. A |
| 44. C | 49. A | 54. A |
| 45. A | 50. C | 55. C |
| 46. E | 51. E | 56. C |
| 47. B | 52. B | |

## Section II: Essay Questions

Essay scoring guides, student essays, and analysis appear beginning on page 265.

## PRACTICE TEST 3 SCORING WORKSHEET

Use the following worksheet to arrive at a probable final AP grade on Practice Test 3. While it is sometimes difficult to be objective enough to score one's own essay, you can use the sample essay answers that follow to approximate an essay score for yourself. You might also give your essays (along with the sample essays) to a friend or relative to score if you feel confident that the individual has the knowledge necessary to make such a judgment and that he or she will feel comfortable in doing so.

### Section I: Multiple-Choice Questions

$$\underset{\substack{\text{right}\\\text{answers}}}{\underline{\hspace{2cm}}} - (\tfrac{1}{4} \text{ or } .25 \times \underset{\substack{\text{wrong}\\\text{answers}}}{\underline{\hspace{2cm}}}) = \underset{\substack{\text{multiple-choice}\\\text{raw score}}}{\underline{\hspace{2cm}}}$$

$$\underset{\substack{\text{multiple-choice}\\\text{raw score}}}{\underline{\hspace{2cm}}} \times 1.20 = \underset{\substack{\text{multiple-choice}\\\text{converted score}}}{\underline{\hspace{2cm}}} \text{ (of possible 67.5)}$$

### Section II: Essay Questions

$$\underset{\substack{\text{question 1}\\\text{raw score}}}{\underline{\hspace{1.5cm}}} + \underset{\substack{\text{question 2}\\\text{raw score}}}{\underline{\hspace{1.5cm}}} + \underset{\substack{\text{question 3}\\\text{raw score}}}{\underline{\hspace{1.5cm}}} = \underset{\substack{\text{essay}\\\text{raw score}}}{\underline{\hspace{1.5cm}}}$$

$$\underset{\substack{\text{essay}\\\text{raw score}}}{\underline{\hspace{2cm}}} \times 3.055 = \underset{\substack{\text{essay}\\\text{converted score}}}{\underline{\hspace{2cm}}} \text{ (of possible 82.5)}$$

### Final Score

$$\underset{\substack{\text{multiple-choice}\\\text{converted score}}}{\underline{\hspace{2cm}}} + \underset{\substack{\text{essay}\\\text{converted score}}}{\underline{\hspace{2cm}}} = \underset{\substack{\text{final}\\\text{converted score}}}{\underline{\hspace{2cm}}} \text{ (of possible 150)}$$

### Probable Final AP Score

| Final Converted Score | Probable AP Score |
|:---:|:---:|
| 150–104 | 5 |
| 103– 92 | 4 |
| 91– 76 | 3 |
| 75– 50 | 2 |
| 49–  0 | 1 |

# ANSWERS AND EXPLANATIONS FOR PRACTICE TEST 3

## SECTION I: MULTIPLE-CHOICE QUESTIONS

### First Passage

From *The Proud Tower* by Barbara Tuchman.

1. (A) The first sentence speaks of the "remorselessly uncompromising opinions" of Robert Cecil (Lord Salisbury), which paradoxically are to be the means of making him Prime Minister or the obstacle that must be overcome. The freedom with which Lord Salisbury will express and act on his opinions is a central issue in the rest of the passage. The notion is not retracted (B) or (D), and although the comment is amusing, it is also relevant (E).

2. (B) The remark is an understatement expressed by using the negative and, in the restraint of its expression, at odds with a phrase like "remarkable for their virulence and insolence." Disraeli's phrase could be called a metaphor ("measure") but not a simile (A). It is directly quoted (C). Although the remark is "to the man" (*ad hominem*), that is, a personal comment, it is not an *ad hominem* argument (D) or a diatribe (E), an abusive attack.

3. (B) There are direct quotations from Disraeli, Lord Morley, and an unnamed fellow member in the first paragraph. The later paragraphs have fewer quotations, although at least one in each of the two following paragraphs. Neither the first paragraph nor the rest of the passage makes noteworthy use of cause and effect reasoning, *ad hominem* argument, or abstract generalizations.

4. (D) The second paragraph and the rest of the passage enlarge the characterization of Lord Salisbury. The second paragraph does give examples of his rudeness and his short attention span

but also discusses his attitudes to the public and his oratorical skills, so (B) and (C) are not quite as accurate as (D). Choices (A) and (E) are untrue.

5. (C) Although he spoke without notes, we know from the first paragraph that his speeches could be "clear and perfect." Choices (A) and (B) cannot be correct. The characterization of Lord Salisbury makes it clear that he didn't fear any audience and wasn't at all reluctant to reveal his real feelings. If his speeches in public were awkward, they were so because he was indifferent to what the public thought and didn't, as he saw it, waste his time in preparation for them.

6. (B) As it is used here, a "tattoo" is a continuous drumming, not the picture on the skin. Choice (D), which is incorrect, probably has "taboo" in mind.

7. (B) The praise of an enemy is praise that is untainted by prejudice so (I) is certainly true. The paragraph does go on to discuss Lord Salisbury's "sympathetic" private self (II). Given Lord Salisbury's indifference to the opinions of others, especially those of the opposing political party, it is far more likely that Salisbury would be equally unconcerned by Gladstone's praise or blame.

8. (D) Since the phrase says "not in the press," there would be no point in adding "not even in *Punch*" if *Punch* were the press (E). We can infer that *Punch* must be some kind of publication even more likely to take liberties with a public figure than the press, pointing to a satirical publication rather than a conservative one.

9. (C) The sentence is loaded with intensifiers: "simply," "in his bones and brain cells," "any," "anyone whatever." If the phrase "no reason" were omitted, the sentence would lack a direct object and make no sense.

10. (E) The sentence contains twelve prepositional phrases. It uses three parallel participial phrases ("having entered . . .," "having

been returned . . .," and "having . . . sat . . ."). The sentence is periodic, reaching its subject, verb, and object only at the end.

11. (A) The last paragraph says that Lord Salisbury revered "up—to the monarchy." The only member of the royal family among these choices is the Prince of Wales, the son of the king or queen.

12. (E) The speaker or author here is a biographer but not a skeptical one. She is not a political supporter or a mordant satirist, the latter phrase being far too strong. The adjective "objective" is more appropriate than "sympathetic," since the passage presents both the strengths and the limitations of its subject.

13. (D) There is no overt use of the judgments of other modern historians, although the author, no doubt, has studied them. An example of (A) is the quotation from Disraeli or from Gladstone, of (C), the quotation in the second paragraph, and of (E), the last sentence in the first paragraph. The conclusion of the third paragraph is a good example of (B).

14. (E) There is no mention of Lord Salisbury's fearing social change (A). He is anything but a hypocrite (C), and although "he was not rank-conscious," he was uninterested in the general populace. The final sentence of the third paragraph insists upon the importance of his consciousness of himself as a Cecil, a distinguished family for centuries.

15. (E) Although the passage implies that Lord Salisbury became Prime Minister and implies that this would be sometime after 1850, it doesn't place the event late in the nineteenth century. The other options can be easily demonstrated by closely reading the passage.

*Second Passage*

From Jean Jacques Rousseau's "On Democracy."

16. (E) Rousseau claims that "nothing is more dangerous than private interest having any influence on public affairs" (lines 13–14). Choices (A), (C), and (D) are not addressed. Choice (B) is indirectly addressed as the author discusses the number of poeple who work efficiently together, but *ineffective* committees are not specifically addressed.

17. (B) The fourth paragaraph asserts that "affairs will be transacted with the greatest ease and expedition in fewest hands" (lines 35–36). Choices (A) and (E) are not addressed. Legislators and private interest groups, (C) and (D), are discussed but are not related to the efficiency of tribunals.

18. (C) This long, complex sentence uses parallel structure to increase its coherence, listing the "circumstances" that "conspire" against democracy. The sentence includes no extended metaphor (A), irony, or hyperbole (E). Whether the tone is persuasive and argumentative is irrelevant to the *coherence* of the sentence (B). Choice (D) is inaccurate for the same reason (irrelevance) and, in addition, contradicts the sense of the essay.

19. (A) All the paragraphs except the fifth suggest reasons that a democracy may not work, but this paragraph outlines what *is* necessary for a democracy. Although Rousseau implies that these conditions are nearly impossible to achieve, he here outlines how a democracy could be possible. "Present democracies" (B) and "traits of a good leader" (E) are not addressed, and there is no use of ridicule (C). Choice (D) is inaccurate because of the word "ease." Rousseau doesn't suggest that democracy is easy to achieve.

20. (A) The last paragraph explains that a democracy would work well in a "nation of gods" but that it will not "agree with men." The other choices list normal people, not the godlike.

21. (D) From the third paragaraph, you can infer that the nature of humanity will not allow a strict democracy to work. Rousseau claims here that a democracy, in the strict sense of the word, "never did, and never will, exist" because it is "against the natural order" that the greater number of people should govern the smaller number. Civil war (A) is addressed, but the author claims only that civil war is a *byproduct* of democracy, not its greatest obstacle. Rousseau doesn't see legislators as a serious obstacle to democracy or claim they are seditious (treasonous) (B). Nor does he imply that capitalists are "avaricious" (greedy) (C). While "inequality among citizens" (E) is a possible answer, it is not the *foremost* obstacle to democracy, since it can perhaps be overcome. Choice (D), however, addresses that in the human condition which Rousseau suggests cannot be changed.

22. (C) The fifth paragraph outlines conditions necessary for a democracy to work. Enthusiastic obedience (II) is not addressed.

23. (B) Each paragraph discusses an aspect of democracy and is clearly unified by discussion of that aspect. The essay employs no comparison and contrast (C). While it may argue strongly and persuasively (D), such arguments do not describe the paragaraphs' *organization*. Argumentation is a *mode* of rhetoric but not a *method* of *organization*. Choice (E) is tempting. The fifth paragraph, for instance, provides examples of "circumstances" which "conspire." But other paragraphs do not follow this supposition/example format, leaving (B) as the best answer.

24. (D) The paradox, or self-contradiction, is that people who inherently act correctly in a society have no need of a government at all; they govern themselves.

25. (B) The author provides clear arguments concerning democracy. The essay is more than expository (A) because it does more than provide information. It doesn't describe democracy (C), narrate a story (D), or demonstrate anything (E).

26. (C) The question asks for an example of the author's condescending attitude, one that demonstrates an air of superiority, of patronization. Choice (C) is the best of those listed because of the word "tedious." Rousseau here speaks of the need for simple manners "to prevent a multiplicity of affairs" and claims that the discussions that ensue concerning these "affairs" would be tedious. The remark can be seen as condescending because the citizens involved in those affairs would not likely think them tedious, but rather meaningful and significant. Rousseau seems to condescendingly imply that he considers these discussions a waste of time.

27. (C) A historical background of democracies could strengthen Rousseau's assertions (both about impediments to democracy and possibilities for its survival) by providing evidence rather than simply opinion. While expert opinions (B) might support Rousseau's contentions, they would not necessarily strengthen them.

28. (D) Rousseau is indeed skeptical, saying that "strict" democracy is "against the natural order" and suggesting that democracy of any type faces great obstacles. "Aggressive" (A) and "vituperative" (B) are too strong. Rousseau's argument is calm and rational. "Moderate" (C) is too weak. "Sanguine" (E), optimistic, is the opposite of Rousseau's attitude.

### Third Passage

From "Meditations upon a Broomstick" by Jonathan Swift.

29. (C) The sentence is not pedantic (overly scholarly). All of the remaining answer choices can be found in this sentence.

30. (E) The broomstick began life in nature in a "flourishing state . . . full of sap, full of leaves, and full of boughs." Man began life in youth "strong and lusty, in a thriving condition." Choices (A), (C), and (D) contradict the passage. (B) is not addressed.

31. (D) The author feels that man, as a youth, is closer to perfection. The older a man gets, the more mistakes he makes. The author also believes that man misuses nature, as he misuses the broomstick, out of selfishness. The author does not believe it is likely that man will take a turn for the better.

32. (B) The broomstick starts life as a flourishing tree, but after man uses it up, he throws it away or burns it. Choices (C) and (E) contradict the passage. Nature does not triumph over man's evil tendencies, and man does not fear nature, but rather destroys it. The evil inherent in man's soul (D) is not addressed.

33. (E) Intemperance is a lack of moderation in behavior, and the "axe of intemperance" is a metaphor for those excesses. It is the "axe" that chops man down like a tree. Before that, man had "green boughs"; after, he has but a "withered trunk." The phrase does not refer to "man's dominance over nature" (A). Nature is not shown as providing much nourishment (B); rather, it is destroyed. "Axe of intemperance" is neither a simile (C) nor hyperbole (D).

34. (A) The author is saddened and disillusioned at man's behavior. Choice (B) is incorrect because man's future is not addressed. (C) and (E) contradict the tone of the passage— there is *no* optimism or praise here. This author is angry with *man* and his nature, not the society man has created (D).

35. (A) The phrase "a flourishing state in a forest" refers to pure, untouched nature (before man chops down trees) and has positive connotations.

36. (D) Swift never suggests that man accomplishes anything magnificent; obviously, a broomstick can't claim such an accomplishment.

37. (A) "*Man*" is the antecedent: "man" *is* a reasoning vegetable to this author.

38. (C) No oxymorons (the juxtaposition of two contradictory terms) appear. All the other literary devices are used.

39. (B) Man *pretends* to solve the problems of the world but only makes them worse. Choice (A) is inaccurate—the broomstick represents decline, not thriving. (C) is also inaccurate; the broomstick is a metaphor for *man,* not society. There is no evidence for choice (D); nature doesn't exert control in this author's world, man does. (E) is obviously incorrect: the broomstick is an analogy for man's physical state, not his intellectual state.

40. (E) It is only man's pretension that allows him to believe that he can correct abuses; in fact, he "raises a mighty dust where there was none before."

41. (C) Swift is cynical toward mankind and all of man's works, believing that mankind is motivated wholly by self-interest and therefore not to be trusted. This author takes a strong position, not a neutral one (A), and while he may be condescending, the condescension is directed toward *man,* not nature (B). "Bellicose" (D) means quarrelsome and warlike and is too strong a term to accurately describe the tone here.

42. (D) Swift appears to concentrate on how inappropriate it is for man to try to reform nature while thinking of himself in such grand terms and, in reality, being the corrupter of nature.

### Fourth Passage

From "Criticism and Fiction" by William Dean Howells.

43. (D) The best term is "critical." The author's purpose is to criticize those who do not think for themselves, imitating older works in pursuit of art. Some examples of this critical tone: "men have been afraid to apply their own simplicity," "seeds of death are planted," "spirit of the wretched pedantry," "decays when it withdraws itself," "they are destitute of the documents," "they are quite ignorant," "you descend . . . in the moral and

social scale," and "you are one to be avoided." "Somber" (A) is too strong, as evidenced by the playful grasshopper analogy and fun the author pokes at old readers. The sentences are not complex enough or the diction flamboyant enough to be called "ornate" (B). The author's purpose is not "didactic" (C), that is, he does not mean to teach, and his diction is not pedantic. Choice (E), "formal," like "ornate," is too strong. The tone is more conversational than formal.

44. (C) Howells feels that the common people don't place enough trust in their own abilities to interpret literature, but rather rely on "some one who professed to know better and who browbeat wholesome common-sense" into them (lines 12–13). Choices (A) and (C) are not mentioned. Choices (B) and (E) contradict the passage. Howells feels that common people *should* attempt to make their own judgments rather than copy anyone's taste.

45. (A) "The seeds of death" is a metaphor for imitative art, art formed from studying older masters who themselves imitated the life of their time. According to Howells, this practice produces dead art, imitative art. The author doesn't deal with the *destruction* of art (B), but with the *imitation* of art. The "seeds of death" do not represent the art of an older age (C), but the tendency to mimic the art.

46. (E) Howells hopes the artist and common person will *reject* the ideal grasshopper in favor of a more natural form of art.

47. (B) While Howells feels that readers who restrict their reading to older literature are narrow-minded, he also finds them "very amusing . . . delightful." The author claims that these old ideas will die out *slowly,* not quickly (A), that "the time is yet far off," and doesn't dismiss these readers as unimportant, suggesting only that they are far too limited in their approach. Howells does attribute harm to them (D), in their narrow approach, and characterizes their knowledge as assumed rather than great (E).

48.  (D) The idealized grasshopper, made of cardboard and wire, is symbolic of the artificial. No quest to merge art and science is mentioned (A); the passage presents only an artist talking to a scientist, and no reference is made to the search for perfection—the cardboard grasshopper is far from perfection. Although this cardboard grasshopper is said by the artist to be indestructible, it will not last through the ages as *art* (C) because it is divorced from reality (although the artist seems to think that it will). Choice (E) is incorrect because the scientist doesn't produce the idealized grasshopper; the artist does.

49.  (A) In the quest for the ideal, the grasshopper is created out of wire, cardboard, and paint, ironically becoming in the process a lesser thing because it does not resemble reality. Even if true (and there is no evidence that they are), choices (B) and (C) are not ironic. Common sense tells us that everyone can tell a cardboard grasshopper from a real one (D), and the passage suggests that the cardboard grasshopper has, indeed, been created (E).

50.  (C) In lines 57–68, Howells claims that the natural, simple grasshopper will eventually be recognized. The remaining choices are types of grasshoppers that he hopes will disappear as the natural one emerges.

51.  (E) Howells urges his readers to read widely from all literary periods and to reach an individual interpretation that is not based on some pedantic notion. Conversely, he feels that it is a mistake to read *only* classical literature.

52.  (B) Howells's satire makes fun of those who believe that they can create an idealized copy of nature when, obviously, nature's product is alive, real, and superior. It is also humorous to think of this silly cardboard grasshopper as a realistic imitation of life. The other answer choices are either stated too strongly or not evident in the passage.

53. (A) The author believes that one should use simplicity, naturalness, and honesty in art and in its appreciation. The remaining answers involve attitudes which Howells criticizes.

54. (A) While the artist creates an idealized version of the grasshopper and the scientist's description (version) of the grasshopper will be based on reality, both of their creations remain artificial, both representations rather than reality. It is true that Howells presents the scientist's creation as preferable because it approaches reality more closely, but the fact remains that neither creation is *itself* reality. There is no evidence in the passage for the remaining answer choices.

55. (C) A motif is a conventional or recurring element in a narrative, a device not found in the passage. The remaining devices are present. Some examples. Irony: the grasshopper analogy (while the artist professes that the cardboard grasshopper is to be preferred to the real, Howells would have the reader understand that the opposite is true). Metaphor: "The seeds of death" (line 21). Allusion: to Shakespeare, Thackeray, Hawthorne, and others. Analogy: extended analogy in the grasshopper segment.

56. (C) The objection to these older readers is that they read and interpret based on only older models. They don't consider comtemporary literary representations based on contemporary reality worthy of attention and consequently remain "quite ignorant." Current critics (A) and middle-class readers (E) are not mentioned in the passage. The lady and gentleman are *not* well-rounded readers (B) or careless readers (D), but narrow readers.

# SECTION II: ESSAY QUESTIONS

## Question 1

### Scoring Guide for Question 1 (Henry James)

8–9 This well-written essay shows clear understanding of how an author's choices, especially in diction and selection of detail, reflect attitude. The writer will have accurately read the passage to identify the author's attitude, and the paper perceptively analyzes several techniques used to communicate that attitude. The essay presents strong, relevant evidence and thoroughly explains how the evidence points to the attitude toward the past and present. While the writing may contain a few minor errors, the paper demonstrates effective and precise communication.

6–7 This essay, also well written, accurately describes the author's attitude but usually less explicitly than do top-scoring essays. Discussion of the author's effective use of literary devices may be less thorough and less specific. Connection between the thesis and the evidence may not be as clear as that of top-scoring essays. Some errors in mechanics may occur, but overall this essay shows satisfactory control of organization, development, and use of language.

5 This average essay demonstrates adequate understanding of the author's attitude but may not present as precise a thesis about that attitude. Attempts to analyze the literary techniques may be simplistic, or evidence offered may be insufficient to prove the thesis. The paper may not provide clear connection between the evidence and the author's attitude. The essay may be clearly organized but may show inconsistent control of language.

3–4 This essay attempts to explain the author's attitude but does so with insufficient evidence or perhaps based on an inaccurate reading of the passage. It may fail to complete all of the tasks set forth in the essay question. This essay may merely catalog the devices used without providing analysis or connection to the thesis. Weak control of the essay format and/or language may be evident, and mechanical errors may be frequent.

1–2 This essay fails to reasonably respond to the question or the passage. It may fail to recognize the author's attitude or may misread the passage so as to distort that attitude. Because little or no evidence is provided for assertions, this essay fails to convince the reader, and the connection between the evidence and the thesis may be shallow or nonexistent. Persistent weaknesses in grammar and/or the basic elements of essay form may be evident.

*High-Scoring Essay*

Elements of style such as diction, imagery, figurative language, and sentence structure are used by Henry James in his short story "The Jolly Corner" to express the author's attitudes of comfort and familiarity towards the past, and confusion towards the present.

James opens the story with an image of Alice Staverton, an older woman, friend to the main character, "in the afternoon of life," living separately from the rest of a fast-paced New York. James chooses such words as "delicately" and "subtly" to slowly sketch Alice's character, while describing her lifestyle and the way in which she has managed to maintain a smooth career in a changing world. This image is sharply contrasted, a few sentences later, with the metaphor of the growing city, a "vast ledger-page, overgrown, fantastic, of ruled and criss-crossed lines and figures." This image of the present, seen in the nervous, complex city, is always pressing the reader as James continues to describe pedestrians' scramble for the street-cars and the chaos that always ensues. This haste and constant movement enforces James' presentation of the present as a hustle-bustle of anonymous people, strangers in the streets who are always hurrying to unknown destinations. James describes the changing times as an "awful modern crush," insinuating pressure and tension, complexity and confusion.

It is to this fast-paced, quickly evolving world that the main character returns, after a 33 year stay in Europe. He returns to visit Alice and is both surprised and relieved to find her unchanged. James describes the main character's perception of Alice in his expression "she stood off" which depicts Alice's ability to remove herself from the modern world. While she does stand apart from the rest of the modern world, James also manages to show Alice as a person well-footed in reality. Alice is not a recluse but "she sallied forth and did battle when the challenge was really to 'spirit,'" showing her acceptance of inevitable change. James' word choice when describing her appearance is very effective as he likens her "slim mystifying grace" to a young troubled-looking woman who also gives the appearance of a "fine smooth older one." In this way James leaves the reader with the impression of a woman who does not age, thus emphasizing a more positive outlook towards the older Alice than the chaotic present-day city. However, throughout the uncertainties of a changing era, Alice represents a stable reminder of a past life, "of the better time." This image of the past is emanated by Alice to the main character, who finds solace in her and her home. This outlook—"her precious reference, above all, to memories and histories into which he could enter"—which holds dear older values from another time and place, allow Alice to remain capable of dealing with change in her world. Her memories and knowledge encompass the main character, helping him to reconcile his own confusion upon returning from Europe. James ends this passage by exemplifying Alice's devotion to the past: "that pious visitation of the spirit from which she had never been diverted."

Word choice, figurative language, imagery and deeper meaning are used by James to express his cherished past and the present to which he is less a part of.

## *Analysis of the High-Scoring Essay*

This essay does an admirable job on a difficult topic. It begins by presenting a relevant thesis that accurately states the author's attitude; his view of the past is seen as positive, one with "comfort and familiarity," but his view of the present is more negative, one with "confusion."

The first body paragraph establishes Alice's character and age, and then contrasts her with the present-day city in which she lives. The student uses language effectively in establishing the author's negative impression of the city through choices like "nervous," "complex," "chaos," and "scramble." Ample evidence is offered from the text for the student's ideas, and clear connections to the thesis and essay topic are given.

The second body paragraph returns to Alice and, through her, reinforces the idea of the author's positive attitude toward the past, toward a comfortable life. However, the student doesn't imply that the author merely paints Alice as a fossil living solely in the past, but rather acknowledges that she may represent an older lifestyle while being "well-footed in reality." By emphasizing the comforting effect that Alice has on the main character, this student accurately discusses the author's positive attitude.

The concluding paragraph appears to have been quickly written and essentially only restates the original thesis. Fortunately, the body paragraphs contain ample insight and enough specific evidence to warrant the high score.

### Medium-Scoring Essay

Henry James manages to effectively create a sense of the familiar past and the complicated present, by his use of tone, diction, and style in his short story, "The Jolly Corner."

James' impresses the image of a familiar, comforting past upon the reader by his diction and sentence structures. The author begins by describing how Alice Staverton, old friend to the main character, has "subtly managed to cling through her almost unbroken New York career." This first glimpse of Alice shows her to be tough, but not tenacious. Wording such as "delicately frugal" add to Alice's characteristics of constancy and endurance. Alice represents an older era now passed by, and to her friend who has just returned from Europe, she is a refreshing, comforting reminder of "their quite far-away and antediluvian social period and order." Alice is an escape for the main character who is subject to a changing world upon his return from a 33 year departure.

James also manages to express the complexities of the modern world, ever growing and changing. His description of the new housing developments which look overgrown and confusing is James' first method by which he shows a distasteful present day. He continues to build this image with diction such as "awful modern crush," and with the simile that likens the scramble for the street cars to the scramble for life boats by people stranded at sea. He refers to any occurrence that happens outside of Alice's haven as "public concussions and ordeals." The author paints a picture of a fast-paced world that forces the main character to find refuge with Alice, away from the complex present, couched within encompassing memories and experiences of the past.

### Analysis of the Medium-Scoring Essay

This essay is a clear example of the medium-socring essay—it makes some points but doesn't expand upon them sufficiently to completely deal with the essay tasks. The student comes close to addressing the author's attitude (but not clearly) and mentions that the past is "familiar" and the present "complicated" but fails to integrate these concepts appropriately in the body of the essay.

The second paragraph offers relevant evidence and attempts to address the topic. The student acknowledges that Alice "represents an older era" while being "refreshing" at the same time, but these insights are not connected to the author's attitude toward the past and present. Unfortunately, this paragraph borders on presenting only simple character analysis rather than an investigation of the author's attitude. The attempt is there, and the student is essentially on the right track, but a high-scoring essay pays closer attention to the essay question tasks.

The third paragraph improves; it directly comments on the negative attitude implied, describing the modern world as "over-grown and confusing" and claiming that the author "shows a distasteful present day." The examples which follow this one are also relevant to the student's point. Once again, however, this paragraph would be improved with greater emphasis on the author's attitude, although it is a definite improvement over the previous paragraph.

The essay as a whole makes valid points and uses some clever wording. Its primary failing is that it needs to connect the evidence to the topic more strongly and directly.

## Question 2

*Scoring Guide for Question 2 (Susan Sontag)*

8–9  This well-written essay shows clear understanding of both Sontag's attitudes toward and use of metaphor. The thesis is thoughtful and articulate. Strong and relevant evidence from the passage combines with intelligent insights connecting the evidence to Sontag's attitudes toward and use of metaphor. Thoroughly convincing, this essay demonstrates a command of essay writing skills. Although it need not be withough errors, the paper is written with mature style and diction.

6–7  This essay demonstrates comprehension of Sontag's attitudes toward and use of metaphor, but its thesis may be less explicit than that of the top-scoring essay. The evidence offered may be less convincing, but the paper still demonstrates clear thinking. The connection between the evidence and Sontag's attitudes toward and use of metaphor may not be as clear as that of the top-scoring essay. Although well written, the paper may show some errors while maintaining satisfactory control over diction and the essay's requirements.

5  This adequately written essay shows some understanding of Sontag's attitudes toward and use of metaphor but may not clearly demonstrate the relationship between details of the passage and those attitudes and use. The writer may merely name the attitudes without effectively discussing them or may not effectively deal with the author's use of metaphor. The thesis may be simplistic and the evidence insufficient to prove the writer's points. Acceptable organization and development may be evident, but the style may not be as sophisticated as that of higher-scoring essays.

3–4  This low-scoring essay fails to convince the reader. The weak presentation may not demonstrate a clear understanding of either Sontag's attitudes toward metaphor or her use of metaphor. The thesis may be unsubstantiated, paragraph development may be weak, and superficial thinking may be evident. Frequent errors in composition that distract the reader may be present.

1–2 This poorly written essay lacks coherence and clarity. It may attempt to identify an attitude or attitudes without mention of the use of metaphor in the passage. The thesis may be overly obvious or absent. Little or no evidence may be offered, and any connection between the evidence and the thesis may be shallow or nonexistent. The paper may be unusually short, and persistent grammatical problems may exist.

*High-Scoring Essay*

In this passage, Sontag uses the metaphor of illness as a nation in which we all must eventually reside. In the face of this inevitability, she suggests that it is best to confront illness face to face rather than through a facade of preconceived ideas. Sontag ironically uses this metaphor to express her dismay with the prevalence of such stereotypes regarding the nature of illness.

The paragraph sequence itself helps to illuminate the insidious nature of the metaphor. The passage begins with such a metaphor, equating illness with a detestable nation. With such descriptions as "the night-side of life" and "onerous citizenship," Sontag firmly implants illness' negative connotations in the reader's mind. Yet the very next paragraph opens up with her intent to describe "not what it is really like to emigrate to the kingdom of the ill . . . but the punitive and sentimental fantasies concocted about that situation: not real geography, but stereotypes of national character." In this statement she establishes the fallacy of the metaphor in general, and specifically of her own opening metaphor by referring to it as "not real geography." In so doing, Sontag alerts the reader to his or her own unquestioning acceptance of such parallels.

Throughout the passage, she continues the use of the geographical metaphor to ironically and effectively show the suggestive power of this literary tool. In her claim "it is hardly possible to take up one's residence in the kingdom of the ill unprejudiced by the lurid metaphors with which it has been landscaped," she subtly weaves in such irony. Her reference to "the kingdom of the ill" is indeed one of the very same "lurid metaphors" against which she cautions the reader. This technique of interweaving irony is very powerful in that the reader, not expecting an author to contradict herself, is forced to reexamine the sentence in closer detail, only to discover the clever subtlety of the author. This forcefully drives home Sontag's implication that the danger in metaphors lies in their unchallenged acceptance.

Sontag's perception of illness metaphors is effectively revealed in the concluding sentence, "It is toward an elucidation of those metaphors that I dedicate this inquiry." By joining the elucidation of metaphor with the liberation from those metaphors, Sontag suggests that close examination will reveal their inaccuracy, thus allowing them to be abandoned by the newly enlightened and astute reader.

Susan Sontag's suspicion of metaphorical approaches to illness is subtly yet clearly conveyed in this passage through irony and implication. The strongest statements are often written between the lines, as Sontag's work clearly demonstrates.

### Analysis of the High-Scoring Essay

The essay's introduction effectively addresses the topic: the analysis of Sontag's attitudes toward and use of the metaphor. The student notes that Sontag uses the metaphor as a tool of irony to "express her dismay" at the use of stereotypes. The student's language is sophisticated, inviting the reader to follow the essay's engaging ideas.

The student then analyzes Sontag's sequence of ideas, noting how she effectively presents the concept of illness as metaphor only to dash it to pieces in her following paragraph. The student's presentation is intelligent, and the writing style is strong. Such phrasing as "helps to illuminate the insidious nature" demonstrates a strong command of language. The student also includes relevant and sufficient evidence from Sontag's writing to prove the essay's points.

The essay continues the effective discussion in the next paragraph by analyzing Sontag's use of metaphor, noting that Sontag contradicts herself and explaining the effect of that contradiction on the reader—that it forces the reader to reexamine preconceived notions about both illness and metaphor.

The third paragraph begins the conclusion by analyzing Sontag's last sentence, suggesting that Sontag's real purpose is to reveal the inaccuracy of metaphors and thus to enlighten her readers. While this paragraph is not as well developed as the previous ones, it is necessary, as it addresses an important part of the topic, Sontag's attitudes toward metaphor. The paragraph could be improved, however, by mention of more than one attitude (the topic specifies "attitudes," plural, which should suggest to the student writer that there may be some ambivalence).

The essay concludes with a summary statement about Sontag's use of metaphor and includes a perceptive comment that readers must read between the lines in order to glean the meaning of an author's writing. Given the essay's thoughtful analysis and sophisticated presentation, it deserves a high score.

### Medium-Scoring Essay

In the introduction to Susan Sontag's book, Illness as Metaphor, she talks about using metaphors to compare illness to something else. She believes that metaphors are too limiting to be used to generalize all illness and that they don't allow for a clear view of sickness itself. This attitude is reflected not only in her direct comments, but also through her own use of a metaphor.

Her negative attitude about metaphors for illness is stated at various places in the excerpt. She very strongly states that "illness is not a metaphor, and that the most truthful way of regarding illness . . . is one most purified of, most resistant to, metaphoric thinking." This shows that since illness isn't a metaphor, people shouldn't try to treat it like one. Sontag feels that using a metaphor to define illness is not truthful because it doesn't necessarily reveal the whole story. Another example where her attitude about metaphors can be seen is in her comment that, "It is toward . . . a liberation from them, that I dedicate this inquiry." Her whole purpose in the book, then, is to draw people away from the metaphor. She wants to get people to confront illness as it is, without a confining metaphor, to be "liberated" from it.

Sontag shows her dislike for metaphor indirectly by in fact using one herself. She describes "the kingdom of the sick" as "the night-side of life." This establishes a clearly defined view of illness. Then she later seems to point out the invalidity of her own metaphor, when she implies that the "kingdom" is "not real geography but stereotypes." This implies that it is not based on reality, but rather ideas. She is referring to metaphors as stereotypes, which expresses her view that they are prejudiced and consequently not very accurate. In a roundabout way, by insulting her own metaphor as a mere stereotype, Susan Sontag conveys the error of metaphors.

In this passage, she claims that metaphors should not be used to describe illness. The reasons she gives are that it is not "the most truthful way" of looking at it, and that they are just stereotypes. She even uses one herself to show you that you can't always trust them to be right. What's true for one person may not necessarily be true for another.

*Analysis of the Medium-Scoring Essay*

This average-scoring essay demonstrates the same faults as do many essays in the medium-score range: it makes some accurate points but without sufficient analysis. In additiion, the presentation lacks the sophistication seen in high-scoring essays. Both the points presented and the style of presentation do not rise above the mundane.

The second paragraph is primarily summary, not analysis. While correct in acknowledging that Sontag has a "negative attitude" toward illness metaphors, the student has nothing more important to say than "since illness isn't a metaphor, people shouldn't treat it like one." The student does acknowledge Sontag's purpose (which wasn't asked for in the topic), "to draw people away from the metaphor," but shows no deeper perception and continues to write mere summary.

The third paragraph is more thoughtful but, once again, lacks strong analysis. The student suggests that Sontag herself makes use of a metaphor, that of the kingdom, but sees only that she is trying to "convey the error of metaphors." This essay points out only what is obvious to most readers.

The conclusion summarizes the essay's main points about Sontag's attitude toward and use of metaphor, but unfortuantely, no new points are presented. Overall, this essay attempts to address the topic, but its ideas are shallow and its presentation simplistic.

## Question 3

*Scoring Guide for Question 3 (Henry David Thoreau)*

8–9  This well-written essay thoroughly explores the accuracy of Thoreau's aphorism in modern society. It articulately and clearly substantiates its points with relevant evidence from contemporary life, connecting that evidence to the thesis with meaningful insight about human nature. Although the paper may contain a few flaws, it demonstrates a command of language, sentence structure, and conventions of essay form.

6–7  This essay explores Thoreau's aphorism but produces a less explicit thesis than that of top-scoring essays. Evidence offered is perhaps less specific or not as clearly connected to the thesis. The paper's ideas may not be as crisply articulated as those in top-scoring essays. Although there may be some errors, the paper is well written and demonstrates mature style and satisfactory command of language.

5  This adequately presented essay has an acceptable thesis and presents some evidence concerning the applicability of the aphorism in modern society but may exhibit flaws in organization, number of examples, or discussion of ideas. In general, this essay is not as effective or convincing because of a pedestrian treatment of the topic, producing commonplace, predictable reading. Inconsistent control of language and sentence structure may be present.

3–4  This essay fails to convince the reader. Superficial thinking and weak evidence may be combined with an uninteresting or obvious thesis. Confused or contradictory thinking may be present, and the essay may lack adequate support to prove its points. Weak organization and paragraph development may be present. Frequent grammatical problems may distract the reader.

1–2 This essay frequently lacks coherence and clarity of thought and may produce an unclear thesis concerning the accuracy of the aphorism. Little or no evidence may be presented for the thesis, and the connection between the evidence and the thesis may be shallow or nonexistent. The essay may exhibit poor organization and paragraph development. Weak syntax and persistent grammatical errors may be present.

### High Scoring Essay

Henry David Thoreau aptly described the nature of mankind by expressing man's tendency to become lost in unimportant pursuits in today's society. Using fish as a symbol for what people believe they are searching for, Thoreau describes a problem of human nature which is seen in all of society: the problem of continually searching while not recognizing what one truly desires in life.

This problem is clouded by the confusing mist of appearances. This shroud hangs over what society has taught one to see as success: money, fancy cars, large houses, to name a few. In the pursuit of what society deems symbolic of success, one is trapped in the conflict of appearance versus reality. All too often someone craves a material object, only to find it boring shortly after it was acquired. This, of course, causes the person to want more possessions, always with the same result. This endless cycle continues, the result being dissatisfaction; as Thoreau might note, this person looks for still more fish, not knowing that fish will not satisfy.

This conflict leads only to the greater problem of getting lost in the race for success and losing sight of life's full meaning. In a society such as America, it is easy to forget that inner happiness cannot be bought with material goods. With so many opportunities for one to flaunt wealth, it is not difficult to understand how people get caught up in trivial pursuits which do not satisfy their actual desire for success. The necessity to discern between needs and wants then becomes apparent within society. Today this confusion of true desire and false success is seen as the divorce rate increases, as drug abuse rises, as people continue to look for permanent happiness and inner success in temporary feelings and actions. Thoreau was accurate as he used this aphorism to describe human tendencies. Sad yet true, Thoreau's comment is still truthful in regard to the earnest search for false success.

### Analysis of the High-Scoring Essay

This essay is articulate in its exploration of Thoreau's aphorism in relation to modern society. It clearly takes a stand and buttresses it with discussion and examples. The student is not side-tracked into irrelevance and keeps the commentary specific.

The second paragraph presents its insights with a nice flair. Phrases like "Clouded by the confusing mist of appearance" and the "shroud [that] hangs over" are negative images appropriate to the writer's assertions and reinforcing the theme of the deceit of "success" as our society defines it. By returning to Thoreau's symbol of fish, the student completes the paragraph logically and effectively links it to the topic.

The third paragaraph continues the philosophical discussion, adding additional relevant, contemporary examples and expanding the notion that people are never satisfied with what they have. Divorce and drugs are especially apt illustrations. The essay would be stronger if it included more such examples, but those used are convincing.

Overall, the essay deserves a fairly high score because it is clearly on topic, is well organized, shows sufficient paragraph development, and demonstrates maturity in style, even if only sporadically. It would earn a higher score if it offered stronger evidence and used more precise language. The repetition of ideas is a problem but one often seen in writing done on philosophical topics under time pressure.

### Medium-Scoring Essay

Thoreau's quote relating to man's futile search for fish is applicable to modern society today. I think this quote especially relates to materialism, which is rampant within our greedy, American, self-centered society. Many values today revolve around selfishness and instant gratification, and the big picture of life isn't really seen. This drive for ownership and power and wealth often materializes itself in the mad rush to buy things. Credit cards only encourage this behavior, and the trip for the fish is not what they need. Materialism is a perfect example of this behavior, since many people feel the need to fill their lives with something, whether it's love or money or things. Thoreau sums up this observation about human nature so well, and this statement related not only to Thoreau's society, but to our society in modern America as well. The difference between needs and wants are easily confused, and those who are consumed by materialism cannot see the forest for the trees. I think Thoreau was reminding people not to forget what the important things in life are, and to express the importance of searching for what really matters in life, not settling for temporary things like material goods.

### Analysis of the Medium-Scoring Essay

This essay has some merit. It does attempt to discuss the topic. The paragraph is acceptable and the points relevant, but the paper falls short of thoroughly convincing a reader. The student's one-paragraph format leads to a rambling, unfocused result here. It isn't the essay's ideas that lower the socre, but the presentation. The writer uses pertinent examples from contemporary life, such as the use of credit cards and "materialism," but lapses into vague terms like "things."

The writer should be commended for trying to connect the essay to Thoreau's "fish" aphorism, but that important connection should be incorporated more smoothly. For example, the sudden jump from "credit cards" to "fish" in the fifth sentence needs a transitional phrase so that the reader can follow the writer's argument. In addition, demonstrating more sophisticated skills in the fundamentals of the essay form and more effective diction would significantly improve this essay.

# Part VI: Suggested Reading List

# SUGGESTED READING LIST

Following is a list of important authors and some of their works that are similar to those used on the AP English language exam. The list is not meant to be all inclusive or required reading for every student, but reading these works extensively and analyzing the authors' use of language will give you excellent preparation for the exam.

## AUTOBIOGRAPHY, BIOGRAPHY, JOURNAL, AND HISTORY

- **Maya Angelou**

    *Gather Together in My Name*
    *The Heart of a Woman*
    *I Know Why the Caged Bird Sings*
    *Singin' and Swingin' and Gettin' Merry Like Christmas*

- **Walter Jackson Bate**

    *John Keats*
    *Samuel Johnson*

- **Charles A. Beard**

    *An Economic Interpretation of the Constitution*
    *The Rise of American Civilization* (with Mary R. Beard)

- **James Boswell**

    *The Life of Samuel Johnson, LL.D.*

- **Van Wyck Brooks**

    *An Autobiography*
    *Days of Phoenix*
    *From a Writer's Notebook*

- **Thomas Carlyle**

  *The French Revolution*
  *Past and Present*

- **Bruce Catton**

  *Mr. Lincoln's Army*
  *A Stillness at Appomattox*

- **Sir Winston Churchill**

  *Blood, Sweat, and Tears*
  *Europe Unite: Speeches 1947 and 1948*
  *A History of the English-Speaking Peoples*
  *In the Balance: Speeches 1949 and 1950*
  *Marlborough*
  *My Early Life*
  *Their Finest Hour*
  *Triumph and Tragedy*

- **Charles Dana**

  (any nonfiction)

- **Thomas De Quincey**

  *Confessions of an English Opium Eater*

- **Frederick Douglass**

  *The Life and Times of Frederick Douglass*
  *My Bondage and My Freedom*
  *Narrative of the Life of Frederick Douglass*

- **Leon Edel**

  *Bloomsbury: A House of Lions*
  *Henry James, A Life*
  *The Stuff of Sleep and Dreams*
  *Telling Lives*

- **Richard Ellmann**

  *Eminent Domain: Yeats among Wilde, Joyce, Pound, Eliot, and Auden*
  *James Joyce*

- **Antonia Fraser**

  *King James I of England*
  *Mary, Queen of Scots*
  *Oliver Cromwell*
  *The Warrior Queens*
  *The Weaker Vessel: Women's Lot in Seventeenth Century England*

- **Edward Gibbon**

  *The History of the Decline and Fall of the Roman Empire*

- **Lillian Hellman**

  *Scoundrel Time*
  *An Unfinished Woman*

- **William Dean Howells**

  *Years of My Youth*

- **Alfred Kazin**

  *New York Jew*
  *Starting Out in the Thirties*
  *A Walker in the City*

- **Helen Keller**

  *The Story of My Life*

- **Maxine Hong Kingston**

  *China Men*
  *The Woman Warrior*

- **T. E. Lawrence**

  *The Revolt in the Desert*
  *Seven Pillars of Wisdom*

- **Gerda Lerner**

  *The Creation of Patriarchy*
  *The Female Experience: An American Documentary*
  *The Majority Finds Its Past: Placing Women in History*

- **Thomas Macaulay**

  *Critical and Historical Essays*
  *History of England from the Accession of James II*

- **Malcolm X**

  *The Autobiography of Malcolm X*

- **Samuel Eliot Morison**

  *Christopher Columbus, Admiral of the Ocean Sea*
  *The Growth of the American Republic*
  *Harrison Gray Otis: Urbane Federalist*

- **John Henry Newman**

  (any nonfiction)

- **Francis Parkman**

  *The Oregon Trail*
  *Pioneers of France in the New World*

- **Samuel Pepys**

  *Diary*

- **Richard Rodriguez**

  *Days of Obligation*
  *Hunger of Memory*

- **Mari Sandoz**

  *The Battle of the Little Big Horn*
  *Old Jules*

- **Arthur M. Schlesinger, Jr.**

  *The Age of Jackson*
  *The Age of Roosevelt*
  *The Bitter Heritage*
  *Robert Kennedy and His Times*
  *A Thousand Days*

- **George Trevelyan**

  *English Social History*

- **Barbara Tuchman**

  *Bible and Sword*
  *A Distant Mirror*
  *The Guns of August*
  *The Proud Tower*

- **Richard Wright**

  *American Hunger*
  *Black Boy*

- **Anzia Yezierska**

  *Bread and Givers*
  *The Open Cage*
  *Red Ribbon on a White Horse*

# ESSAY, FICTION, AND CRITICISM

- **Joseph Addison**
  selections from the *Tatler* and the *Spectator*

- **James Agee**
  *Collected Short Prose*
  *A Death in the Family*
  *Let Us Now Praise Famous Men*

- **Michael Arlen**
  *An American Verdict*
  *The Camera Age: Essays on Television*
  *Exiles*

- **Matthew Arnold**
  (any criticism)

- **Margaret Atwood**
  *Cat's Eye*
  *The Handmaid's Tale*

- **Sir Francis Bacon**
  *The Advancement of Learning*
  *The New Atlantis*

- **James Baldwin**
  *Another Country*
  *The Devil Finds Work*
  *The Evidence of Things Not Seen*
  *The Fire Next Time*
  *Go Tell It on the Mountain*
  *If Beale Street Could Talk*
  *Notes of a Native Son*

- **G. K. Chesterton**

  *Heretics*
  *St. Francis of Assisi*
  *St. Thomas Aquinas*
  *The Victorian Age in Literature*

- **Kenneth Clark**

  *Another Part of the Wood*
  *Civilisation*
  *The Other Half*

- **Samuel Taylor Coleridge**

  (any criticism)

- **Arlene Croce**

  (any criticism)

- **Joan Didion**

  *A Book of Common Prayer*
  *Salvador*
  *Slouching Toward Bethlehem*
  (any essays)

- **Ralph Waldo Emerson**

  *The Journals and Miscellaneous Notebooks*
  (any essays)

- **Northrop Frye**

  *Anatomy of Criticism*
  *Fearful Symmetry*
  *Fools of Time*

- **Paul Fussell**

  *Bad, or the Dumbing of America*
  *The Great War and Modern Memory*
  *Thank God for the Atom Bomb and Other Essays*

- **Nadine Gordimer**

  *Face to Face*
  *My Son's Story*
  *Not for Publication*
  (any essays)

- **William Hazlitt**

  (any criticism)

- **Zora Neale Hurston**

  *Dust Tracks on a Road*
  *Jonah's Gourd Vine*
  *Their Eyes Were Watching God*

- **Ruth Prawer Jhabvala**

  *Heat and Dust*
  *In Search of Love and Beauty*

- **Samuel Johnson**

  *The Lives of the Poets*
  selections from the *Idler* and the *Rambler*

- **Pauline Kael**

  *5001 Nights at the Movies*
  *I Lost It at the Movies*
  *State of the Art*

- **William Hugh Kenner**

  *A Colder Eye*

- **Charles Lamb**

  *Tales from Shakespeare*
  (any essays)

- **Stephen Leacock**

  *Last Leaves*
  *Winnowed Wisdom*

- **Norman Mailer**

  *Ancient Evenings*
  *The Armies of the Night*
  *The Naked and the Dead*
  *Pieces and Pontifications*

- **Mary McCarthy**

  *Cannibals and Missionaries*
  *Ideas and the Novel*
  *Memories of a Catholic Girlhood*
  *The Writing on the Wall*

- **Scott Momaday**

  *The Names: A Memoir*
  *The Way to Rainy Mountain*

- **Montaigne**

  (any essays)

- **Vladimir Nabokov**

  *Lectures on Literature*
  *Pnin*
  *Speak, Memory*

- **V. S. Naipaul**

  *Among the Believers: An Islamic Journey*
  *The Return of Eva Peron*

- **Joyce Carol Oates**

  *Contraries: Essays*
  *The Edge of Impossibility*
  *First Person Singular*
  *New Heaven, New Earth*
  *On Boxing*
  *Woman Writer*

- **Tillie Olsen**

  *Mother to Daughter, Daughter to Mother*
  *Silences*
  *Tell Me a Riddle*
  *Yonnonido*

- **George Orwell**

  *Down and Out in Paris and London*
  *Shooting an Elephant*

- **Cynthia Ozick**

  *Art and Ardor*
  *The Cannibal Galaxy*

- **Walter Pater**

  (any criticism)

- **Adrienne Rich**

  *Of Woman Born*
  *On Lies, Secrets, and Silence*

- **John Ruskin**

  *Modern Painters*
  *Praeterita*
  (any other criticism)

- **George Santayana**

  *The Life of Reason, or, The Phases of Human Progress*
  *The Sense of Beauty*

- **George Bernard Shaw**

  *The Intelligent Woman's Guide to Socialism and Capitalism*
  (any criticism)

- **Susan Sontag**

  *Against Interpretation*
  *Aids and Its Metaphors*
  *Illness as Metaphor*
  *Styles of Radical Will*

- **Richard Steele**

  selections from the *Spectator* and the *Tatler*

- **John Updike**

  *Assorted Prose*
  *Hugging the Shore: Essays and Criticism*
  *Self Consciousness*

- **Gore Vidal**

  *Matters of Fact and Fiction*
  *Reflections upon a Sinking Ship*
  *Rocking the Boat*
  *Views from a Window*

- **Alice Walker**

  *In Love and Trouble*
  *You Can't Keep a Good Woman Down*

- **Eudora Welty**

  *The Eye of the Story: Selected Essays and Reviews*
  *The Golden Apples*
  *Losing Battles*
  *One Writer's Beginnings*

- **E. B. White**

  *The Essays of E. B. White*
  *One Man's Meat*

- **Oscar Wilde**

  (any criticism)

- **Edmund Wilson**

  *Axle's Castle: A Study in the Imaginative Literature of 1870 to 1930*
  *The Devils and Canon Barham: Ten Essays on Poets, Novelists, and*
      *Monsters*
  *Letters on Literature and Politics*
  *Patriotic Gore: Studies in the Literature of the American Civil War*
  *The Shores of Light*

- **Virginia Woolf**

  *The Common Reader*
  *The Death of a Moth*
  *The Moment*
  *Roger Fry*
  *A Room of One's Own*
  *Three Guineas*
  *A Writer's Diary*

## POLITICAL WRITING AND JOURNALISM

- **Roger Angell**

  *Five Seasons: A Baseball Companion*
  *Late Innings*
  *Once More Around the Park*

- **Hannah Arendt**

  *Between Past and Future*
  *The Human Condition*
  *On Revolution*
  *The Origins of Totalitarianism*

- **Simone de Beauvoir**

  *The Coming of Age*
  *The Prime of Life*
  *The Second Sex*

- **William F. Buckley**

  *God and Man at Yale*
  *The Governor Listeth*
  *On the Firing Line*

- **Michel de Crèvecoeur**

  *Letters from an American Farmer*

- **Elizabeth Drew**

  *American Journal: The Events of 1976*
  *Washington Journal: The Events of 1973–1974*

- **W. E. B. Du Bois**

  *Autobiography*
  *The Philadelphia Negro*
  *The Souls of Black Folk*
  *Worlds of Color*

- **Nora Ephron**

  *Crazy Salad: Some Things About Women*
  *Wallflower at the Orgy*

- **Frances Fitzgerald**

  *America Revisited*
  *Cities on a Hill*
  *Fire in the Lake*

- **Janet Flanner**

  *Janet Flanner's Uncollected Writings*
  *Men and Monuments*
  *Paris Was Yesterday: 1925–1939*

- **John Kenneth Galbraith**

  *The Affluent Society*
  *Ambassador's Journal*
  *The Anatomy of Power*
  *The Nature of Mass Poverty*

- **Charlotte Perkins Gilman**

  *The Charlotte Perkins Gilman Reader*
  *Herland*

- **Ellen Goodman**

  *At Large*
  *Close to Home*
  *Keeping in Touch*
  *Making Sense*

- **Thomas Hobbes**

  *Leviathan*
  *Philosophical Rudiments*

- **Thomas Jefferson**

  (any writings)

- **George Kennan**

  *American Diplomacy 1900–1950*
  *Democracy and the Student Left*
  *Sketches from a Life*

- **Martin Luther King, Jr.**

  *Stride Toward Freedom*
  *A Testament of Hope*
  *The Trumpet of Conscience*

- **John Locke**

  *An Essay Concerning Human Understanding*
  *Two Treatises on Government*

- **Andy Logan**

  *The Man Who Robbed the Robber Barons*

- **Machiavelli**

  *The Prince*

- **John McPhee**

  *Headmaster*
  *A Sense of Who You Are*

- **H. L. Mencken**

  *The Bathtub Hoax and Other Blasts and Bravos from the Chicago*
      *Tribune*
  *A Choice of Days*
  *H. L. Mencken's Smart Set Criticism*
  *In Defense of Women*
  *Selected Prejudices*

- **John Stuart Mill**

  *On Liberty*
  *The Subjection of Women*
  *Utilitarianism*

- **Sir Thomas More**
  *Utopia*

- **Jan Morris**
  *Destinations: Essays from Rolling Stone*

- **Olive Schreiner**
  *The Story of an African Farm*

- **William L. Shirer**
  *Berlin Diary*
  *The Nightmare Years*
  *20th Century Journey*

- **Red Smith**
  *The Red Smith Reader*
  *To Absent Friends*

- **Lincoln Steffens**
  *Autobiography*
  *The Shame of the Cities*
  *The Upbuilders*

- **Jonathan Swift**
  (any essays)

- **Alexis de Tocqueville**
  *Democracy in America*
  *The Old Regime and the Revolution*

- **Calvin Trillin**
  *American Fried*
  *An Education in Georgia*
  *Third Helpings*
  *Uncivil Liberties*

- **T. H. White**

  *Breach of Faith*
  *Fire in the Ashes*
  *In Search of History*
  *The Making of the President: 1960*

- **Tom Wolfe**

  (any essays)

## SCIENCE AND NATURE WRITING

- **Isaac Asimov**

  *The Exploding Suns*
  *In Joy Still Felt* (autobiography)
  *In Memory Yet Green* (autobiography)
  *Until the Sun Dies*

- **Jacob Bronowski**

  *The Origins of Knowledge and Imagination*
  *A Sense of the Future*

- **Annie Dillard**

  *An American Childhood*
  *Holy the Firm*
  *Living by Fiction*
  *Pilgrim at Tinker Creek*
  *Teaching a Stone to Talk: Expeditions and Encounters*
  *The Writing Life*

- **Gretel Ehrlich**

  *The Solace of Open Spaces*

- **Stephen Jay Gould**

  *Ever Since Darwin*
  *Hen's Teeth and Horse's Toes*
  *The Mismeasure of Man*
  *Time's Arrow, Time's Cycle*
  *An Urchin in the Storm*

- **Peter Matthiessen**

  *At Play in the Fields of the Lord*
  *Far Tortuga*
  *In the Spirit of Crazy Horse*
  *The Snow Leopard*
  *The Tree Where Man Was Born*

- **Margaret Mead**

  *And Keep Your Powder Dry: An Anthropologist Looks at America*
  *Blackberry Winter*
  *Coming of Age in Samoa*

- **Carl Sagan**

  *The Dragons of Eden*
  *A Path Where No Man Thought*

- **Lewis Thomas**

  *The Fragile Species*
  *Late Night Thoughts on Listening to Mahler's 9th Symphony*
  *The Lives of a Cell: The Notes of a Biology Watcher*
  *The Medusa and the Snail*

# FINAL PREPARATION: "THE FINAL TOUCHES"

1. Spend your last week of preparation on general review of key concepts, test-taking strategies, and techniques.
2. Don't cram the night before the test! It's a waste of time.
3. Remember to bring the proper materials: three or four sharpened Number 2 pencils, an eraser, several ballpoint pens, and a watch.
4. Start off crisply, answering the questions you know first and then coming back to the harder ones.
5. If you can eliminate one or more of the answer choices, make an educated guess.
6. Mark in reading passages, underline key words, jot down important information. Take advantage of being permitted to write in the test booklet.
7. Make sure that you're answering "what is being asked" and that your answer is reasonable.
8. Cross out incorrect choices immediately in the test booklet in order to avoid reconsidering a choice you've already eliminated.
9. Plan your essays carefully and monitor your timing.

# Think Quick

Now there are more Cliffs Quick Review® titles, providing help with more introductory level courses. Use Quick Reviews to increase your understanding of fundamental principles in a given subject, as well as to prepare for quizzes, midterms and finals.

Do better in the classroom, and on papers and tests with Cliffs Quick Reviews.

Publisher's ISBN Prefix 0-8220

| Qty. | ISBN | Title | Price | Total | Qty. | ISBN | Title | Price | Total |
|---|---|---|---|---|---|---|---|---|---|
| | 5309-8 | Accounting Principles I | 9.95 | | | 5330-6 | Human Nutrition | 9.95 | |
| | 5302-0 | Algebra I | 7.95 | | | 5331-4 | Linear Algebra | 9.95 | |
| | 5303-9 | Algebra II | 9.95 | | | 5333-0 | Microbiology | 9.95 | |
| | 5300-4 | American Government | 9.95 | | | 5326-8 | Organic Chemistry I | 9.95 | |
| | 5301-2 | Anatomy & Physiology | 9.95 | | | 5335-7 | Physical Geology | 9.95 | |
| | 5304-7 | Basic Math & Pre-Algebra | 7.95 | | | 5337-3 | Physics | 7.95 | |
| | 5306-3 | Biology | 7.95 | | | 5327-6 | Psychology | 7.95 | |
| | 5312-8 | Calculus | 7.95 | | | 5349-7 | Statistics | 7.95 | |
| | 5318-7 | Chemistry | 7.95 | | | 5358-6 | Trigonometry | 7.95 | |
| | 5320-9 | Differential Equations | 9.95 | | | 5360-8 | United States History I | 7.95 | |
| | 5324-1 | Economics | 7.95 | | | 5361-6 | United States History II | 7.95 | |
| | 5329-2 | Geometry | 7.95 | | | 5367-5 | Writing Grammar, Usage, & Style | 9.95 | |

*Prices subject to change without notice.*

Available at your booksellers, or send this form with your check or money order to **Cliffs Notes, Inc., P.O. Box 80728, Lincoln, NE 68501** http://www.cliffs.com

☐ Money order ☐ Check payable to Cliffs Notes, Inc.

☐ Visa ☐ Mastercard Signature_____

Card no. _____ Exp. date_____

Name _____

Address _____

City _____ State_____ Zip_____

Telephone (_____)_____